Measuring economic welfare: new methods

Measuring economic welfare

New methods

GEORGE W. McKENZIE

Reader in International Economics
University of Southampton

CAMBRIDGE UNIVERSITY PRESS

Cambridge
London   New York   New Rochelle
Melbourne   Sydney

Published by the Press Syndicate of the University of Cambridge
The Pitt Building, Trumpington Street, Cambridge CB2 1RP
32 East 57th Street, New York, NY 10022, USA
296 Beaconsfield Parade, Middle Park, Melbourne 3206, Australia

First published 1983

Printed in the United States of America

Library of Congress Cataloging in Publication Data
McKenzie, George W.
Measuring economic welfare.
Bibliography: p.
Includes index.
1. Welfare economics. 2. Consumption
(Economics) – Mathematical models. 3. Demand
functions (Economic Theory) I. Title.
HB846.M37   330.15′5   82–4422
ISBN 0 521 24862 0   AACR2

Contents

Preface

The origins of this work can be traced back to the spring of 1964, when I was a teaching assistant at the University of California at Berkeley. I was giving a class on the topic of consumer demand to a group of students taking an introductory economics course. In the process of my presentation I attempted to show the link between the demand function and consumer satisfaction by resorting to the use of a consumer surplus diagram. I had thought this to be a useful pedagogic device, particularly in that it enabled, I believed, the student to better understand marginal analysis. It was easy to show that the consumer would increase consumption up to the point where marginal utility in terms of the surplus just equaled price. The loss of satisfaction due to a price rise could then be illustrated in a straightforward manner. However, simplicity has a cost, as I was soon to learn. Near the end of the discussion, one student inquired as to how the consumer surplus analysis could be utilized if more than one price was varied. If two commodities were involved, then the demand curve for each would shift according to the degree of complementarity or substitutability. My answer consisted of two parts. First, I argued that my analysis was purely partial and was presented as a pedagogic device. General problems would have to wait until discussion of indifference curves. Second, we need not worry about the interaction between demand functions if the goods are independent, that is, if the cross-price effects are zero. Neither argument satisfied the inquisitive student. If the concept of consumer surplus was not general, he argued, why discuss it at all? Previous class sessions had been spent emphasizing the empirical significance of complementarity and substitutability. The inconsistency in my attempt to rationalize consumer surplus was too apparent.

Unfortunately, I could think of no alternative argument. I was aware of the important points raised by Samuelson in his studies of the marginal utility of money and the problem of integrability (1942, 1950). But neither discussion could be translated into suitable language for the first-year student. Indeed, if anything, those issues would simply have forced me to point out in more sophisticated terms the limitations of consumer surplus techniques. As a result, I decided to abandon the concept as a pedagogic tool, and I gave it no further thought until the autumn of 1970.

I had just arrived in England on sabbatical and almost immediately became interested in studying the economic effects of the United Kingdom's proposed entry into the European Economic Community. I had previously undertaken some empirical work on the relationship between international trade patterns and relative price movements, and I thought that the procedures I had developed would be of considerable use in measuring the trade effects of the proposed membership. However, in the course of my work I became more and more involved in a thoroughgoing examination of the procedures that had been used by previous researchers to evaluate the costs and benefits of tariff protection. This interest was renewed to a large extent by several papers presented at the Department of Economics staff seminars at Southampton during 1971. Inevitably, these involved very crude, back-of-the-envelope calculations based on consumer surplus procedures. My mind drifted back to that economics class at Berkeley: Had I been wrong to reject this concept so readily?

As it turned out, the answer was no. A comprehensive review of consumer surplus analysis confirmed all the restrictions that I had been aware of several years earlier. It was likely to be a highly inaccurate measure. Indeed, it was clear that Alfred Marshall himself had rejected this tool as an operational procedure, although he continued to use it as a pedagogic device to illustrate the marginal analysis contained in his *Principles* (1890).

The use of the consumer surplus procedures, however, involves more than technical problems. Most studies of the costs of tariff protection (and the costs of monopolies) have concluded that the losses involved in such distortions are likely to be quite small. However, such aggregate calculations are likely to mask significant income redistribution effects, with some groups in society enjoying gains, whereas others appear to suffer losses. Thus, not only did the consumer surplus calculations contain inherent errors; in addition, they were undertaken in such a way as to mask the most important effects of any policy variations.

In the spring of 1971 I decided to remain in England, taking up the offer of a permanent position at Southampton. This enabled me to begin an important and fruitful collaboration with Ivor Pearce. My initial efforts had been devoted to the construction of a rigorous critique of consumer surplus procedures. Pearce, however, impressed on me that it was useless to criticize unless a superior alternative procedure could be developed. Indeed, the response of consumer surplus advocates to any criticism has been that nothing better exists. We thus embarked on an intellectual fishing expedition to determine whether or not there was an alternative basis for building a theory of applied welfare economics.

The results of this collaboration led us to devise a numerical representation of consumer preferences that could be expressed in monetary units and written in terms of the parameters of ordinary demand functions. No special assumptions over and above those usually made explicit in econometric demand analysis are required. The purpose of this volume is to explore the underlying measure in detail and to contrast the approach with contemporary thinking in the area of applied welfare economics.

An important debt of gratitude is owed to my colleagues, past and present, in the Department of Economics at the University of Southampton. The environment has been such that constructive criticism has been encouraged and sought. I would particularly like to thank Ivor Pearce, John Wise, John Driffill, and Steve Thomas for their helpful comments and suggestions as this work proceeded. Peter Wagstaff provided substantial assistance in clarifying many of the arguments in the penultimate draft of the manuscript. Brian Orman of the Department of Mathematics assisted in formulating some of the examples that appear in Chapter 3. A particular debt of gratitude is owed to David Ulph of University College, London, who acted as the referee for Cambridge University Press. His extensive comments led to substantial revisions in the first draft of the manuscript. Of course, neither he nor any other person can be held responsible for any errors that remain. That burden must remain with me.

Some of the analysis contained in this volume has been drawn from articles I have previously published in the *Review of Economic Studies,* the *Journal of Political Economy,* the *Oxford Economic Papers,* the *American Economic Review,* and *Economic Theory of Natural Resources* (edited by W. Eichhorn). Early formulations of the material were presented at two different meetings of the International Economics Study Group sponsored by the Social Science Research Council (U. K.).

I also owe a great debt to the Social Science Research Council for providing me research funds to pursue this topic in its early stages and the Nuffield Foundation for awarding me a fellowship to draw this work to a conclusion. Their assistance enabled me to utilize that scarcest of all resources, time, more efficiently than would otherwise have been possible.

Finally, I would like to thank the secretarial staff of the Department of Economics at Southampton. In particular, I would like to mention Frances Edwards and Carole Sherman, who cheerfully and carefully prepared this manuscript.

CHAPTER 1

An introduction to the money-metric

1.1 Introduction

The basic objective of applied welfare economics is to determine if the introduction of a specific project or economic policy will make an individual or group of consumers better off or worse off than will the available alternatives, including the status quo. The tasks involved are the same, whether we are concerned with evaluating the consequences of some policy that affects the entire economy (e.g., a variation in the level of tariffs on imports) or the effects of a project involving only a small community (e.g., the construction of a road that bypasses a congested urban center). In both instances a procedure is required that will enable the economist to work with observable data about consumer preferences, as revealed in the associated demand functions, in order to draw inferences about how the consumer is affected by changes in relative prices and/or income. The objective of this book is to explain the steps required to utilize such information so as to create an operational welfare measure.

This problem has taxed economists now for over a century. At the microeconomic level of project evaluation, the concept of consumer surplus, based on the area beneath a consumer demand curve, continues to attract widespread interest. At the macroeconomic level, many types of index numbers have been formulated and classified. Yet current thinking hardly yields hopeful conclusions. Many economists deny that it is possible to construct an applied welfare indicator at all. Others have argued that it is possible only in very special and limited circumstances. Still others, perhaps agreeing with that latter body of thought, have claimed that the problems are unimportant, because "reasonable" approximate welfare indicators are available. Subsequent chapters will examine each of these viewpoints in detail. At this point, however, it is sufficient to note that in the past, considerable controversy has surrounded discussions of consumer surplus and index-number techniques. For this reason it is extremely important that it be clear at the outset what we are going to be talking about and what we hope to achieve. The best way to do this is to state five basic criteria that any operational welfare indicator must meet:

1

1. For an individual or homogeneous group of individuals (i.e., a group possessing identical tastes and expenditure levels) the measure must be capable of ranking all relevant price/quantity situations according to the preferences of the individual or homogeneous group.
2. The measure must take the form of a single metric or scale.
3. The metric or scale must be expressed in monetary units.
4. The welfare indicator must be amenable to calculation in terms of the parameters of ordinary, observable demand functions.
5. Once an indicator meeting the preceding four criteria is constructed, it must be such that it can be aggregated across individuals or homogeneous groups so as to obtain an overall measure of the social desirability of the project or policy under consideration.

Why these criteria? To answer this question, it is necessary to emphasize that the evaluation of any project or policy involves two fundamental steps. First, it is necessary to determine which individuals (or homogeneous groups) appear to gain and which appear to lose as a result of any policy action. Second, given this information about the redistribution of income and consumer satisfaction, it is necessary to decide on the basis of value judgments whether the proposed policy should or should not be undertaken. Criteria 1 through 4 are directed toward taking the first step. Criterion 5 concerns the second step.

Criterion 1 underlies all of modern consumer theory and involves the assumption that all consumers have well-defined tastes. Thus, if we possessed complete information about each individual's preference for one situation over another, we would be able to determine qualitatively whether a project or policy has made that individual worse off or better off. That is, the first criterion establishes the fact that we are interested in the sign of any change in the level of consumer satisfaction. Although many theoretical discussions of economic policy have been confined to this qualitative plane, applied economists require something more. For them, it is necessary to be able to rank all changes on the same scale (criterion 2). This has two effects. First, if we are comparing, say, eight alternative situations, we require eight numbers that will enable us to order the several possibilities. As we shall see, some approaches allow only binary or pairwise comparisons. From an operational point of view, this is extremely cumbersome, because it requires $\sum_{i=2}^{n} (i - 1)$ calculations to be made, where n represents the number of alternatives. In our earlier example, 28 such pairwise comparisons would have to be made. Second, we should be able to determine not only whether or not A and B have gained but also whether A has gained more or less than B. *We require a metric or scale with which to characterize (on a uniform basis) every individu-*

al's set of preferences. As we shall see later in this volume, there are infinitely many possible metrics that could be used. However, from a pragmatic point of view, it is necessary to express the metric in terms that can be easily interpreted by lay economists and the general public. The most obvious approach is to seek a measure that can be expressed in monetary units (criterion 3). This property has considerable pedagogic value and will enable us to make the direct, quantitative comparisons that we seek to undertake. In addition, it represents a significant step toward the achievement of criterion 5. If we are interested in calculating social welfare functions, it is a straightforward matter to attach weights (however complicated) to the money-metric indicators associated with each individual or homogeneous group so as to obtain an overall aggregate index. The weights, of course, become an explicit representation of value judgments and enable one to compare the policy recommendations that will arise when alternative weighting schemes (i.e., alternative value judgments) are assumed. This topic will be discussed in Chapter 8.

Now let us turn to the fourth criterion. The theory of consumer behavior tells us that there is a one-to-one correspondence between the ordinal structure of consumer preferences and the structure of consumer demand functions. This result obviously must play a central role in the construction of an operational welfare indicator. It means that there is, in principle, a link between the observable data contained in the demand functions and economic welfare. Unfortunately, by itself, this fact turns out to be of little assistance in applied welfare economics. Until now, economists have not been able to devise a straightforward, manageable procedure for expressing the link between the demand functions and preferences in terms of *elementary* mathematical functions. An elementary function is one that can be constructed from "polynomials, exponentials, logarithms, trigonometric or inverse trigonometric functions in a finite number of steps by using the operations of addition, subtraction, multiplication, division or composition" (Apostol, 1967). Such elementary relationships are fundamental if we are to systematically characterize available price and expenditure data by means of modern econometric techniques. The use of consumer surplus represents a heroic attempt to achieve this objective. Unfortunately, it suffers from two serious defects: (a) Its logical underpinnings are extremely weak. (b) Its performance, in practice, is bound to be subject to substantial error. These points will be discussed in detail in subsequent chapters.

Faced with this situation, we may be tempted to conclude that we should not concern ourselves with this particular criterion and, instead, should simply follow the methodology of the theorist and base any evaluation procedures on the assumption that we know the ordinal preference function describing consumer behavior. However, this approach is not entirely satisfactory either. As we shall determine in the next chapter, there are many circumstances in which it is not possible to express the money-metric in terms of elementary mathematical functions, even though we may possess a function that exactly characterizes consumer preferences. Thus, the problem facing those who desire to start from demand functions reemerges, albeit in a slightly different guise. However, the solution is the same. As we shall see in Chapter 3, it is possible to derive a money-metric in terms of the parameters of ordinary demand functions by using some very basic numerical procedures. The elusive task of trying to express a money measure of welfare in terms of simple algebraic formulas will therefore be abandoned in favor of more complex but more fruitful techniques.

1.2   Some basic assumptions

Considerable effort has been expended by economists in formalizing the properties that characterize consumer preferences and, in particular, in identifying very general conditions under which they can exist. The analysis contained in this book will fall short of the most general treatment, however, because it is not possible to subject it to the techniques of applied econometric demand analysis. Preferences exhibiting satiation or kinks will be assumed away, as will lexicographic orderings. To be explicit, we shall assume that the problems with which we deal in subsequent chapters exhibit the following properties: *Property 1.* The services generated in the process of consuming commodities can be expressed as nonnegative real numbers. This condition will also be placed on commodity prices and total expenditure. Thus, certain commodities or services that have a zero nominal price are ruled out, as are those commodities for which no consumption takes place. Given the level of aggregation that characterizes even the best available data, it is not likely that this assumption could be avoided, even if that were believed to be crucial (which it is not) to the analysis of this volume.

Let X_i represent the quantity consumed for commodity i. Then the approach to be adopted assumes that each individual consumer possesses a preference function

$$U = U(X_1, \ldots, X_n) \tag{1.1}$$

which possesses the following properties:

Property 2. The consumer is capable of ordering all possible combinations or market baskets of commodities. Thus, for every possible pair of such baskets, denoted as Z_i and Z_j, one of the following relationships must hold:

1. Z_i is preferred to Z_j.
2. Z_j is preferred to Z_i.
3. The consumer is indifferent between Z_i and Z_j.

Property 3. For all possible market baskets, if Z_i is preferred to Z_j and Z_j is preferred to Z_k, then Z_i is preferred to Z_k. This has the effect of eliminating the possibility that the three situations listed under Property 2 could exist simultaneously.

Property 4. The preference function U that orders the various market baskets is continuous. That is, no gaps exist in the ordering.

Property 5. The preference function U is increasing over the various commodities. More is preferred to less.

Property 6. The *marginal rate of substitution* indicates the rate at which one commodity substitutes for another along any indifference surface, if the quantities of all other commodities are held constant. Thus, for any pair of commodities, i and j, we shall assume that the marginal rate of substitution of i for j decreases as X_j increases. The interpretation is that as the ratio of X_i to X_j decreases, the consumer becomes more reluctant to give up X_i so as to maintain his level of satisfaction constant. That is, the consumer is willing to give up fewer and fewer units of X_i to obtain one additional unit of X_j.

Finally, we need to make two assumptions that will be of crucial significance for the computational procedures to be discussed in Chapter 3. First, we shall assume that consumer preferences can be represented by a function that is analytic over the region of price and income variation. That is, we shall assume that any preference function to be considered possesses derivatives of all orders for all values of prices and total expenditure to be considered. However, the main characteristic of an analytic function is that it may be represented by a Taylor series expansion that is covergent as its order approaches infinity. A Taylor series of infinite order is of little operational significance until it is truncated. Because there is always the possibility that a series of order k will neglect the impact of very large derivatives of order greater than k, we shall restrict the functions to be studied by making one further assumption: The absolute value of the remainder term associated with any kth-order Taylor series expansion monotonically tends to zero as k approaches infinity.

Although these two assumptions do restrict the domain of mathematical functions to be considered, it is not unreasonable to conjecture that human behavior does tend to satisfy the conditions noted. Both Kannai (1974) and Mas-Colell (1974) have examined the mathematical properties of such functions and have concluded that they are not unreasonable. With respect to the assumption of monotonic convergence of the Taylor series, it is highly unlikely that human behavior will be heavily dominated by a high-order derivative of a consumer preference function with respect to its arguments. Indeed, for realistic values of prices and income, the various preference functions underlying econometric estimation of demand systems all possess the properties stated in the following composite assumption:

Property 7. Consumer preferences can be expressed as an analytic function. Further, the absolute value of the remainder term of any Taylor series monotonically tends toward zero as the order of the series tends toward infinity.

Thus, the framework that we shall adopt is not completely general. Nevertheless, these assumptions provide the basis for contemporary work in the field of applied demand analysis and for most discussions of consumer surplus or index-number techniques. Equally important from the point of view of this volume is the fact that these assumptions enable us to focus very clearly on the basic problem: It is one thing to be able to draw an indifference map such as that in Figure 1.1; it is quite another thing to be able to express it in terms of elementary functions.

1.3   The money-metric

Although the search for a monetary representation of consumer preferences has generated considerable controversy over the past 100 years or so, such a measure is really quite simple to visualize. Indeed, the concept is already widely known, but, unfortunately, widely neglected and/or misinterpreted. Consider Figure 1.1, which depicts (a) several representative indifference surfaces satisfying the assumptions previously discussed, (b) budget lines (on the assumption of constant prices), and (c) the associated income expansion path. Suppose also that the incomes represented in the diagram are those shown in Table 1.1. It is fairly easy to appreciate that we may adopt any numerical ordering pattern for the indifference surfaces provided that the chosen representation is always monotonic and increasing. That is, suppose $\phi = \phi(X_1, \ldots, X_n)$ is some function describing the indifference surfaces in Figure 1.1. Then any transformation

Table 1.1 *Transformation*

Indifference surface	Expenditure level (constant prices)	R	S	T
I	100	100	100	100
II	200	170	220	200
III	300	220	370	300
IV	400	250	550	400

$U = U[\phi(X_1,\dots,X_n)]$ will also do, provided that $\partial U/\partial\phi$ is greater than zero. The points of tangency of the indifference surfaces with the budget lines remain unchanged irrespective of the transformation chosen. Consumer behavior remains unaffected. This property is extremely important. In the past, many economists thought that satisfaction could be quantified in terms of measured units of pain or pleasure. However, the fact that we can represent a given preference system by any arbitrary increasing monotonic transformation implies that a cardinal representation of consumer satisfaction is not necessary. An ordinal approach is all that is required. Although this is true, it does not necessarily exclude the possibility that some cardinal representation may be of interest in its own right. To appreciate that this is so, again consider Table 1.1, which shows three alternative numbering schemes R, S, and T that might be used to characterize the indifference surfaces shown in Figure 1.1.

Under transformation R we note that although the utility indicator chosen increases as money expenditure increases, it does so at a decreasing rate. That is, the marginal utility of money decreases as total expenditure increases. Under transformation S, the utility indicator increases at an increasing rate. The marginal utility of money increases as total expenditure increases. However, under transformation T, the marginal utility of money remains constant as expenditure increases. The latter representation immediately suggests a money-metric interpretation. Suppose that the slopes of the budget lines indicate the prices that hold in some initial situation, say that labeled 1 in Figure 1.1. Then it is possible to order all alternatives in the following way. Suppose that some policy change enables the price/quantity situation at point 3 to be achieved. Then we can say that this new situation generates a level of satisfaction that is equivalent to a move from point 1 to point 2 brought about solely by a change in money income. The same can also be said for point 5. It is immediately obvious that all price/quantity situations can be ranked in this way,

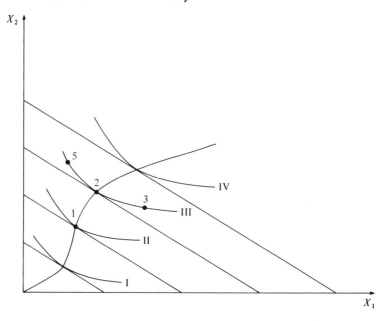

Figure 1.1

because it is always possible to find some level of expenditure, given initial prices, that generates the same level of satisfaction as the policy change. This scale is identical with the transformation T shown in Table 1.1. The metric used to characterize consumer preferences is the level of expenditure required to achieve any level of satisfaction given initial prices. The difference between this level of expenditure and the initial level is called the *equivalent variation*. Thus, a move from situation 1 to situation 3 is equivalent to an income gain of 100 dollars. By calculating this measure for all situations of interest, the alternatives can be ranked not just ordinally but in terms of a monetary unit (i.e., in terms of a metric) that is easily understood.

The advantage of this particular formulation is that it allows the policymaker or project analyst to compare the monetary gains or losses accruing to consumers with the monetary cost of financing that project or policy. In other words, the approach to be developed in this volume is capable of forming a meaningful basis for what is conventionally called cost – benefit analysis. For example, consider the situation illustrated in Figure 1.2. Let us suppose that a project is contemplated that will lead to an increase in the consumption of X_1 and X_2. Suppose also that the funds required to undertake this project

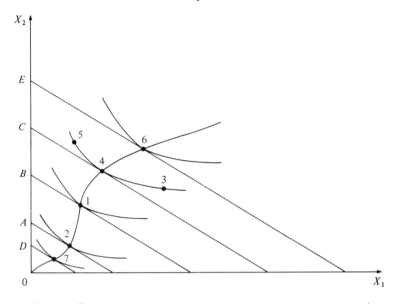

Figure 1.2

are raised by a lump-sum income tax. Given that the initial situation is depicted as point 1 in Figure 1.2, the imposition of the tax, *ceteris paribus*, lowers welfare to point 2. If we normalize the price of X_2, so that its initial value is one, then the value of the tax is calculated by the distance AB. The funds having been raised, the project is now introduced, with the result that the economy moves from point 2 to point 3. This is equivalent to an increase in expenditure equal to AC such that the economy moves from point 2 to point 4. In other words, at a cost of AB, the economy enjoys gains equivalent to AC, thereby producing net gains of BC.

If several projects are under consideration, then similar calculations of costs and benefits can be made for each, and the results can be compared so as to reveal which is best. Consider, for example, one alternative (a move from 1 to 7) that costs an amount equal to BD and generates gains equivalent to DE (a move from 7 to 6). The net gain is thus BE, which is greater than the BC associated with the project discussed earlier.

To many readers, this result will appear quite surprising. Yet the concept of the equivalent variation is well known in the literature dealing with various aspects of welfare economics. It was first defined as such by Hicks as part of a discussion that took place in the 1940s as economists attempted to clarify his celebrated rehabilitation of consumer surplus. The major analytical issues involved will be examined in Chapters 4 and 5. In 1949, Allen used this measure as the basis for an exact quantity index. Its properties were pointed out in a well-known study by Hurwicz and Uzawa (1971) on the important problem of the integrability of demand functions. Yet, it is only in recent years, following Samuelson's labeling of the measure as the "money-metric" and the attempts by McKenzie and Pearce (1976) to characterize it in terms of the parameters of demand functions, that greater interest has been shown in this concept.

However, if a full understanding of the issues involved is to be achieved, numerous misconceptions must be clarified. Despite widespread awareness of the equivalent variation, economists have not fully appreciated the relationship of this measure to consumer preferences. For example, Debreu (1951, p. 273) wrote that a basic problem in applied welfare economics "comes from the fact that no meaningful metrics exists in the satisfaction space." Boadway (1974), summarizing the conclusions of Silberberg (1972), Mohring (1971), and Burns (1973), concluded that "there can be no measure of welfare change in monetary units which is independent of the path of integration." This is a very strong result that in subsequent chapters will be shown to be mathematically incorrect. That it is intuitively incorrect can be appreciated from the diagrammatic analysis of the equivalent variation previously discussed. Yet, having determined that a money measure exists, another misconception must be cleared away. As we shall determine in the next chapter, Willig's claim (1976, p. 589) that the equivalent variation is "unobservable" is clearly wrong.

Much discussion has also been confused by the preference of most cost−benefit analysts and index−number theorists for the conceptually identical notions of "willingness to pay" and the *compensating variation*. This indicates the amount of money that a consumer will be willing to pay, following some policy change, so as to return to the initial level of satisfaction. It is important that the compensating variation and equivalent variation not be confused. For one thing, the reference points for the two are entirely different. For the equivalent variation, an arbitrarily chosen vector of prices serves to define the base situation, whereas with the compensating variation it is an arbitrarily chosen base level of satisfaction. The latter will be consistent with a large number of alternative price vectors. More important, however, is the fact that, unlike the equivalent variation, the compensating variation cannot be used to construct a metric that meets the first criterion set out earlier in this chapter. The compensating variation is not an ordinal welfare metric. It is true, as several writers have pointed out, that it could conceivably be used for binary comparisons. However, this involves an extremely cumbersome procedure. As we have already noted, if there are n alternatives, $\sum_{i=2}^{n} (i - 1)$ pairwise calculations will have to be made if the compensating variation is to be used. The results will have to be presented in matrix form. In contrast, if the equivalent variation is used, only n calculations will be required, and the results can be presented in vector notation in the same way that index numbers are presented in statistical abstracts. In other words, the equivalent variation is a money-metric, whereas the compensating variation is not.

1.4   Summary

Two objectives have been achieved in this chapter. First, we have listed a set of assumptions characterizing consumer behavior. Second, we have shown that, in principle, consumer preferences can be characterized by a money-metric and that this is related to the well-known equivalent variation.

CHAPTER 2

The marginal utility of money as an integrating factor

2.1 Introduction

In this chapter we have two objectives. First, we need to determine the properties that consumer demand functions must possess when they are generated on the basis of the consumer maximizing a preference function satisfying the conditions discussed in Chapter 1. Second, we need to devise procedures for actually retrieving information about consumer preferences in the form of the money-metric from the aforesaid demand functions. Unfortunately, the analytic tools required to achieve this second objective receive scant attention in most modern economics texts. In particular, we need to make clear the relationship between the marginal utility of money expenditure and the mathematical concepts of (a) the Lagrange multiplier and (b) the integrating factor. The significance of these three variables (which, in fact, are conceptually identical) is that they provide the crucial linkage that will enable us to derive the money-metric from consumer demands. In the parlance of the mathematician, we shall need to determine an integrating factor in order to form an expression from which the demand functions can be integrated to create a utility function and, more specifically, the money-metric function. For this reason it is important that we examine the roles of these variables in rather basic terms. This approach has the added advantage that it will enable us to easily identify some of the difficulties into which consumer surplus theorists and index-number theorists have fallen in the past.

2.2 The Lagrange multiplier

Assume that each individual consumer is maximizing a preference function, which can be written generally as

$$U = U[\phi(X_1, \ldots, X_n)] \tag{2.1}$$

where the function ϕ satisfies the assumptions stated in Chapter 1 and U is any increasing, monotonic function of ϕ. Further assume that U is maximized subject to a budget constraint

$$Y = \sum_{i=1}^{n} p_i X_i \tag{2.2}$$

13

where Y is fixed income and p_i is the price of the ith commodity, where all prices are assumed to be given. The constraint (2.2) implies that the consumer always exhausts his current income. A more sophisticated approach would assume that the individual could be a net saver or net debtor. However, this would involve us in a discussion of the theory of portfolio behavior, a subject beyond the scope of this volume. In any case, no additional points of principle are involved. In essence, we assume that if for some reason the consumer does possess idle funds, he can always improve his satisfaction by spending these balances until they are completely depleted.

The conditions that characterize this maximum can be derived by first eliminating one of the commodities from the list of arguments in (2.1) through substitution of (2.2). Let us choose the nth commodity (the choice is arbitrary) so that we obtain

$$U = U\left[\phi\left(X_1, \ldots, X_{n-1}, \frac{Y - \sum_i^{n-1} p_i X_i}{p_n}\right)\right] \tag{2.3}$$

The function (2.3) can now be maximized with respect to the remaining commodities to obtain the following necessary first-order conditions:

$$\frac{(\partial U/\partial \phi)(\partial \phi/\partial X_i)}{(\partial U/\partial \phi)(\partial \phi/\partial X_n)} = \frac{\partial \phi/\partial X_i}{\partial \phi/\partial X_n} = \frac{p_i}{p_n} \quad (i = 1, \ldots, n-1) \tag{2.4}$$

where $\partial U/\partial X_i$ indicates the marginal utility associated with additional consumption of X_i. It is easy to see that this ratio condition (2.4) applies to all commodity pairings. Hence, consumers will appear to maximize their satisfaction when the ratio of the marginal utilities for any two commodities equals the ratio of the respective prices. It is important to note that this condition is independent of the monotonic transformation chosen for the preference function, and hence the diagrammatic discussion in Chapter 1 is reinforced.

Although there is nothing wrong with the foregoing approach, economists have generally used a somewhat different technique to derive the conditions under which consumers maximize their levels of satisfaction subject to their budget constraints. This alternative procedure involves the introduction of an additional variable to the analysis, the *Lagrange multiplier*.

Any relationship written in ratio form, such as the set of equations (2.4), can be rewritten linearly by introducing a factor of proportionality that is independent of the variables X_i. This factor can be written as a function of income and prices

$$\lambda = \lambda(Y, p_1, \ldots, p_n) \tag{2.5}$$

because these variables are assumed to be given to the consumer. Hence, we can rewrite the conditions for the maximization of welfare (2.4) as

$$\frac{\partial U}{\partial \phi}\frac{\partial \phi}{\partial X_i} + \lambda(Y, p_1, \ldots, p_n) \cdot p_i = 0 \quad (i = 1, \ldots, n) \tag{2.6}$$

where λ, the factor of proportionality, is called the Lagrange multiplier.

The set of conditions (2.6) is consistent with a maximization problem that is somewhat different from the one previously considered. They can be derived by first forming a new expression

$$\mathcal{L} = U(X_1, \ldots, X_n) + \lambda(Y, p_1, \ldots, p_n) \cdot \left(\sum p_i X_i - Y\right) \tag{2.7}$$

and then maximizing this with respect to the X_i. This yields the first-order conditions that, together with the budget constraint, can be solved for the n unknown variables X_i and the Lagrange multiplier associated with the optimal X_i, all in terms of prices and total expenditure. In other words, in principle, we should be able to construct a set of demand functions from the first-order conditions and the budget constraint.

It should be emphasized that the first-order conditions for utility maximization, whether written in the form (2.4) or (2.6), are necessary but not sufficient. In general, such conditions can also be consistent with the minimization of a function. Hence, we must check to ensure that certain second-order conditions are fulfilled. These may be expressed in several ways. However, for the moment we shall simply note that the following bordered Hessian determinants must alternate in sign:

$$|U_{ii}| < 0$$

$$\begin{vmatrix} U_{11} & U_{12} & U_1 \\ U_{21} & U_{22} & U_2 \\ U_1 & U_2 & 0 \end{vmatrix} > 0$$

$$\begin{vmatrix} U_{11} & U_{12} & U_{13} & U_1 \\ U_{21} & U_{22} & U_{23} & U_2 \\ U_{31} & U_{32} & U_{33} & U_3 \\ U_1 & U_2 & U_3 & 0 \end{vmatrix} < 0 \tag{2.8}$$

and so forth, where U_{ij} is the second derivative $\partial^2 U/\partial X_i \partial X_j$ associated with the preference function. For the algebraic details underlying this condition, the reader is referred to the work of Samuelson (1947), Pearce (1964), or Henderson and Quandt (1958).

2.3   An example

To appreciate the Lagrange multiplier approach and also to set the stage for subsequent analysis, it is useful to consider a concrete example. Suppose that an individual's preferences are described by the function

$$U = \prod_i^n (X_i - c_i)^{g_i} \tag{2.9}$$

where the g_i and c_i are parameters of the function, and X_i, as before, indicates the quantity consumed. We then form the Lagrangian expression

$$\mathcal{L} = \prod_i^n (X_i - c_i)^{g_i} + \lambda\left(\sum p_i X_i - Y\right) \tag{2.10}$$

which is then maximized with respect to the X_j and λ to yield the following first-order conditions:

$$\frac{\partial \mathcal{L}}{\partial X_j} = \frac{g_j}{(X_j - c_j)} \prod_i^n (X_i - c_i)^{g_i} + \lambda p_j = 0 \tag{2.11}$$

$$\frac{\partial \mathcal{L}}{\partial \lambda} = \sum p_i X_i - Y = 0 \tag{2.12}$$

Solving the $n + 1$ equations represented by (2.11) and (2.12) for the $n + 1$ unknowns will, in general, be fairly tedious. However, in this instance the following systematic procedure may be adopted. Suppose that we are interested in deriving the demand function for the ith commodity. Then we take the first-order condition associated with this good,

$$\frac{g_i}{(X_i - c_i)} \prod_j (X_j - c_j)^{g_i} + \lambda p_i = 0 \tag{2.13}$$

and substitute it into the remaining $n + 1$ first-order conditions so as to eliminate λ. This forms a set of expressions that are equivalent to equation (2.4), indicating that, at the optimum, the ratio of marginal utilities for any two commodities should equal their price ratio; that is,

$$\frac{g_i/(X_i - c_i)}{g_j/(X_j - c_j)} = \frac{p_i}{p_j} \quad (j = 1, \ldots, n) \tag{2.14}$$

For our purposes, it is more convenient to rearrange the various terms of (2.14) so as to yield the set of equations

$$g_i p_1 (X_1 - c_1) = g_1 p_i (X_i - c_i)$$
$$g_i p_2 (X_2 - c_2) = g_2 p_i (X_i - c_i)$$
$$g_i p_n (X_n - c_n) = g_n p_i (X_i - c_i) \tag{2.15}$$

If these are then added together, we obtain

$$g_i \sum p_j X_j - g_i \sum c_j p_j = p_i X_i \sum g_j - c_i p_i \sum g_j \tag{2.16}$$

Two simplifications can now be made. First, we know from the budget constraint that $\sum p_j X_j = Y$. Hence, (2.15) can be rewritten as

$$p_i X_i = \frac{g_i Y}{\sum g_j} + c_i p_i - \frac{g_i}{\sum g_j} \sum c_j p_j \tag{2.17}$$

Second, we can derive expressions similar to (2.17) for each of the n commodities. It is easy to see that the budget constraint will always be satisfied if all of the n equations are added together, because $\sum_i (g_i / \sum g_j) = 1$ suggests the following simplification. Define a new parameter b_i, where $b_i = g_i / \sum g_j$ and $\sum b_i = 1$. Thus, (2.17) can be written finally as

$$p_i X_i = b_i Y_i + c_i p_i - b_i \sum c_j p_j \tag{2.18}$$

This expression has been called the linear expenditure system. It was originally derived by Klein and Rubin (1947–8), although not by the method used here. It has been widely discussed and used as a basis for a considerable amount of applied econometric research. The demand function associated with (2.18) is easily obtained by dividing through by p_i to obtain

$$X_i = b_i \frac{Y}{p_i} + c_i - b_i \sum c_j \frac{p_j}{p_i} \tag{2.19}$$

The properties of this interesting function, together with a generalization, will be discussed in subsequent sections.

It would be extremely convenient if consumer demand functions could be obtained from the first-order conditions for utility maximization in the straightforward manner followed for the linear expenditure system. Unfortunately, things are not so simple. The ordinary demand functions associated with most direct utility functions are not expressible in terms of elementary functional forms. An example is the so-called direct addilog function (see Houthakker, 1960):

$$U = \alpha_1 X_1{}^{\beta_1} + \alpha_2 X_2{}^{\beta_2} + \ldots + \alpha_n X_n{}^{\beta_n} \tag{2.20}$$

where the α_i and β_i are parameters. If (2.20) is maximized by the usual method, we obtain as first-order conditions

$$\alpha_j \beta_j X_j{}^{\beta_j - 1} + \lambda p_j = 0 \quad (j = 1, \ldots, n) \tag{2.21}$$

$$Y - \sum_j p_j X_j = 0 \tag{2.22}$$

It should be immediately obvious that problems exist, because the equations represented by (2.21) involve exponential functions, whereas (2.22) is linear. Indeed, the most that has been accomplished is a pairwise expression. If we take the logarithm of (2.21) and combine the results for any two commodities, say i and k, so as to eliminate λ, we obtain

$$(\beta_i - 1) \ln X_i - (\beta_k - 1) \ln X_k$$
$$= \ln(\alpha_k \beta_k) - \ln(\alpha_i \beta_i) + \ln\left(\frac{Y}{p_k}\right) - \ln\left(\frac{Y}{p_i}\right) \tag{2.23}$$

Although it is not possible to derive simple expressions for the ordinary demand functions associated with (2.20), it is possible to derive the so-called inverse demand functions. That is, it is possible to solve (2.21) and (2.22) for prices in terms of the quantities demanded and total expenditure:

$$p_i = p_i(X_1, \ldots, X_n, Y) \quad (i = 1, \ldots, n) \tag{2.24}$$

Thus, if a consumer were faced with purchasing a given market basket of commodities and if his total income were Y, then the functions (2.24) would indicate those prices consistent with (a) the maximization of satisfaction and (b) the consumption of all items in the market basket. The inverse demand functions associated with (2.20) can be derived by first multiplying (2.21) through by X_j:

$$\alpha_j \beta_j X_j{}^{\beta_j} + \lambda p_j X_j = 0 \quad (j = 1, \ldots, n) \tag{2.25}$$

These relationships are then summed over all commodities and solved for λ:

$$\lambda = -\frac{\sum_j \alpha_j \beta_j X_j{}^{\beta_j}}{Y} \tag{2.26}$$

Substitution of (2.26) into (2.21) yields the inverse demand function

$$p_j = Y \frac{\alpha_j \beta_j X_j^{\beta-1}}{\sum \alpha_j \beta_j X_j^{\beta_j}} \quad (j = 1, \dots, n) \tag{2.27}$$

Additonal discussion of these relationships will be undertaken in Chapter 4 and 5.

2.4   Two restrictions on consumer behavior

As we proceed to develop the linkage between consumer preferences and demands, it will become apparent that the assumptions we have made imply certain restrictions on the set of demand functions. Two such properties should be noted at this juncture. The first is the so-called *adding-up condition,* that is, the sum of expenditures on all individual commodities must equal total expenditure [see equation (2.2)]. This relationship implies two fundamental results that we shall require for our subsequent work. First, differentiate the budget constraint with respect to total expenditure Y:

$$p_1 \frac{\partial X_1}{\partial Y} + p_2 \frac{\partial X_2}{\partial Y} + \dots + p_n \frac{\partial X_n}{\partial Y} = 1 \tag{2.28}$$

In other words, the sum of the marginal propensities to consume the several commodities must equal one. Second, differentiate the budget constraint with respect to any price, p_j:

$$p_1 \frac{\partial X_1}{\partial p_j} + p_2 \frac{\partial X_2}{\partial p_j} + \dots + p_n \frac{\partial X_n}{\partial p_j} = -X_j \tag{2.29}$$

The sum of the various cross-price effects on the left-hand side of (2.29) must equal the negative of the quantity consumed of the jth commodity.

The second restriction implied by the analysis thus far is that the consumer demand functions are homogeneous of degree zero; that is, proportional increases in all prices and total expenditure have a zero effect on all quantities demanded. This result can be determined by first rewriting the budget constraint (2.2) as

$$\sum \frac{p_i}{p_n} X_i = \frac{Y}{p_n} \tag{2.30}$$

As it stands, an infinite number of demand patterns could satisfy this identity, given prices and total expenditure. However, because p_i/p_n equals the ratio of the respective marginal utilities [see equation (2.4)], which remains unchanged for all pairings when prices are varied proportionally, it is clear that only one set of X_i can satisfy (2.30) given an equal proportional change in Y as well. Consequently, if we differentiate any demand function with respect to prices and income and then alter these variables by a proportion θ, we obtain

$$\frac{\partial X_i}{\partial p_1}p_1 + \frac{\partial X_i}{\partial p_2}p_2 + \ldots + \frac{\partial X_i}{\partial p_n}p_n + \frac{\partial X_i}{\partial Y}Y \equiv 0 \qquad (2.31)$$

2.5   Roy's identity and the marginal utility of money

In the discussion in Section 2.2 we treated the Lagrange multiplier basically as a mathematical device for characterizing the maximization process that the consumer is presumed to undertake. However, it has an important economic interpretation in its own right. Consider the following reasoning.

The analysis of the previous sections was carried out in terms of what has come to be called a *direct utility function*. That is, consumer satisfaction is assumed to depend directly on the quantities of goods consumed, as in equations (2.1) and (2.9). However, there is an alternative representation of consumer preferences that will prove to be extremely useful not only for interpreting the Lagrange multiplier but also for understanding more clearly the relationship between consumer preferences and demands. Consider the direct utility function

$$U = U[\phi(X_1, \ldots, X_n)]$$

and the associated demand functions

$$X_i = X_i(Y, p_1, \ldots, p_n) \quad (i = 1, \ldots, n) \qquad (2.32)$$

Each of the functions represented by (2.32) can be substituted into the direct utility function so as to form an expression for consumer preferences in terms of prices and income:

$$U = U\{\phi[X_1(Y, p_1, \ldots, p_n), \ldots, X_n(Y, p_1, \ldots, p_n)]\} \qquad (2.33)$$

$$= U[F(Y, p_1, \ldots, p_n)] = v(Y, p_1, \ldots, p_n) \qquad (2.34)$$

Equation (2.34) is called an *indirect utility function*, because it does not appear to be determined from the X_i, from which satisfaction is directly obtained, but from the Y and p_i, which, by affecting the X_i, indirectly affect consumer satisfaction. It should be emphasized that the indirect utility function (2.34) already embodies the assumption that consumer satisfaction has been maximized. This follows from the fact that the demand functions required to formulate (2.33) are themselves derived on the basis of the maximization process. Consequently, the indirect utility function has the following interpretation: It represents the maximum satisfaction that a consumer can receive from a given income (which is exhausted) and a given set of commodity prices. The question immediately arises: Why not start with the indirect form and use it as a basis for deriving consumer demand functions? Indeed, it was exactly this procedure that René Roy suggested in 1941. To determine what is involved, let us differentiate the utility function (2.34) with respect to prices and income and then use the first-order conditions (2.6) so as to obtain

$$\frac{\partial v}{\partial p_i} = \frac{\partial U}{\partial F}\frac{\partial F}{\partial p_i} = \sum \frac{\partial U}{\partial \phi}\frac{\partial \phi}{\partial X_j}\frac{\partial X_j}{\partial p_i} = \lambda \sum p_j \frac{\partial X_j}{\partial p_i} \quad (i = 1,\ldots,n)$$

(2.35)

$$\frac{\partial v}{\partial Y} = \frac{\partial U}{\partial F}\frac{\partial F}{\partial Y} = \sum \frac{\partial U}{\partial \phi}\frac{\partial \phi}{\partial X_j}\frac{\partial X_j}{\partial Y} = \lambda \sum p_j \frac{\partial X_j}{\partial Y} \tag{2.36}$$

Substitution of (2.28) and (2.29), respectively, into (2.35) and (2.36) enables us to determine that

$$\frac{\partial v}{\partial Y} = \lambda > 0 \tag{2.37}$$

and

$$\frac{\partial v}{\partial p_i} = -\lambda X_i < 0 \quad (i = 1,\ldots,n) \tag{2.38}$$

The sign condition on (2.37) follows from (a) the fact that an increase (decrease) in income represents an expansion (contraction) of the set of feasible consumption patterns available to the individual and (b) the assumption that the consumer never attains a condition of satiation. That is, the greater the level of consumption, the greater the level of satisfaction enjoyed. Because zero or negative consumption is ruled out by assumption, the sign condition (2.38) follows immediately.

The first thing we must notice before proceeding is that if we substitute equation (2.37) into (2.38), we obtain

$$X_i = -\frac{\partial v/\partial p_i}{\partial v/\partial Y} = \frac{(\partial U/\partial F)(\partial F/\partial p_i)}{(\partial U/\partial F)(\partial F/\partial Y)} = \frac{\partial F/\partial p_i}{\partial F/\partial Y} \tag{2.39}$$

an expression widely known as *Roy's identity*. It is an extremely powerful result, for it enables us to postulate a functional form for the indirect utility function(2.34) (on the assumption that its direct counterpart is being maximized) and then derive the associated demand functions directly via equation (2.39). These functions will be completely independent of any monotonic, increasing transformation of the preference system described by F, a result that can be directly seen from (2.39). No matter what form we choose for the transformation U, it will leave the demand functions unchanged.

Equation (2.37) indicates that the Lagrange multiplier, which forms the denominator of the demand function (2.33), can be interpreted as the *marginal utility of money expenditure*. Unfortunately, this widely used title gives the impression that it refers to a very objective, scientific measure. Indeed, over the years there have been several attempts to quantify this term. However, no pursuit could be more fruitless. From equation (2.36) we see that we could have written the marginal utility of expenditure as

$$\frac{\partial v}{\partial Y} = \frac{\partial U}{\partial F}\frac{\partial F}{\partial Y} = \lambda \tag{2.40}$$

In other words, there exists another marginal utility of expenditure λ' such that

$$\lambda = \frac{\partial U}{\partial F}\lambda' \tag{2.41}$$

and λ' is associated with the function $F(Y, p_1, \ldots, p_n)$. Because this is true for any monotonic, increasing transformation U of F, there exists a virtual infinity of marginal utility of expenditure expressions that are associated with any preference system and its related set of demand functions. This does not mean, however, that we can arbitrarily pick just any constant number to serve as a Lagrange multiplier. Although λ depends on an arbitrary transformation, it also depends on the relationship between the utility function and total expenditure, under the assumption, of course, that the consumer is maximizing his level of satisfaction subject to the budget constraint. This is easily seen from (2.40).

We are now in a position to state a number of properties possessed by the marginal utility of money:

1. $\lambda > 0$. This follows from (2.37). This result is not modified by a monotonic, increasing transformation of U, because $\partial U/\partial F > 0$, as in (2.41).
2. λ is homogeneous of degree minus one. This is due to the fact that the consumer preference system is homogeneous of degree zero.
3. The derivative of the marginal utility of income may be of any sign; that is,

$$\frac{\partial \lambda}{\partial Y} \lesseqgtr 0 \tag{2.42}$$

This last result has already been established from the diagrammatic discussion presented in Chapter 1. However, it also becomes apparent when (2.41) is differentiated with respect to income:

$$\frac{\partial \lambda}{\partial Y} = \frac{\partial U}{\partial F}\frac{\partial \lambda'}{\partial Y} + \frac{\partial^2 U}{\partial F^2}\left(\frac{\partial \lambda'}{\partial Y}\right)^2 \tag{2.43}$$

It is frequently assumed that the marginal utility of income declines as income increases (see Frisch, 1959, p. 189). Let us suppose that this is indeed the case for the utility function associated with λ'. Thus, $(\partial U/\partial F)(\partial \lambda'/\partial Y)$ will also be negative. However, there is no such sign constraint on the second derivative $\partial^2 U/\partial F^2$. This can be positive or negative, and consequently so can the second term on the right-hand side of (2.43). If $\partial^2 U/\partial F^2$ is sufficiently large and positive, then $\partial \lambda/\partial Y$ can be positive even though $\partial \lambda'/\partial Y$ is negative. The same reasoning also enables us to determine that $\partial \lambda/\partial p_i$ can take on any sign.

2.6   The integrating factor and the marginal utility of money

In the preceding section we have shown that demand functions can be derived from direct or indirect preference systems. In addition, we have shown how preference and demand functions are directly related to the Lagrange multiplier or marginal utility of expenditure, even though the latter are, of course, not invariant under monotonic, increasing transformations of consumer preference functions. We are now in a position to reverse this process and inquire into the procedures necessary to derive a preference ordering from information contained in consumer demand functions.

For suitably small changes in prices and expenditure, there is, in principle, no difficulty in achieving this aim. If preferences are described by any general indirect function (2.34), then we can express a change in the level of satisfaction as

$$dU = \frac{\partial U}{\partial F}\sum \frac{\partial F}{\partial p_i}dp_i + \frac{\partial U}{\partial F}\frac{\partial U}{\partial Y}dY \tag{2.44}$$

Because $(\partial U/\partial F)\cdot(\partial F/\partial p_i) = -\lambda X_i$ and $(\partial U/\partial F)\cdot(\partial F/\partial Y) = \lambda$ from the first-order conditions for utility maximization, we can rewrite (2.44) as

$$dU = \lambda[dY - \sum X_i(Y, p_1, \ldots, p_n)\,dp_i] \tag{2.45}$$

As we have just seen in the preceding section, the marginal utility of total expenditure λ is not invariant under any monotonic transformation of the consumer preference function. However, it is always positive. In addition, the first-order conditions hold exactly. Thus, for any price/quantity situation, the change in satisfaction will have the same sign as

$$dW = dY - \sum X_i(Y, p_1, \ldots, p_n)\, dp_i \tag{2.46}$$

an indicator involving observable information about prices and quantities. For the economic theorist, an expression such as (2.46) is capable of providing a good deal of information about local conditions. However, a considerable jump in reasoning is required if we are to say that this differential equation is also acceptable when expressed in terms of discrete changes, namely,

$$\Delta W = \Delta Y - \sum X_i \Delta p_i \tag{2.47}$$

Indeed, the terms on the right-hand side of (2.47) can be thought of as the first-order terms of a Taylor series approximation. The problem then arises that the higher-order terms that go to make up the "remainder" may be sufficiently important to render this expression useless as an approximation. It is simply that the magnitude of this expression may be wrong; it is possible, and indeed likely, that it will yield the incorrect sign. This is a matter of some considerable importance, and it will be examined thoroughly in Chapter 6.

Our aim here, however, is more ambitious than determining the sign of welfare change: We are actually concerned with the construction of an identifiable functional form representing consumer preferences. The most straightforward way of approaching this task is to calculate any non-small changes in satisfaction by means of a line integral formed from the differential equation (2.44). Thus, we can write

$$\Delta \nu = \int_c \left(\sum \frac{\partial \nu}{\partial p_i}\, dp_i + \frac{\partial \nu}{\partial Y}\, dY \right) \tag{2.48}$$

Because this is no ordinary integral, some explanation is in order. Let us suppose that we partition our calculation of the change in utility due to price and income variations into a series of steps. First, let us calculate the change in ν due to the change in Y:

$$\Delta \nu_Y = \int_{Y^0}^{Y^1} \frac{\partial \nu}{\partial Y}(Y, p_1^0, \ldots, p_n^0)\, dY \tag{2.49}$$

Next we calculate the change in money-metric satisfaction due to a change in p_1, but on the assumption that expenditure is now at its new level Y^1:

$$\Delta \nu_1 = \int_{p_1^0}^{p^1} \frac{\partial \nu}{\partial p_1} (Y^1, p_1, p_2^0, \dots, p_n^0) \, dp_1 \tag{2.50}$$

Third, we calculate the change in money-metric satisfaction due to a change in p_2, but on that assumption that both Y and p_1 are at their new levels:

$$\Delta \nu_2 = \int_{p_2^0}^{p_2^1} \frac{\partial \nu}{\partial p_2} (Y^1, p_1^1, p_2, p_3^0, \dots, p_n^0) \, dp_1 \tag{2.51}$$

Next, we calculate the change in satisfaction due to a variation in p_3, but on the assumption that now Y, p_1, and p_2 are at their new levels. And so forth for all price variations. We can then add up all the constituent parts to obtain the total change in satisfaction:

$$\Delta \nu = \Delta \nu_Y + \sum \Delta \nu_i \tag{2.52}$$

In terms of a two-dimensional example, as illustrated in Figure 2.1, we might have a change in satisfaction from A to B due to an increase in total expenditure; then we have a change in satisfaction from B to C due to an increase in the price of commodity 1; and finally we have the change from C to D due the reduction in the price of commodity 2. The sum of these component changes is exactly equal to the change in satisfaction that would be calculated if we moved directly from A to D rather than in the stepwise fashion just described. It should be noted that both moves are equivalent to an increase in income equal to GH, where we have chosen to normalize the price of X_1 at one. This calculation is independent of the path of integration. In the general case, we could have first integrated with respect to p_n, then p_{n-1}, and so forth. Or we could have chosen any other sequence or path to carry out the calculation. It makes no difference. However, this is not a general result that can be applied to all differential equations without restriction. In mathematical terms, the procedure is applicable if the differential equation under examination is exact. This will occur if and only if

$$\frac{\partial(\partial \nu / \partial p_i)}{\partial p_j} = \frac{\partial(\partial \nu / \partial p_j)}{\partial p_i} \tag{2.53}$$

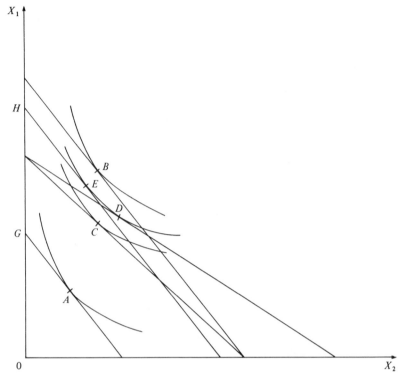

Figure 2.1

and

$$\frac{\partial(\partial v/\partial Y)}{\partial p_i} = \frac{\partial(\partial v/\partial p_i)}{\partial Y} \tag{2.54}$$

We then say that the differential equation (2.46) is integrable and that there exists an integrating factor such that (2.45) is exact. Hence, any change in utility v can be expressed as an integral such as (2.48). This terminology is simply a way of indicating that we need not worry about the path of integration.

To a mathematician, the analysis presented thus far in this section probably will appear to be superfluous. After all, we have assumed to begin with that the function $v = v(p_1, \dots, p_n, Y)$ does exist. Thus, having expressed it in terms of a differential equation, there is no difficulty in retrieving the original function U. The differential equation (2.45) is exact by definition.

Nevertheless, we have established some important principles that enable us to approach the following problem: Suppose that we do not know the form of the consumer preference system but that we set out by positing a set of demand functions. (As we hinted in Section 2.1, these functions cannot take any arbitrary form, a point we shall continue to develop in the remainder of this chapter.) The problem then becomes one of finding an expression for the marginal utility of total expenditure λ such that we can use the demand functions to form the exact differential equation given by (2.45). The importance of determining a form for this term is apparent if we rewrite the integrability conditions (2.53) and (2.54):

$$\frac{\partial(\lambda X_i)}{\partial p_j} = \frac{\partial(\lambda X_j)}{\partial p_i} \tag{2.55}$$

$$\frac{\partial \lambda}{\partial p_i} = -\frac{\partial(\lambda X_i)}{\partial Y} \tag{2.56}$$

The problem is that without knowledge of the utility function, the search for an expression for the marginal utility of total expenditure becomes a hit-or-miss exercise. In mathematical terms, we are searching for an *integrating factor* equal to the marginal utility of expenditure λ. Unfortunately, no mathematician has been able to devise a systematic procedure for discovering this factor that will work in all circumstances. In point of fact, it may not be possible to express the integrating factor in terms of elementary functions, even though, in principle, such a factor may exist. In addition, even though we may know λ, it still may not be possible to undertake the desired integration, except by numerical methods. This issue will be discussed in the next chapter.

Because of this difficulty, many economists have attempted to determine the conditions that would have to exist for the integrating factor to be independent of the variables under consideration. In general, this is equivalent to requiring that equation (2.46) rather than (2.45) be exact. Others, such as Hause (1975), Burns (1973), and Willig (1976), have claimed that the problem of path independence is a theoretical problem rather than a practical problem and hence need not be of concern in applied welfare economics. These two approaches will be critically evaluated in subsequent chapters.

2.7 Restrictions on the parameters of consumer demand functions imposed by integrability

The integrability conditions derived in the preceding section impose very definite restrictions on the parameters of consumer demand functions. These can be derived in the following manner: First, carry out the differentiation indicated by (2.55) and (2.56):

$$\frac{\partial \lambda}{\partial p_j} X_i + \lambda \frac{\partial X_i}{\partial p_j} = \frac{\partial \lambda}{\partial p_i} X_j + \lambda \frac{\partial X_j}{\partial p_i} \tag{2.57}$$

$$\frac{\partial \lambda}{\partial p_i} = -\frac{\partial \lambda}{\partial Y} X_i - \lambda \frac{\partial X_i}{\partial Y} \tag{2.58}$$

Substitution of (2.58) into (2.57) yields

$$-X_i\left(\frac{\partial \lambda}{\partial Y} X_j + \lambda \frac{\partial X_j}{\partial Y}\right) + \lambda \frac{\partial X_i}{\partial p_j} = -X_j\left(\frac{\partial \lambda}{\partial Y} X_i + \lambda \frac{\partial X_i}{\partial Y}\right) + \lambda \frac{\partial X_j}{\partial p_i} \tag{2.59}$$

which simplifies into the expression

$$-X_i \frac{\partial X_j}{\partial Y} + \frac{\partial X_i}{\partial p_j} = -X_j \frac{\partial X_i}{\partial Y} + \frac{\partial X_j}{\partial p_i} \tag{2.60}$$

Hence, a relationship of the form (2.60) must exist between all quantities demanded and the income and price effects. It should be noted that the integrating factor or marginal utility of expenditure is not involved in this revised form of the integrability condition.

Equation (2.60) has an alternative interpretation that is of considerable historical interest. Let us suppose that the price of a particular commodity, say the jth, changes and that in response we vary total expenditure so as to maintain the level of consumer satisfaction constant. We then inquire as to the net effect this procedure has on the quantity demanded of any particular commodity, say the ith. If we differentiate the demand function for X_i so as to reflect the foregoing action, we obtain

$$\frac{dX_i}{dp_j} = \frac{\partial X_i}{\partial p_j} + \frac{\partial X_i}{\partial Y}\frac{dY}{dp_j}\bigg|_{v=c} \tag{2.61}$$

The first component on the right-hand side is an ordinary price effect indicating the response of X_i to a change in p_j, *ceteris paribus*. The second term on the right is an income effect indicating the response of X_i to the change in income designed to maintain the level of satisfaction v constant. If we now differentiate the indirect utility function with respect to p_j and Y and set $dv = 0$, we obtain

$$dv = \frac{\partial v}{\partial p_j} dp_j + \frac{\partial v}{\partial Y} dY = 0 \tag{2.62}$$

Making use of Roy's identity and rearranging terms, we find an expression for $dY/dp_j|_{v=c}$ as follows:

$$\left.\frac{dY}{dp_j}\right|_{v=c} = -\frac{\partial U/\partial p_j}{\partial U/\partial Y} = X_j\Big|_{v=c} \qquad (2.63)$$

Hence, equation (2.61) can be rewritten as

$$\sigma_{ij} = \frac{\partial X_i}{\partial p_j} + X_j\frac{\partial X_i}{\partial Y} = \left.\frac{dX_i}{dp_j}\right|_{v=c} \quad (i,j = 1,\ldots,n) \qquad (2.64)$$

This is the so-called *compensated price effect* (for X_i given a change in p_j). It is also known as the Slutsky equation, after the Russian economist who developed it in 1915.

If we rearrange the terms in the integrability condition (2.60), we find that there must be perfect symmetry of these price effects. In other words,

$$\sigma_{ij} = \sigma_{ji} \quad (i = j; \, i,g = 1,\ldots,n) \qquad (2.65)$$

where this condition simply represents an alternative statement of the integrability condition.

Another important property of these substitution effects follows from the second-order condition associated with the maximization of consumer satisfaction (2.08): The matrix of Slutsky substitution effects must be negative semidefinite. This implies that the principal minors of this matrix must alternate in sign. That is,

$$\sigma_{ii} < 0$$

$$\begin{vmatrix} \sigma_{ii} & \sigma_{ij} \\ \sigma_{ji} & \sigma_{jj} \end{vmatrix} > 0$$

$$\begin{vmatrix} \sigma_{ii} & \sigma_{ij} & \sigma_{ik} \\ \sigma_{ji} & \sigma_{jj} & \sigma_{jk} \\ \sigma_{ki} & \sigma_{kj} & \sigma_{kk} \end{vmatrix} < 0 \qquad (2.66)$$

and so forth. Stated in this way, this restriction is very tedious to check. However, (2.66) means that the matrix of substitution effects is negative semidefinite, and hence

$$\sum_i \sum_j \sigma_{ij}z_i z_j \leq 0 \qquad (2.67)$$

where $(z_1,\ldots,z_n)$ is any vector of real variables not equal to zero. For a formal discussion of (2.66) and (2.67) and their relationship to the second-order conditions for utility maximization, the reader is referred to the work of Pearce (1964, especially Chapter 1).

Of particular interest in the preceding discussion is the result that the diagonal elements of the matrix of substitution effects must be negative. Thus, whenever a price increases and the consumer is compensated so that his level of satisfaction remains unchanged, it is still the case that the consumer will purchase less of the commodity whose price has increased.

No such strong sign conditions can be placed on the off-diagonal substitution terms. However, the following result does impose a restriction on the possible sign patterns that the σ_{ij} can take. Calculate the following sum:

$$\sum p_i \sigma_{ij} = \sum p_i \frac{\partial X_i}{\partial p_j} + X_j \sum p_i \frac{\partial X_i}{\partial Y}$$
$$= -X_j + X_j = 0 \tag{2.68}$$

a result that follows immediately from (2.23) and (2.24). Because $\sigma_{ii} < 0$, it must then be true that

$$\sum_{i \neq j} p_i \sigma_{ij} > 0 \tag{2.69}$$

This imposes the further restriction that at least one σ_{ij} must be positive.

In this section, two important results have come to the fore. First, if we are interested in drawing welfare implications from consumer demand functions, it is not sufficient to posit any arbitrary function without restriction. By way of summary, it is necessary that the functions possess the following characteristics. The first two were derived in Section 2.4.

1. Consumer demands must add up so as to exhaust the expenditure available for consumption.
2. The demand functions must be homogeneous of degree zero.
3. The integrability conditions must hold. This amounts to saying that the matrix of Slutsky substitution terms should be symmetric.
4. The matrix of Slutsky substitution terms should be negative semi-definite. This implies that $\sigma_{ii} < 0$.
5. The condition

$$\sum_i p_i \sigma_{ij} = 0$$

must hold.

But this is only half the solution. Once we have written down a set of demand functions that satisfy the properties 1 to 5, we must still determine an expression for the integrating factor or marginal utility of expenditure. As we have already noted, this probably will not be an easy task. However, we shall leave the solution of this problem for the next chapter.

2.8   The equivalence or money-metric function

On the basis of the analysis carried out thus far in this chapter, we are now in a position to deal with the issue of expressing consumer preferences in the form of a money-metric. Consider again the indirect preference function (2.34). Because utility is a monotonic, increasing function of total expenditure, we can invert this function so as to obtain a new relationship, which we shall name a *cost-of-utility function:*

$$C = C(v, p_1, \ldots, p_n) \tag{2.70}$$

This relationship indicates the amount of money income (equal to total expenditure) required to achieve the level of satisfaction U given any set of prices $(p_1, \ldots, p_n)$. Because v is the satisfaction generated by expenditure Y and the set of commodity prices $(p_1, \ldots, p_n)$, it must be the case that C equal to Y represents the cost or expenditure level required to sustain v, given commodity prices.

At this stage the reader should be warned that there is the potential for confusing some of the uses to which the cost-of-utility function can be put. A clear understanding of what is involved can be achieved only by adopting clear and straightforward terminology. For one thing, equation (2.70) often is referred to as an *expenditure function*. In this volume we shall avoid this usage. First of all, the term *cost-of-utility function* indicates reasonably clearly what is being calculated. Second, the term *expenditure function* appears to be somewhat ambiguous in view of the two measures that are based on (2.70).

The first and most important relationship from the point of view of this volume is the *equivalence function* or *money-metric*. Choose any set of prices, say those currently existing, as a base or reference set $(p_1^0, \ldots, p_n^0)$. Then

$$M = C[v(Y, p_1, \ldots, p_n); p_1^0, \ldots, p_n^0] \tag{2.71}$$

indicates the cost of achieving any level of satisfaction v, as generated by Y and the set of prices $(p_1, \ldots, p_n)$, but given the base set of prices. This is exactly the money-metric referred to in Chapter 1.

The equivalence or money-metric function possesses several important and useful properties:

1.   If we subtract the level of expenditure associated with the base or reference situation Y_0, we obtain the equivalent variation EV:

$$EV = M - Y^0 \tag{2.72}$$

To repeat the definition presented in Chapter 1, we note that the equivalent variation indicates the change in total expenditure, given base prices, required to generate the same change in satisfaction as generated by a set of prices different from those holding in the base situation.

2.   It is easy to see that M is a monotonic, increasing transformation of v and hence is a welfare indicator in its own right. Thus, we have established that a monetary measure of satisfaction does exist, provided, of course, that consumers do act according to a preference function. As such, it must possess all the properties of such a function. The same is also true for the equivalent variation, which differs from M only by the scalar Y^0. However, both the money-metric and the equivalent variation are invariant under increasing, monotonic transformations of the underlying preference function.

3.   As a consequence of property 2, it is obvious that the equivalence function possesses all the characteristics of an indirect preference function. That is,

$$\frac{\partial M}{\partial p_i} < 0 \tag{2.73}$$

and

$$\frac{\partial M}{\partial Y} > 0 \tag{2.74}$$

In addition, the equivalence function is homogeneous of degree 0 in prices and total expenditure.

4.   The transformation involved in the preceding formulation implies very specific values for the marginal utility of expenditure and its derivatives with respect to expenditure *when these are evaluated at the base set of prices*. It is immediately obvious that the cost of utility associated with the level of satisfaction generated by Y and $(p_1^0, \ldots, p_n^0)$, that is, by

$$v(Y, p_1^0, \ldots, p_n^0) \tag{2.75}$$

is Y itself. And, quite obviously, any change in income is equivalent to itself in money-metric terms, given initial prices. This means that the following relationships must hold:

$$\lambda(Y, p_1^0, \ldots, p_n^0) \equiv 1 \tag{2.76}$$

and

$$\frac{\partial^r \lambda}{\partial Y^r}(Y, p_1^0, \ldots, p_n^0) \equiv 0 \quad (r = 1, \ldots, \infty) \tag{2.77}$$

It should be emphasized that this result holds true only at initial prices. The particular transformation of preferences we have chosen implies that we are in a position to interpret λ now as the marginal money-metric utility of income. However, we shall retain the more traditional usage of marginal utility of money or income for ease of exposition.

The equations represented by (2.76) and (2.77) will play an important role in the numerical analysis to be developed in the next chapter. To set the stage for that discussion, it is helpful to recast the discussion of integrability contained in Section 2.6 in terms of the money-metric. First, let us consider the effect of a variation in total expenditure on consumer satisfaction. The integral expression (2.49) can now be rewritten

$$\Delta M_Y = \int_{Y^0}^{Y^1} \frac{\partial M}{\partial Y}(Y, p_1^0, \ldots, p_n^0) \, dY \tag{2.78}$$

Because we know that $\partial M / \partial Y$ equals one when evaluated at base prices, ΔM_Y must equal total expenditure ΔY. However, the remaining expressions to be evaluated in (2.48),

$$\Delta M_i = \int_{p_i^0}^{p_i^1} \frac{\partial M}{\partial p_i}(Y^1, p_1^1, \ldots, p_{i-1}^1, p_i, p_{i+1}^0, \ldots, p_n^0) \, dp_i$$

$$(i = 1, \ldots, n) \tag{2.79}$$

do not reduce to such a simple analysis and must await the application of numerical procedures. However, once the expressions described by (2.79) are evaluated, then the total change in the money-metric (equal to the equivalent variation) can be calculated as

$$\Delta M = \Delta Y + \sum \Delta M_i \tag{2.80}$$

2.9   The compensation function

Although most of our analysis will be in terms of the money-metric, it is important to consider an alternative measure that can be constructed from the cost-of-utility function (2.70). Consider any level of satisfaction defined by the expenditure level and set of prices holding in the base or reference situation, that is, $\nu^0 = \nu\ (Y^0, p_1^0, \ldots, p_n^0)$. Then

$$H = C[\nu(Y^0, p_1^0, \ldots, p_n^0); p_1, \ldots, p_n] \tag{2.81}$$

indicates the cost of achieving ν^0 on the basis of any alternative set of prices $(p_1, \ldots, p_n)$.

Like the equivalence function, the compensation function is a monetary measure. But there the similarity ends: The most important difference is that H is not an ordinal welfare metric. This should be intuitively obvious from the fact that the compensation function is defined with respect to a given level of satisfaction, and hence it is not immediately obvious how we can rewrite (2.81) in such a way that it appears as an increasing, monotonic transformation of the underlying preference function. Before establishing that this is not possible, in general, we note the following properties:

  1. The compensating variation CV is defined as

$$\begin{aligned}
\mathrm{CV} &= C(\nu^0, p^j) - C(\nu^0, p^0) \\
&= C(\nu^0, p^j) - Y^0
\end{aligned} \tag{2.82}$$

That is, this amount represents the difference between the cost of achieving some reference level of satisfaction ν^0 given any vector of prices p^j and the initial level of expenditure Y^0 (i.e., the cost of maintaining ν^0 at prices p^0). This measure indicates the compensation that would have to be paid (if there was a gain) or received (if there was a loss) for the initial level of satisfaction to be maintained following some variation in prices. As we have already noted, this measure forms the basis for a good deal of applied welfare economics and will be the subject of detailed scrutiny in subsequent chapters. For the moment, we note the following important property:

  2. The compensation function is an ordinal money-metric if and only if preferences are homothetic. To show this, we note first that an ordinal indicator should generate the same value of H along any indifference surface. Hence, it follows that having chosen a base or initial set of prices and total expenditure $(Y^0, p_1^0, \ldots, p_n^0)$, a movement from that situation to any point along another indifference surface should always generate the same change in the value of H. That is, the compensating variation associated with a move from one indifference

surface to another should remain constant irrespective of the price vectors that generate the two alternative levels of satisfaction. Thus, we may write

$$\frac{C(v^i, p^j)}{C(v^i, p^k)} = 1 \quad (i, j, k = 0, \ldots, s) \tag{2.83}$$

where s represents the number of alternatives being compared. In addition,

$$CV = C(v^i, p^j) - C(v^0, p^j) = C(v^i, p^k) - C(v^0, p^k) \tag{2.84}$$

where v is any level of satisfaction different from v^0. If we now combine (2.83) and (2.84) and rearrange terms, we obtain the condition that

$$\frac{C(v^i, p^j)}{C(v^i, p^k)} = \frac{C(v^0, p^j)}{C(v^0, p^k)} \quad (i, j, k = 0, \ldots, s) \tag{2.85}$$

In other words, the ratios appearing in (2.85) must be independent of the level of satisfaction. That is,

$$\partial \left[\frac{C(v; p^j)}{C(v; p^k)} \right] \Big/ \partial v = 0 \tag{2.86}$$

This implies that $C = \phi(v) \cdot \theta(p)$ or, equivalently, that

$$V = \phi(v) = Y/\theta(p) \tag{2.87}$$

where $\theta(p)$ is homogeneous of degree one in prices. It is immediately obvious that

$$\theta(p^j) = \theta(p^k) \quad (j, k = 0, \ldots, s) \tag{2.88}$$

along any indifference surface on the assumption that Y remains constant.

That preferences should be of the form indicated by (2.87) is a necessary and sufficient condition for homotheticity; that is, all income expansion paths or Engel curves should be linear and pass through the origin. An alternative way of stating this definition is that the ratio of consumption of any two commodities is independent of the level of income. Hence,

$$\frac{\partial(x_j/x_k)}{\partial Y} = \frac{\partial[\partial v/\partial p_j/(\partial v/\partial p_k)]}{\partial Y} = 0 \tag{2.89}$$

A necessary and sufficient condition for (2.89) to equal zero is that preferences be of the form (2.87).

3.   The compensation function is homogeneous of degree one in prices. This follows immediately from the fact that the indirect preference function is homogeneous of degree zero in prices and total expenditure. Hence, if prices double, the original level of satisfaction can be supported only if total expenditure, as indicated by H, also doubles.

4.   The derivative of the compensation function (2.81) with respect to any price p_j indicates the amount of money to be paid or received following a variation in p_j. Hence, from (2.63),

$$\frac{dH}{dp_j} = \frac{\partial H}{\partial p_j} = \frac{dY}{dp_j}\bigg|_{u=c} = X_j\bigg|_{u=c} > 0 \tag{2.90}$$

This result is frequently referred to as Shephard's lemma (1953), and it indicates that any price increase (decrease) will require compensation to be received (to be paid) so as to maintain ν at a constant level. This procedure also provides a straightforward method for deriving the so-called compensated demand function that played such an important role in Hicks's attempt to rehabilitate consumer surplus procedures. This topic will be developed in further detail in Chapter 5.

5.   The matrix of second-order derivatives $\partial^2 H/\partial p_i \partial p_j$ is negative semidefinite. This follows immediately from the fact that these derivatives represent the compensated or Slutsky price effects

$$\sigma_{ij} = \frac{\partial X_j}{\partial p_i}\bigg|_{u=c} = \frac{\partial^2 H}{\partial p_j \partial p_i}$$

discussed in Section 2.7. This property also follows from the fact that the compensation function is concave. [For a clear discussion of this point, see the work of Varian (1978).] A particular implication of negative semidefiniteness is that as compensation increases as a result of a rise, say in p_1, this will occur only at a diminishing rate. That is, the marginal compensation decreases as prices rise, and conversely. This result follows immediately from the fact that the second derivative $\partial^2 H/\partial p_j^2$ equals the Slutsky own-price effect σ_{jj}. Thus,

$$\frac{\partial^2 H}{\partial p_j^2} = \frac{\partial X_j}{\partial p_j}\bigg|_{u=c} = \sigma_{jj} < 0 \quad (j = 1,\dots,n) \tag{2.91}$$

The sign condition follows immediately from (2.66).

2.10   The relationship between the equivalent and compensating variations

The most important difference between the equivalence function and the compensation function is that the former produces an ordinal money-metric, whereas the latter does not, except in the case of homo-thetic preferences. However, the fact that the two are both derived from the cost-of-utility function does impart a certain similarity that is capable of generating some misunderstanding. Consider the following argument. It is apparent that the cost of today's satisfaction level evaluated at today's prices is simply today's total expenditure, namely,

$$Y^0 = C[\nu(Y^0, p^0), p^0] \tag{2.92}$$

$$Y^1 = C[\nu(Y^1, p^1), p^1] \tag{2.93}$$

Consequently, by adding and subtracting Y^1, we can rewrite the expression for the equivalent variation (2.72) as

$$\begin{aligned}
\text{EV} &= C[\nu(Y^1, p^1), p^0] - Y^0 \\
&= C[\nu(Y^1, p^1), p^0] - Y^1 + (Y^1 - Y^0) \\
&= C[\nu(Y^1, p^1), p^0] - C[\nu(Y^1, p^1), p^1] + (Y^1 - Y^0)
\end{aligned} \tag{2.94}$$

The difference between the two cost-function expressions on the right-hand side of (2.94) indicates the compensation required to maintain the new level of satisfaction $\nu(Y^1, p^1)$ following a move from situation 1 to situation 0. Thus, if, for example, total expenditure remains unchanged, the equivalent variation associated with a move from situation 0 to situation 1 is exactly equal to the negative of the compensating variation associated with a move from 1 to 0. However, the latter is not equal to the compensating variation as traditionally defined, that is, the amount of money required to maintain the initial level of satisfaction following a variation in prices, equation (2.82). Thus, (2.94) is simply another way of writing the equivalent variation or money-metric; it is not the same as (2.82), the compensating variation.

These considerations enable us to expand on an important point raised in Chapter 1. Both the equivalent and compensating variations are suitable for binary welfare comparisons. For example, if a particular project or policy is equivalent to a reduction in income, it is also true that positive compensation will have to be paid in order to maintain the initial level of satisfaction. However, as the analysis contained in Sections 2.8 and 2.9 has highlighted, only the equivalent variation is capable of performing the role of a money-metric. From a practical point of view, it is this consideration that is paramount. Many, if not most, problems of interest involve the comparison of several options, not just two. In these circumstances it is economically sensible to wish to construct a scale against which all possibilities can be compared. The equivalent variation fulfills this objective.

2.11   An example

In order to appreciate the important results derived in the previous
sections, it will be useful to illustrate them by means of a straightforward example. Earlier in this chapter we posited a particular preference function, equation (2.9), that was used as a basis for deriving
a set of linear expenditure equations (2.18). In point of fact, the
original work on this system by Klein and Rubin took the expenditure
system as the starting point and then determined the parameter restrictions necessary to satisfy the theory of consumer behavior. Subsequently, Geary (1950) derived the utility function associated with
this system. Because this is the procedure in which we are interested,
it is useful to review the steps involved.

Consider the unconstrained linear expenditure system

$$p_i X_i = \beta_i Y + \sum_j \alpha_{ij} p_j \quad (i = 1, \dots, n) \tag{2.92}$$

It is easy to see that the demand function for X_i is homogeneous of
degree zero by dividing (2.92) through by p_i. In addition, the adding-
up condition is met provided that $\sum \beta_i = 1$. However, the restrictions implied by the symmetry of the matrix of Slutsky compensated
price effects (2.65) are more difficult to determine. From (2.92) we
know that

$$\frac{\partial X_i}{\partial p_j} = \frac{\alpha_{ij}}{p_i} \tag{2.93}$$

$$\frac{\partial X_i}{\partial Y} = \frac{\beta_i}{p_i} \tag{2.94}$$

Therefore, equation (2.65) implies

$$\frac{\alpha_{ij}}{p_i} + X_j \frac{\beta_i}{p_i} = \frac{\alpha_{ji}}{p_j} + X_i \frac{\beta_j}{p_i} \tag{2.95}$$

If we multiply (2.95) through by $p_k p_j$, substitute the expenditure equations defined by (2.92), and rearrange terms, we obtain

$$\beta_i \sum_{\substack{k \neq i \\ k \neq j}} \alpha_{jk} p_k + \alpha_{ij}(1 - \beta_j) p_j + \beta_i \alpha_{jj} p_j$$

$$= \beta_j \sum_{\substack{k \neq i \\ k \neq j}} \alpha_{ik} p_k + \alpha_{ji}(1 - \beta_i) p_i + \beta_j \alpha_{ii} p_i \tag{2.96}$$

The only general restriction that will hold for all pairs of commodities and all prices is the one where

$$\alpha_{ij} = -\beta_j \gamma_j \quad (i = j) \tag{2.97}$$

$$\alpha_{ii} = (1 - \beta_i)\gamma_i \tag{2.98}$$

where the γ_i are parameters defined by (2.97) and (2.98). If we now substitute these conditions back into (2.92), we obtain the system as discovered by Klein and Rubin:

$$p_i X_i = \beta_i Y + \gamma_i p_i - \beta_i \sum \gamma_k p_k \tag{2.99}$$

[The β_i and γ_i parameters are, respectively, identical with the b_i and c_i parameters of (2.18).] In order to be able to derive a functional representation of this system, we need to be able to find an integrating factor such that

$$\frac{\partial(\lambda X_i)}{\partial p_j} = \frac{\partial(\lambda X_j)}{\partial p_i}$$

or, equivalently, such that

$$
\gamma_i \frac{\partial \lambda}{\partial p_j} - \frac{\lambda \beta_i \gamma_j}{p_i} + \frac{\beta_i(Y - \sum \gamma_k p_k)}{p_i} \frac{\partial \lambda}{\partial p_j}
$$
$$
= \gamma_j \frac{\partial \lambda}{\partial p_i} - \frac{\lambda \beta_j \gamma_i}{p_j} + \frac{\beta_j(Y - \sum \gamma_k p_k)}{p_j} \frac{\partial \lambda}{\partial p_i} \tag{2.100}
$$

One such integrating factor is

$$\lambda = \prod_k^n \left(\frac{\beta_k}{p_k}\right)^{\beta_k} \tag{2.101}$$

where

$$\frac{\partial \lambda}{\partial p_i} = -\frac{\beta_i}{p_i} \prod_k^n \left(\frac{\beta_k}{p_k}\right)^{\beta_k} = -\frac{\beta_i}{p_i}\lambda \quad (i = 1, \ldots, n) \tag{2.102}$$

Substituting (2.102) for $\partial \lambda / \partial p_i$ and $\partial \lambda / \partial p_j$ in (2.100), we see that the condition for integrability is met. Hence,

$$
\nu = \int_c \frac{\partial \nu}{\partial p_i} dp_i = -\int_c \sum \lambda X_i \, dp_i
$$
$$
= -\int_c \sum \left[\gamma_i + \beta_i \frac{(Y - \sum \gamma_k p_k)}{p_i}\right] \prod_k^n \left(\frac{\beta_k}{p_k}\right)^{\beta_k}
$$
$$
= \left[Y - \sum \gamma_k p_k\right] \prod_k^n \left(\frac{\beta_k}{p_k}\right)^{\beta_k} \tag{2.103}
$$

The indirect preference function (2.103) can now be inverted to solve for the level of total expenditure or income necessary to support any particular level of satisfaction. Consequently, the cost-of-utility function associated with the Klein-Rubin system is

$$C = v \Big/ \prod_k^n \left(\frac{\beta_k}{p_k}\right)^{\beta_k} + \sum \gamma_j p_j \qquad (2.104)$$

Hence, the *money-metric* can be written as

$$M = \prod_i^n \left(\frac{p_i^0}{p_i}\right)^{\beta_i} \left(Y - \sum \gamma_j p_j\right) + \sum \gamma_j p_j^0 \qquad (2.105)$$

and the *compensation function* as

$$H = \prod_i^n \left(\frac{p_i}{p_i^0}\right)^{\beta_i} \left(Y^0 - \sum \gamma_j p_j^0\right) + \sum \gamma_j p_j \qquad (2.106)$$

It is easily seen that the marginal utility of total expenditure associated with the money-metric M is

$$\lambda = \frac{\partial M}{\partial Y}(Y, p_1^0, \dots, p_n^0) = \prod_i^n \left(\frac{p_i^0}{p_i}\right)^{\beta_i} \qquad (2.107)$$

which equals one when evaluated at base prices. In addition,

$$\frac{\partial^r C}{\partial Y^r}(Y, p_1^0, \dots, p_n^0) = 0 \quad (r = 1, \dots, \infty) \qquad (2.108)$$

For the functional form chosen for this example, equation (2.108) holds for all possible prices. However, for more complex relationships, it will be true only for the initial or base price levels.

2.12   Summary

In this chapter we have developed the basic tools of analysis necessary to study the relationship between observable consumer demands and a monetary representation of consumer preferences. Several of the concepts that have been discussed will play crucial roles in the analysis of subsequent chapters. First, the integrating factor in the form of the marginal utility of money expenditure provides the link between demands and preferences. Second, the cost-of-utility function provides the desired monetary representation of consumer preferences. As we shall determine in the next chapter, the path of integration discussed in Section 2.6 offers an operational basis on top of which these concepts can be combined to yield a simple method for calculating the money-metric.

CHAPTER 3

Calculation of the money-metric

3.1 Introduction

In Chapter 2 we placed considerable emphasis on the role that the marginal utility of money or integrating factor plays as the linchpin between consumer preferences and the associated system of demand functions. Of particular importance was the result that there exists a particular form for this integrating factor such that the underlying preference function can be expressed in the form of a money-metric. In this chapter we exploit this linkage in order to develop some simple, operational procedures for calculating this metric directly from the consumer demand functions. These methods will be seen to be direct descendents of the approach we developed earlier (McKenzie and Pearce, 1976). In Appendix 3.1 at the end of this chapter, a computer program is provided that will enable us to approximate the money-metric to a high degree of accuracy.

Virtually all the difficulties that plague economists working in this area could be avoided if it were possible to adopt the approach that econometricians have used to formulate complete, estimatable demand systems. In general, researchers in this area start by assuming a preference function and then deriving the associated demand systems. More recently, Deaton (1978), Muellbauer (1976), and Deaton and Muellbauer (1980) have begun directly with the cost-of-utility function and used this as a basis for constructing the demand relationships. In this respect, two cost-of-utility functions have attracted attention:

1. *The price-independent generalized linear (PIGL) function*

$$C = \{v[b(p^*)]^\lambda + [a(p^*)]^\lambda\}^{1/\lambda} \tag{3.1}$$

where the associated utility function can be written as

$$v = \frac{Y^\lambda - [a(p)]^\lambda}{[b(p)]^\lambda} \tag{3.2}$$

and $a(p)$ and $b(p)$ represent functions of prices that are homogeneous of degree one. As before, C indicates the cost of achieving v, but given the vector of prices p^*.

41

2. *The price-independent generalized logarithmic (PIGLOG) function*

$$\ln C = (1 - \nu) \ln[a(p^*)] + \nu \ln[b(p^*)] \tag{3.3}$$

where

$$\nu = \frac{\ln Y - \ln[a(p)]}{\ln[b(p)] - \ln[a(p)]} \tag{3.4}$$

As with any properly specified indirect utility function, it is a simple matter to apply Roy's identity to explicit representations of (3.2) or (3.4) to obtain demand functions that can, in principle, be estimated. Clearly, if this procedure could be established as general, there would be no problem in calculating the money-metric (3.1) or (3.3) from the estimated parameters.

Unfortunately, however, the class of cost-of-utility functions that can be expressed in terms of elementary mathematical functions is rather small. There exists a virtual infinity of cost-of-utility functions for which no simple expression can be written down, even though the associated system of demand equations is easily derived. This much broader class of cost-of-utility functions can be calculated only by means of numerical methods.

Basically, two issues are involved. First, even if we are able to write an indirect preference function exactly, it still may not be possible to invert it so as to obtain the cost-of-utility function in terms of the elementary mathematical functions. However, in the case of the functions (3.2) and (3.4) this operation is relatively straightforward. Second, and perhaps more fundamental, is the problem that even though we may possess a system of well-specified demand functions that satisfy the basic assumptions of the theory of consumer behavior, we may not be able to express the preference system, let alone the cost-of-utility function, in terms of elementary relationships.

These two issues can best be examined by using the following approach. We know from Roy's identity that the system of consumer demand functions can be written as

$$X_i = -\frac{\partial \nu / \partial p_i}{\lambda} \tag{3.5}$$

where $\partial \nu / \partial p_i$ is the derivative of the indirect utility function and λ is the marginal utility of money. If we multiply (3.5) by p_i, sum overall commodities, and rearrange terms, we obtain a general expression for the required integrating factor, or marginal utility of money, λ, as follows:

$$\lambda = -\left(\sum p_j \frac{\partial \nu}{\partial p_j}\right) \Big/ Y \tag{3.6}$$

Hence, the system of demand functions can be rewritten as

$$X_i = \frac{Y(\partial v/\partial p_i)}{\sum p_j(\partial v/\partial p_j)} \tag{3.7}$$

or, more conveniently, as a budget shares equation

$$w_i = \frac{p_i X_i}{Y} = \frac{p_i(\partial v/\partial p_i)}{\sum p_j(\partial v/\partial p_j)} \tag{3.8}$$

In other words, an alternative to positing a preference function or cost-of-utility function and then deriving a demand function is to start with a set of expressions for $p_i(\partial v/\partial p_i)$. Of course, as the analysis of Chapter 2 has shown, not just any set of expressions will do. Certain restrictions must be satisfied, most notably:

1. The term $p_i(\partial v/\partial p_i)$ must be homogeneous of degree zero. This follows automatically from the fact that v is homogeneous of degree zero.

2. The matrix of second derivatives, $\partial^2 v/\partial p_i \partial p_j$, must be symmetric. This ensures that the matrix of Slutsky substitution effects is also symmetric. Of course, all the restrictions on these effects must also hold as well. Finally, it should be noted that the sum of the budget shares (3.8) automatically equals one. This approach has been used by McKenzie and Thomas (1982) to estimate composite demand systems.

The greater generality of this procedure, as compared with more traditional methods, can be clearly appreciated by considering the following example. For simplicity, let us suppose that preferences are additively separable and that

$$\frac{\partial v}{\partial p_i} = f_i = \frac{\beta_{ii}}{Y} \ln\left[\left(\frac{p_i}{Y}\right)^2 + \phi_i\left(\frac{p_i}{Y}\right) + \eta_i\right] \quad (i = 1, \ldots, n) \tag{3.9}$$

where β_{ii}, ϕ_i, and n_i are parameters. It is a simple matter to derive an expression for λ from (3.6):

$$\lambda = \frac{1}{Y^2} \sum_j \beta_{jj} p_j \ln\left[\left(\frac{p_j}{Y}\right)^2 + \phi_j\left(\frac{p_j}{Y}\right) + \eta_j\right] \tag{3.10}$$

Hence, the related budget shares equation is

$$w_i = \frac{\beta_{ii} p_i \ln[(p_i/Y)^2 + \phi_i(p_i/Y) + \eta_i]}{\sum_j \beta_{jj} p_j \ln[(p_j/Y)^2 + \phi_j(p_j/Y) + \eta_j]} \quad (i = 1, \ldots, n) \tag{3.11}$$

Equation (3.9) and the associated budget shares equations (3.11) are relatively simple. Yet it is unlikely that an economist would initiate his work on the basis of the associated preference function

$$U = \sum_j \beta_{ij} \left[\left(\frac{p_j}{Y} + \frac{\phi_j}{2} \right) \ln\left(\frac{p_j^2}{Y^2} + \phi_j \frac{p_j}{Y} + \eta_j \right) - 2\frac{p_j}{Y} \right.$$
$$\left. + \frac{2\eta_j - \phi_j^2/2}{(\eta_j - \phi_j^2/4)^{1/2}} \tan^{-1}\left(\frac{(p_j/Y) + (\phi_j/2)}{(\eta_j - \phi_j^2/4)^{1/2}} \right) \right] \qquad (3.12)$$

It is clearly impossible to invert this so as to express the cost-of-utility function in terms of elementary mathematical functions.

Let us pursue this line of reasoning somewhat further. Suppose that the derivatives of the preference system with respect to prices are of the following form:

$$\frac{\partial U}{\partial p_i} = \frac{\alpha_i}{p_i} + \beta_{ii} \frac{1}{p_i} \cot^{-1}\left(\frac{p_i}{Y} \right) \qquad (i = 1, \ldots, n) \qquad (3.13)$$

where the sum of the parameters α_i equals one. In this case it is simply impossible to express the underlying preference or cost-of-utility expressions as a finite expression, because

$$\frac{1}{p_i} \cot^{-1}\left(\frac{p_i}{Y} \right) = \frac{\pi}{2} \ln p_i - \frac{p_i}{Y} + \frac{p_i^3}{3^2 Y^3} - \frac{p_i^5}{5^2 Y^5}$$
$$+ \frac{p_i^7}{7^2 Y^7} - \ldots \qquad (i = 1, \ldots, n)$$

Yet the budget shares equation can be written simply as

$$w_i = \frac{\alpha_i + \beta_{ii} \cot^{-1}(p_i/Y)}{1 + \sum_j \beta_{jj} \cot^{-1}(p_j/Y)} \qquad (i = 1, \ldots, n) \qquad (3.14)$$

Many other examples of such functions can be constructed. In particular, it will be noted that those discussed thus far involve preference functions that are additively separable in the ratios p_i/Y.

3.2   The Taylor series representation of the money-metric

In this section we shall want to make explicit use of the assumption introduced as Property 7 at the end of Section 1.2. There we noted that a consumer preference function that was analytic could be represented exactly by an infinite Taylor series expansion. Because we shall truncate this series in practice, we also assume that we are dealing with

functions where the absolute value of the remainder term monotonically tends toward zero as the order of the Taylor series approaches infinity. The practice of expressing a preference function in
such a manner is not new (e.g., Harberger, 1971; Reaume, 1973;
Dixit, 1976). However, the full implications of this formulation have
not been drawn out. The objective of this section is to do just that. For
any price and expenditure changes, we can write the change in value
of an indirect utility function written in money-metric form as

$$
\begin{aligned}
\Delta M = {} & \sum \frac{\partial M}{\partial p_i} \Delta p_i + \frac{\partial M}{\partial Y} \Delta Y + \frac{1}{2} \sum \sum \frac{\partial^2 M}{\partial p_i \partial p_j} \Delta p_i \Delta p_j \\
& + \sum \frac{\partial^2 M}{\partial p_i \partial Y} \Delta p_i \Delta Y + \frac{1}{2} \frac{\partial^2 M}{\partial Y^2} (\Delta Y)^2 \\
& + \frac{1}{6} \sum \sum \sum \frac{\partial^3 M}{\partial p_i \partial p_j \partial p_k} \Delta p_i \Delta p_j \Delta p_k \\
& + \frac{1}{2} \sum \sum \frac{\partial^3 M}{\partial p_i \partial p_k \partial Y} \Delta p_i \Delta p_k \Delta Y \\
& + \frac{1}{2} \sum \frac{\partial^3 M}{\partial p_i \partial Y^2} \Delta p_i (\Delta Y)^2 + \frac{1}{6} \frac{\partial^3 M}{\partial Y^3} (\Delta Y)^3 + \dots \quad (3.15)
\end{aligned}
$$

where all derivatives are evaluated at the initial values of prices and
total expenditure. Although the preceding expansion is shown only
up to the third order, it can be extended to as many terms as we wish
provided that the two conditions mentioned earlier are fulfilled. Although these assumptions mean that our presentation does lack complete generality, it is likely that this will not prove to be a great problem. There are several reasons for this. First, the procedures to be
discussed represent a considerable improvement over those currently
being discussed in the literature. Second, most preference functions
used in applied economics are analytic in the region of price and
expenditure variation. Third, the assumptions simply reflect the not
unreasonable belief that consumers act in a "smooth," not schizo-
phrenic, manner. Hence, high-order rates of change in human behavior diminish in magnitude as the order increases. This does not imply
that cumulatively the second-order and higher-order expressions in
the Taylor series expansion will be unimportant. Quite the contrary.
As we shall see, these terms are quite important quantitatively. Rather,
the assumptions rule out functions where most of the variation in a
Taylor series expansion would be accounted for by the nth-order
term. Casual observation of human behavior appears to rule out this
possibility.

In order to put the Taylor series formulation to use in calculating the money-metric, we need to express each of the derivatives in (3.15) in terms of observable information. Immediately, it would appear that we must deal with the same problem raised in the preceding chapter: How do we cope with the integrating factor or marginal utility of money? Even if we follow the procedure outlined in Section (3.1) and construct a set of demand functions on the basis of assumed partial derivatives $\partial v/\partial p_i$ and knowledge that there exists a $\lambda = -[\sum p_j(\partial v/\partial p_j)]/Y$, this relationship will not be one capable of generating the money-metric. Some unknown transformation of this λ will be required. Fortunately, however, there is no problem. Each of the terms in the Taylor series is evaluated at the initial values of total expenditure and prices. Further, it will be recalled from Chapter 2 that the marginal utility of money, λ, associated with the money-metric equals one, *given initial prices*. And all the higher-order derivatives of λ with respect to total expenditure equal zero, again *given initial prices*. That is,

$$\lambda(Y,p^0) \equiv 1 \tag{3.16}$$

$$\frac{\partial^r \lambda}{\partial Y^r}(Y,p^0) \equiv 0 \quad (r = 1,\ldots,\infty) \tag{3.17}$$

This fact provides us with the key to retrieving the money-metric directly from consumer demand functions. To show this, let us first derive general expressions for the derivatives of the Taylor series expansion (3.15). This is achieved by differentiating the first-order conditions

$$\frac{\partial M}{\partial p_i} = -\lambda X_i \tag{3.18}$$

$$\frac{\partial M}{\partial Y} = \lambda \tag{3.19}$$

with respect to prices and total expenditure so as to obtain

$$\frac{\partial^2 M}{\partial p_i \partial Y} = \frac{\partial \lambda}{\partial p_i} = -\lambda \frac{\partial X_i}{\partial Y} - X_i \frac{\partial \lambda}{\partial Y} \tag{3.20}$$

$$\frac{\partial^2 M}{\partial p_i \partial p_j} = -\lambda \frac{\partial X_i}{\partial p_j} - X_i \frac{\partial \lambda}{\partial p_j} \tag{3.21}$$

$$\frac{\partial^3 M}{\partial p_i \partial p_j \partial p_k} = -\lambda \frac{\partial^2 X_i}{\partial p_j \partial p_k} - \frac{\partial \lambda}{\partial p_k} \frac{\partial X_i}{\partial p_j} - X_i \frac{\partial^2 \lambda}{\partial p_j \partial p_k} - \frac{\partial X_i}{\partial p_k} \frac{\partial \lambda}{\partial p_j} \tag{3.22}$$

$$\frac{\partial^3 M}{\partial Y \partial p_j \partial p_k} = \frac{\partial^2 \lambda}{\partial p_j \partial p_k} = -\lambda \frac{\partial^2 X_j}{\partial Y \partial p_k} - \frac{\partial \lambda}{\partial p_k} \frac{\partial X_j}{\partial Y}$$

$$- X_j \frac{\partial^2 \lambda}{\partial Y \partial p_k} - \frac{\partial X_j}{\partial p_k} \frac{\partial \lambda}{\partial Y} \tag{3.23}$$

$$\frac{\partial^3 M}{\partial p_k \partial Y^2} = \frac{\partial^2 \lambda}{\partial p_k \partial Y} = -\lambda \frac{\partial^2 X_k}{\partial Y^2} - 2 \frac{\partial X_k}{\partial Y} \frac{\partial \lambda}{\partial Y} - X_k \frac{\partial^2 \lambda}{\partial Y^2} \tag{3.24}$$

$$\frac{\partial^3 M}{\partial Y^3} = \frac{\partial^2 \lambda}{\partial Y^2} \tag{3.25}$$

and so forth for higher-order terms. Although each of the terms (3.18) through (3.25) involves either the marginal utility of money or its higher-order derivatives with respect to prices and total expenditure, these are easily eliminated *without loss of generality* by making use of the properties of the money-metric utility indicator (3.16) and (3.17). Thus, the first-order terms (3.18) and (3.19) become

$$\frac{\partial M}{\partial p_i} = -X_i \tag{3.26}$$

$$\frac{\partial M}{\partial Y} = 1 \tag{3.27}$$

Because $\partial \lambda / \partial Y$ equals zero at initial prices,

$$\frac{\partial^2 M}{\partial p_i \partial Y} = \frac{\partial \lambda}{\partial p_i} = -\frac{\partial X_i}{\partial Y} \tag{3.28}$$

Then substitution of (3.27) and (3.28) into (3.21) yields

$$\frac{\partial^2 M}{\partial p_i \partial p_j} = -\frac{\partial X_i}{\partial p_j} + X_i \frac{\partial X_j}{\partial Y} \tag{3.29}$$

Before proceeding further, the reader should check that (3.29) is *not* the Slutsky compensated price effect [see equation (2.72)].

Expressions for the third-order derivatives in terms of observable demand effects can be obtained in a similar fashion. We first note that $\partial^2 \lambda / \partial Y^2$ equals zero. Then, from (3.27),

$$\frac{\partial^3 M}{\partial p_k \partial Y^2} = \frac{\partial^2 \lambda}{\partial p_k \partial Y} = -\frac{\partial^2 X_k}{\partial Y^2} \tag{3.30}$$

Substitution of (3.30) and (3.28) into (3.23) yields

$$\frac{\partial^3 M}{\partial Y \partial p_j \partial p_k} = \frac{\partial^2 \lambda}{\partial p_j \partial p_k} = -\frac{\partial^2 X_j}{\partial Y \partial p_k} + \frac{\partial X_k}{\partial Y} \frac{\partial X_j}{\partial Y} + X_j \frac{\partial^2 X_k}{\partial Y^2} \tag{3.31}$$

This equation, along with (3.28), can then be substituted into (3.22) as follows:

$$\frac{\partial^3 M}{\partial p_i \partial p_j \partial p_k} = -\frac{\partial^2 X_i}{\partial p_j \partial p_k} + \frac{\partial X_k}{\partial Y}\frac{\partial X_i}{\partial p_j}$$
$$- X_i\left(\frac{\partial X_k}{\partial Y}\frac{\partial X_j}{\partial Y} - \frac{\partial^2 X_j}{\partial Y \partial p_k} + X_j\frac{\partial^2 X_k}{\partial Y^2}\right)$$
$$+ \frac{\partial X_i}{\partial p_k}\frac{\partial X_j}{\partial Y} \tag{3.32}$$

The term $\partial^3 M/\partial Y^3$ is, of course, zero. This basic procedure can be repeated for all higher-order terms in the Taylor series expansion until the degree of accuracy established by some *a priori* criterion is met. Unfortunately, it is probably the case that most of the economics data with which we deal are not very accurate beyond two or three digits. Thus, a reasonable operational approach would be to continue to extend the Taylor series expansion until there is no change in, say, the third digit of the money-metric indicator.

This, of course, may appear to be a highly tedious procedure. Indeed, it would be if all calculations had to be undertaken by hand. However, most economists and government officials have access to simple computers that can easily be programmed to undertake the necessary calculations once the functional form for the demand functions has been chosen.

Finally, as a check on our previous discussion, it is useful to note that in the case where only total expenditure varies, the expansion

$$\Delta M = \frac{\partial M}{\partial Y}\Delta Y + \frac{1}{2}\frac{\partial^2 M}{\partial Y^2}(\Delta Y)^2 + \frac{1}{6}\frac{\partial^3 M}{\partial Y^3}(\Delta Y)^3 + \ldots \tag{3.33}$$

simply reduces to ΔY. Thus, if $\Delta Y = f$ generates the same level of satisfaction as an alternative situation where prices vary, $\Delta M = f$ is the equivalent variation.

The particular monotonic, increasing transformation we have chosen to use as a money-metric representation is, as we have frequently emphasized, only one of an infinity of transformations that could be used. To increase the reader's understanding of the basic thrust of the argument presented here, it will be instructive to experiment with alternative transformations. However, only two possibilities will be discussed here. The first represents an attempt to construct an exact utility indicator that "looks like" the area under a conventional demand curve. The second is mainly of historical interest, in that it was the initial approach I. F. Pearce and I took in an attempt to solve the problem of constructing a welfare indicator on the basis of the parameters of ordinary demand functions.

3.3   Some alternative transformations

Instead of normalizing our utility indicator so that, given initial prices, $\partial^r \lambda / \partial Y^r \equiv 0$, let us normalize with respect to the jth price given the initial level of total expenditure and the initial levels of all other prices:

$$\frac{\partial^r \lambda}{\partial p_j^r} (Y^0, p_1^0, \ldots, p_j, \ldots, p_n^0) \equiv 0 \quad (r = 1, \ldots, \infty) \tag{3.34}$$

If we use the foregoing first-order derivative, substitute it into equation (3.20), and rearrange terms, we find

$$\frac{\partial \lambda}{\partial Y} = -\frac{1}{X_j} \frac{\partial X_j}{\partial Y} \tag{3.35}$$

Then, for all prices but the jth,

$$\frac{\partial^2 \nu}{\partial p_k \partial Y} = \frac{\partial \lambda}{\partial p_k} = -\frac{\partial X_k}{\partial Y} + \frac{X_k}{X_j} \frac{\partial X_j}{\partial Y} \quad (k \neq j) \tag{3.36}$$

This last equation can then be substituted into (3.21) to obtain

$$\frac{\partial^2 \nu}{\partial p_k \partial p_j} = -\frac{\partial X_k}{\partial p_j} \tag{3.37}$$

and

$$\frac{\partial^2 \nu}{\partial p_i \partial p_k} = -\frac{\partial X_i}{\partial p_k} + X_i \left(\frac{\partial X_k}{\partial Y} - \frac{X_k}{X_j} \frac{\partial X_j}{\partial Y} \right) \quad (k \neq j) \tag{3.38}$$

The third-order terms can be obtained by first solving

$$\frac{\partial^3 \nu}{\partial Y \partial p_j^2} \equiv 0 = -\frac{\partial^2 X_j}{\partial Y \partial p_j} = X_j \frac{\partial^2 \lambda}{\partial Y \partial p_j} + \frac{1}{X_j} \frac{\partial X_j}{\partial p_j} \frac{\partial X_j}{\partial Y} \tag{3.39}$$

for

$$\frac{\partial^2 \lambda}{\partial Y \partial p_j} = -\frac{1}{X_j} \frac{\partial^2 X_j}{\partial Y \partial p_j} + \frac{1}{X_j} \frac{\partial X_j}{\partial p_j} \frac{\partial X_j}{\partial Y} = \frac{\partial^3 \nu}{\partial p_j \partial Y^2} \tag{3.40}$$

This, in turn, can be combined with (3.30) to yield

$$\frac{\partial^2 \lambda}{\partial Y^2} = \frac{\partial^3 \nu}{\partial Y^3} = \frac{1}{X_j^2} \frac{\partial^2 X_j}{\partial Y \partial p_j} - \frac{1}{X_j^3} \frac{\partial X_j}{\partial p_j} \frac{\partial X_j}{\partial Y} + \frac{1}{X_j} \frac{\partial^2 X_j}{\partial Y^2} - \frac{2}{X_j^2} \left(\frac{\partial X_j}{\partial Y} \right)^2 \tag{3.41}$$

Equation (3.41) can then be substituted back into (3.22) through (3.24) to obtain expressions for the remaining derivatives, which are with respect to prices other than jth. These calculations turn out to be quite tedious and hence will not be presented. However, in the special case where only one price, the jth, varies, the welfare indicator implied by this transformation is the ordinary consumer surplus measure. In this case, we have, from (3.32),

$$\frac{\partial^3 v}{\partial p_j^3} = -\frac{\partial^2 X_j}{\partial p_j^2} \tag{3.42}$$

Hence,

$$\Delta v = -X_j \Delta p_j - \frac{1}{2}\frac{\partial X_j}{\partial p_j}(\Delta p_j)^2 - \frac{1}{6}\frac{\partial^2 X_j}{\partial p_j^2}(\Delta p_j)^3 + \dots \tag{3.43}$$

which, of course, is a Taylor series representation of the change in the area under the demand schedule for the ith product when its price varies. This is merely a very complex method of stating something we already know. If a single price goes up, it is hardly surprising to learn that the consumer is worse off. Hence, in this instance, changes in the area under an ordinary demand schedule fulfill the role of a utility indicator.

The next transformation to be discussed is one that I. F. Pearce and I originally considered, and it involves normalizing the marginal utility of money, given initial prices, such that

$$\frac{\partial^r \lambda}{\partial Y^r}(Y^0, p_1^0, \dots, p_n^0) \equiv 1 \quad (r = 1, \dots, \infty) \tag{3.44}$$

This simply adds to the complexity of the derivatives of the utility function, as can be seen, for example, by examining (3.20) and (3.21), which became

$$\frac{\partial^2 v}{\partial p_k \partial Y} = \frac{\partial \lambda}{\partial p_i} = -\frac{\partial X_i}{\partial Y} - X_i \tag{3.45}$$

and

$$\frac{\partial^2 v}{\partial p_i \partial p_j} = -\frac{\partial X_i}{\partial p_j} + X_i\frac{\partial X_j}{\partial Y} + X_i X_j \tag{3.46}$$

Nothing is gained by following this procedure. Indeed, quite a bit is lost, because the resulting utility indicator is not a money-metric. This becomes immediately clear when we examine the expansion that results when only total expenditure varies:

$$\Delta v = \Delta Y + \frac{1}{2}(\Delta Y)^2 + \frac{1}{6}(\Delta Y)^3 + \dots \tag{3.47}$$

However, given initial prices, this implies that (3.47) equals

$$\Delta v = e^{\Delta Y} - 1 \tag{3.48}$$

3.4 Improved numerical methods for calculating the money-metric

In this chapter we have expressed the money-metric utility indicator in the form of a generalized Taylor series expansion. This has the merit of allowing the measure to be written in terms of an index with fixed weights, these being determined by the initial values of total expenditure and prices. Indeed, a first-order Taylor series will yield the well-known Laspeyres quantity variation. However, from a practical point of view, this approach suffers from the considerable disadvantage of involving tedious, complex, time-consuming manipulations and calculations. This problem became particularly apparent to me when I attempted to write a general computer program that would enable the user to calculate the money-metric for any number of price changes and in terms of any particular set of well-behaved demand functions. Fortunately, there are several alternative procedures that are relatively straightforward and easy to put into practice. In particular, the repetitiveness of the calculations involved in these methods makes them especially well suited to manipulation by a computer. Outlines of suitable programs are contained in Appendix 3.1.

From the first two chapters we know that because M itself is a utility indicator, the differential

$$dM = \frac{\partial M}{\partial Y} dY + \sum \frac{\partial M}{\partial p_i} dp_i = \lambda \, dY - \lambda \sum X_i \, dp_i \tag{3.49}$$

is exact and can be integrated *without regard to the path taken*. This latter property is the key to understanding the procedures to be discussed next. Let us suppose that M is a function of total expenditure and only three prices, all of which vary. Then the following calculation is valid:

$$
\begin{aligned}
\Delta M = Y^1 - Y^0 &= \int_c \sum \frac{\partial M}{\partial p_i} dp_i \\
&= Y^1 - Y^0 - \Delta M_1(p_1, p_2^0, p_3^0, Y^1) \\
&\quad - \Delta M_2(p_1^1, p_2, p_3^0, Y^1) \\
&\quad - \Delta M_3(p_1^1, p_2^1, p_3, Y^1)
\end{aligned}
\tag{3.50}
$$

where

$$\Delta M_1(p_1^0, p_2^0, p_3^0, Y^1) = - \int_{p_1^0}^{p_1^1} \lambda(p_1, p_2^0, p_3^0, Y^1) X_1(p_1, p_2^0, p_3^0, Y^1) \, dp_1 \tag{3.51}$$

$$\Delta M_2(p_1^1, p_2, p_3^0, Y^1) = - \int_{p_2^0}^{p_2^1} \lambda(p_1^1, p_2, p_3^0, Y^1) X_2(p_1^1, p_2, p_3^0, Y^1) \, dp_2$$

(3.52)

$$\Delta M_3(p_1^1, p_2^1, p_3, Y^1) = - \int_{p_3^0}^{p_3^1} \lambda(p_1^1, p_2^1, p_3, Y^1) X_3(p_1^1, p_2^1, p_3, Y^1) \, dp_3$$

(3.53)

In other words, first let us vary total expenditure. Because no price variations have occurred, it is still the case that the fundamental initial conditions hold:

$$\lambda(p^0, Y) = 1$$

(3.54)

and

$$\frac{\partial^i \lambda}{\partial Y^i}(p^0, Y) = 0$$

(3.55)

Thus, no adjustments to ΔY are required. The next step is to allow p_1 to vary and hence to calculate ΔM_1, *given the new level of total expenditure* Y^1. This result is then added to ΔY. Then we calculate ΔM_2, given both Y^1 and the new level of p_1, and so forth in a step-by-step recursive path. This is the basic plan. Next we need to consider actual numerical procedures for calculating each of the integrals in (3.50). In the following sections, two alternative approaches will be discussed. In each instance, information about consumer demand functions and their derivatives up to the third order is required. This would seem to permit approximations of a degree of accuracy sufficient for most problems. However, if the reader believes that the margins of error are not good enough, still more complex procedures are available, although they will not be discussed.

3.5   Method 1

Method 1 involves estimating each of the integrals in (3.50) in terms of a Taylor series expansion, in much the same way as if only one price had been varied. However, the key to understanding the procedure involved is that we do not calculate each integral on the basis of a starting point involving all prices at their initial base levels. Let us run through what is involved. Most of the following manipulations have been carried out already. However, they are repeated here for two reasons. First, it enables us to introduce notation that will be used in the computer programs contained in Appendix 3.1. Second, it enables us to make explicit all the steps involved and the order in which they must take place.

In developing the procedures outlined in this section, we have chosen to calculate each integral by means of a fourth-order Taylor series expansion. This requires information about the demand functions and all their derivatives up to the third order, as follows:

$$U_1 = \frac{\partial M}{\partial p_i} = -\lambda X_i \tag{3.56}$$

$$U_2 = \frac{\partial^2 M}{\partial p_i^2} = -\frac{\partial \lambda}{\partial p_i} X_i - \lambda \frac{\partial X_i}{\partial p_i} \tag{3.57}$$

$$U_3 = \frac{\partial^3 M}{\partial p_i^3} = -\frac{\partial^2 \lambda}{\partial p_i^2} X_i - 2\frac{\partial \lambda}{\partial p_i}\frac{\partial X_i}{\partial p_i} - \lambda \frac{\partial^2 X_i}{\partial p_i^2} \tag{3.58}$$

$$U_4 = \frac{\partial^4 M}{\partial p_i^4} = -\frac{\partial^3 \lambda}{\partial p_i^3} X_i - 3\frac{\partial^2 \lambda}{\partial p_i^2}\frac{\partial X_i}{\partial p_i} - 3\frac{\partial \lambda}{\partial p_i}\frac{\partial^2 X_i}{\partial p_i^2} - \lambda \frac{\partial^3 X_i}{\partial p_i^3} \tag{3.59}$$

All of the terms involving λ and its derivatives will need to be calculated on the basis of the appropriate variable values involved in the particular integration. The general forms are shown in Table 3.1. The far right-hand column indicates the simpler forms that are used to calculate the first integral in the sequence. These will, of course, form the basis for calculating the money-metric where there is only one price variation under evaluation.

On calculating the parameters B_1 through B_6 for the first price change, we then substitute these values into equations (3.56) through (3.59). The latter form the basis for calculating the approximation

$$\Delta M_1 = U_1 \Delta p_1 + \frac{1}{2} U_2 (\Delta p_1)^2 + \frac{1}{6} U_3 (\Delta p_1)^2 + \frac{1}{24} U_4 (\Delta p_1)^4 \tag{3.60}$$

As we have already emphasized, once a price varies we can no longer make use of (3.54) and (3.55), the initial conditions for the marginal utility of money and its derivatives. These, it must be emphasized again, are purely initial conditions. This problem immediately becomes apparent when we seek to calculate the second integral in equation (3.50), that is, equation (3.52). The values of λ and its derivatives with respect to income have varied as a result of the change in p_1.

Table 3.1

Derivative	Symbol	General form	Form taken for first integration
$\dfrac{\partial \lambda}{\partial p_i}$	B_1	$-\lambda \dfrac{\partial X_i}{\partial Y} - X_i \dfrac{\partial \lambda}{\partial Y}$	$-\dfrac{\partial X_i}{\partial Y}$
$\dfrac{\partial^2 \lambda}{\partial p_i \partial Y}$	B_2	$-2\dfrac{\partial \lambda}{\partial Y}\dfrac{\partial X_i}{\partial Y} - \lambda \dfrac{\partial^2 X_i}{\partial Y^2} - X_i \dfrac{\partial^2 \lambda}{\partial Y_i^2}$	$-\dfrac{\partial^2 X_i}{\partial Y^2}$
$\dfrac{\partial^2 \lambda}{\partial p_i^2}$	B_3	$-\dfrac{\partial X_i}{\partial p_i}\dfrac{\partial \lambda}{\partial Y} - \dfrac{\partial \lambda}{\partial p_i}\dfrac{\partial X_i}{\partial Y} - \lambda \dfrac{\partial^2 X_i}{\partial Y \partial p_i} - X_i \dfrac{\partial^2 \lambda}{\partial Y \partial p_i}$	$\left(\dfrac{\partial X_i}{\partial Y}\right)^2 - \dfrac{\partial^2 X_i}{\partial Y \partial p_i} + \dfrac{\partial^2 X_i}{\partial Y^2} X_i$
$\dfrac{\partial^3 \lambda}{\partial p_i \partial Y^2}$	B_4	$-3\dfrac{\partial^2 \lambda}{\partial Y^2}\dfrac{\partial X_i}{\partial Y} - 3\dfrac{\partial \lambda}{\partial Y}\dfrac{\partial^2 X_i}{\partial Y^2} - \lambda \dfrac{\partial^3 X_i}{\partial Y^3} - X_i \dfrac{\partial^3 \lambda}{\partial Y^3}$	$-\dfrac{\partial^3 X_i}{\partial Y^3}$
$\dfrac{\partial^3 \lambda}{\partial p_i^2 \partial Y}$	B_5	$-2\dfrac{\partial^2 \lambda}{\partial p_i \partial Y}\dfrac{\partial X_i}{\partial Y} - \dfrac{\partial \lambda}{\partial p_i}\dfrac{\partial^2 X_i}{\partial Y^2} - \lambda \dfrac{\partial^3 X_i}{\partial Y^2 \partial p_i}$ $-2\dfrac{\partial \lambda}{\partial Y}\dfrac{\partial^2 X_i}{\partial Y \partial p_i} - \dfrac{\partial X_i}{\partial p_i}\dfrac{\partial^2 \lambda}{\partial Y^2} - X_i \dfrac{\partial^3 \lambda}{\partial Y^2 \partial p_i}$	$2\dfrac{\partial^2 X_i}{\partial Y^2}\dfrac{\partial X_i}{\partial Y} + \dfrac{\partial X_i}{\partial Y}\dfrac{\partial^2 X_i}{\partial Y^2} - \dfrac{\partial^3 X_i}{\partial Y^2 \partial p_i} + 2\dfrac{\partial X_i}{\partial Y}\dfrac{\partial^2 X_i}{\partial Y \partial p_i}$ $- X_i \dfrac{\partial^3 X_i}{\partial Y^3}$
$\dfrac{\partial^3 \lambda}{\partial p_i^3}$	B_6	$-\dfrac{\partial^2 \lambda}{\partial p_i^2}\dfrac{\partial X_i}{\partial Y} - 2\dfrac{\partial \lambda}{\partial p_i}\dfrac{\partial^2 X_i}{\partial Y \partial p_i} - \lambda \dfrac{\partial^3 X_i}{\partial Y \partial p_i^2} - \dfrac{\partial^2 X_i}{\partial p_i^2}\dfrac{\partial \lambda}{\partial Y}$ $-2\dfrac{\partial X_i}{\partial p_i}\dfrac{\partial^2 \lambda}{\partial Y \partial p_i} - \dfrac{\partial X_i}{\partial p_i}\dfrac{\partial^2 \lambda}{\partial p_i \partial Y} - X_i \dfrac{\partial^3 \lambda}{\partial Y \partial p_i^2}$	$-\dfrac{\partial X_i}{\partial Y}\left[\left(\dfrac{\partial X_i}{\partial Y}\right)^2 - \dfrac{\partial^2 X_i}{\partial Y \partial p_i} + X_i \dfrac{\partial^2 X_i}{\partial Y^2}\right]$ $+ 2\dfrac{\partial X_i}{\partial Y}\left(\dfrac{\partial^2 X_i}{\partial Y \partial p_i}\right) - \dfrac{\partial^3 X_i}{\partial Y \partial p_i^2} - X_i[B5]$ $+ 2\dfrac{\partial X_i}{\partial p_i}\dfrac{\partial^2 X_i}{\partial Y^2}$

However, the changes involved may be approximated by the following expressions:

$$\lambda(p_1^1, p_2^0, p_3^0, Y^1) = \lambda(p_1^0, p_2^0, p_3^0, Y^1) + \frac{\partial \lambda}{\partial p_1}(p_1^0, p_2^0, p_3^0, Y^1) \cdot \Delta p_1$$

$$+ \frac{1}{2} \frac{\partial^2 \lambda}{\partial p_1^2}(p_1^0, p_2^0, p_3^0, Y^1) \cdot (\Delta p_1)^2$$

$$+ \frac{1}{6} \frac{\partial^3 \lambda}{\partial p_1^3}(p_1^0, p_2^0, p_3^0, Y^1) \cdot (\Delta p_1)^3 \qquad (3.61)$$

$$\frac{\partial \lambda}{\partial Y}(p_1^1, p_2^0, p_3^0, Y^1) = \frac{\partial \lambda}{\partial Y}(p_1^0, p_2^0, p_3^0, Y^1)$$

$$+ \frac{\partial^2 \lambda}{\partial Y \partial p_1}(p_1^0, p_2^0, p_3^0, Y^1)(\Delta p_1)$$

$$+ \frac{1}{2} \frac{\partial^3 \lambda}{\partial Y \partial p_1^2}(p_1^0, p_2^0, p_3^0, Y^1)(\Delta p_1)^2 \qquad (3.62)$$

$$\frac{\partial^2 \lambda}{\partial Y^2}(p_1^1, p_2^0, p_3^0, Y^1) = \frac{\partial^2 \lambda}{\partial Y^2}(p_1^0, p_2^0, p_3^0, Y^1)$$

$$+ \frac{\partial^3 \lambda}{\partial Y^2 \partial p_1}(p_1^0, p_2^0, p_3^0, Y^1)(\Delta p_1) \qquad (3.63)$$

$$\frac{\partial^3 \lambda}{\partial Y^3}(p_1^1, p_2^0, p_3^0, Y^1) = \frac{\partial^3 \lambda}{\partial Y^3}(p_1^0, p_2^0, p_3^0, Y^1) \qquad (3.64)$$

Because $(\partial^3 \lambda / \partial Y^3)(p^0, Y^1)$ is zero, this derivative will always take up this value irrespective of the levels of prices and expenditure. Effectively, this means that we are approximating ΔM by a function that possesses the property that the third-order and higher-order derivatives of the marginal utility of money with respect to expenditure are always zero.

Equations (3.61) through (3.64) can now be used as a basis for determining new values of B_1 through B_6 and these, in turn, for new values of U_1 through U_4, so as to permit an approximation of the second integral. This pattern of calculations can then be repeated in recursive fashion until all price variations have been accounted for. Although at first glance these manipulations are seen to be tedious, they are also repetitive and hence can easily be translated into a simple computer program. The key, as can be seen from the foregoing outline, is that we do not require any cross-price effects. These have been automatically taken into account via the chosen path of integration. Hence, the computations are considerably simpler than those involved in the generalized Taylor series expansion as discussed in Section 3.2.

3.6   An alternative procedure based on Simpson's rule

Because the preceding Taylor series approach is based on derivatives evaluated at the initial price/quantity situation, there is the possibility that for large price changes or for particularly "sensitive" functions, a very high order expansion may be required before an acceptable approximation is obtained. Thus, a technique that uses information over part or all of the range of price variation would seem to be preferable to the one just discussed. One possibility that requires no more information than that used in the preceding exercise involves the introduction of Simpson's rule.

Let us begin again with the case of a single price variation. If we start from the initial set of prices, the problem is to calculate the area under the curve describing marginal money-metric utility $\partial M/\partial p_i$ as a function of p_i. In terms of Figure 3.1, this involves calculating the area under AA. The method we shall use here involves approximating this area by an alternative function described by the dash line. This can be achieved by adopting a two-step approximation procedure. First, provided that M has a continuous fifth derivative, then the integral

$$\Delta M_i = \int_{p_i^0}^{p_i^1} \frac{\partial M}{\partial p_i} \, dp_i$$

can be written exactly as

$$\Delta M = \frac{p_i^1 - p_i^0}{6} \left(\frac{\partial M}{\partial p_i}(p_i^0) + 4\frac{\partial M}{\partial p_i}(p_i^m) + \frac{\partial M}{\partial p_i} p_i^1 \right)$$
$$- \frac{(p_i - p_i^0)^5}{2880} \frac{\partial^5 M}{\partial p_i^5}(p_i^c) \tag{3.65}$$

where $p_i^m = (p_i^1 + p_i^0)/2$ and p_i^c lies between p_i^1 and p_i^0. This formula is known as *Simpson's rule*. The first three terms on the right-hand side of (3.65) form the basis for an approximation. The last term, involving the fifth derivative $(\partial^5 M/\partial p_i^5)(p_i^c)$, is not known, because we do not know the value of p_i^c.

Unfortunately, we cannot apply Simpson's rule in a straightforward manner to the problem at hand because we do not possess an exact representation of the function $\partial M/\partial p_i = -\lambda X_i$. We do know the functional form for X_i, but we do not, of course, know the form of λ associated with the money-metric. However, in the spirit of the preceding section, we can use a third-order Taylor series to approximate

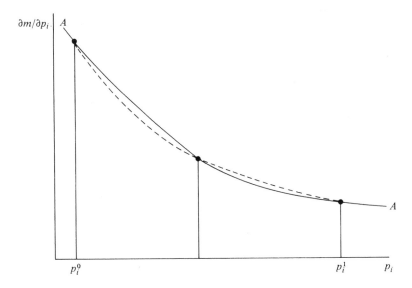

Figure 3.1

the values of λ required in the application of Simpson's rule. Thus, to approximate (3.65), we calculate

$$\Delta M_i \approx -\frac{p_i^1 - p_i^0}{6}[\hat{\lambda}(p_i^0)X_i(p_i^0) + 4\hat{\lambda}(p_i^m) + \hat{\lambda}(p_i^1)X_i(p_i^1)]$$

(3.66)

Because our initial situation is one where all prices are at their base values, we know that $\hat{\lambda}(p_i^0) = 1$. We can then use a third-order Taylor series approximation for $\hat{\lambda}(p_i^m)$:

$$\hat{\lambda}(p_i^m) = 1 + \frac{\partial\lambda}{\partial p_i}(p_i^0)\left(\frac{\Delta p_i}{2}\right) + \frac{1}{2}\frac{\partial^2\lambda}{\partial p_i^2}(p_i^0)\left(\frac{\Delta p_i}{2}\right)^2$$
$$+ \frac{1}{6}\frac{\partial^3\lambda}{\partial p_i^3}(p_i^0)\left(\frac{\Delta p_i}{2}\right)^3$$

(3.67)

and similarly for $\hat{\lambda}(p_i^1)$:

$$\hat{\lambda}(p_i^1) = \hat{\lambda}(p_i^m) + \frac{\partial\lambda}{\partial p_i}(p_i^m)\left(\frac{\Delta p_i}{2}\right) + \frac{1}{2}\frac{\partial^2\lambda}{\partial p_i^2}(p_i^m)\left(\frac{\Delta p_i}{2}\right)^2$$
$$+ \frac{1}{6}\frac{\partial^3\lambda}{\partial p_i^3}\left(\frac{\Delta p_i}{2}\right)^3$$

(3.68)

This procedure can now be extended to problems involving more than one price variation by adapting the procedure discussed earlier with respect to Method 1. For example, if there are three price variations, then we can approximate the total change in money-metric utility by the recursive or stepwise calculation:

$$\Delta M = Y^1 - Y^0 + \Delta M_1 + \Delta M_2 + \Delta M_3 \tag{3.69}$$

where each ΔM_i is calculated on the basis of the previously modified Simpson's rule.

3.7   Difficulties involved in determining error bounds

Unfortunately, the fact that the numerical procedures outlined in this chapter represent a considerable simplification over those discussed previously does not enable us to improve our knowledge of either (a) the convergence properties of the series being considered or (b) likely margins of error. However, this revised framework does enable us to clearly understand the problems involved.

Basically, there are two propositions relating to the Taylor series that would be helpful if we could make use of them. Let us consider them in relation to Method 1. First, assume (a) that M is continuously differentiable in the range of price variation under consideration and (b) that there is some positive constant A such that

$$\left| \frac{\partial^n M}{\partial p_i^n} \right| \leq A_i^n \tag{3.70}$$

Then we know that the Taylor series generated by M converges to M for every price level in the range being considered.

The second proposition of interest concerns the estimation of the remainder. For example, we know that for any fourth-order Taylor series (such as we have been working with in this chapter), the error can be written exactly in the so-called Lagrange form:

$$R_4^i = \frac{1}{5!} (p_i - p_i^0)^5 \frac{\partial^5 M}{\partial p_i^5} (p_i^c) \tag{3.71}$$

where p_i^c lies between p_i^1 and p_i^0. In general, the value of p_i^c will be unknown. However, if we denote the minimum and maximum values of $\partial^5 M / \partial p_i^5$ (over a range of p_i under consideration) as m_5^i and M_5^i, then we can establish the following bounds:

$$m_5^i \frac{(p_i^1 - p_i^0)^5}{5!} \leq R_4^i \leq M_5^i \frac{(p_i^1 - p_i^0)^5}{5!} \quad \text{if} \quad p_i > p_i^0 \tag{3.72}$$

and

$$m^i \frac{(p_i^0 - p_i^1)^5}{5!} \geq R_4^i \geq M_5^i \frac{(p_i^0 - p_i^1)}{5!} \quad \text{if} \quad p_i^0 < p_i \qquad (3.73)$$

The basic difficulty with applying either (3.71) or (3.72) and (3.73) is that we simply do not possess enough information to carry out the comparisons involved. Numerical methods based on Taylor series expansions, Simpson's rule, or other procedures presume that we possess information about the functional form whose value we are attempting to calculate. In general, however, this will not be the case. It is true that we know the relevant demand functions. However, the fact that we do not know, except in a few special cases, the necessary integrating factor or marginal utility of money means that we can evaluate λ and its various derivatives only at the initial price/expenditure situation. That is, we know the exact value for $\partial^n M / \partial p_i^n$ only at the initial or base situation. To apply (3.69) as part of the first proposition stated earlier requires that we know the relevant derivative exactly over the full range of price variation. The identical information is required to calculate m_5^i and M_5^i. It is true that we could approximate values of $\partial^n M / \partial p_i^n$ at other values of prices and expenditure. However, this does not help, because the two key propositions under discussion here both require exact, not approximate, relationships.

The same problem arises with respect to the second method based on Simpson's rule. First of all, we require an upper bound for $\partial^5 M / \partial p_i^n$ in order to establish an upper limit for the error associated with (3.65). In addition, because we are using Taylor series to approximate λ and its derivatives, we will require knowledge of λ itself. But here again we return to the fundamental problem of applied welfare economics.

3.8   An example

All is not entirely lost, however. Experiments with situations in which the cost-of-utility functions have been known have confirmed that the procedures discussed in this chapter are highly accurate (see Chapter 9). In addition, there is one situation in which we know the exact value of the cost-of-utility function, even though we cannot express the result in terms of elementary functions. Because the money-metric is homogeneous of degree zero in prices and total expenditure, we know that any proportional changes in these variables will leave the welfare indicator unaffected. Because we do not need to know an exact functional form to ascertain this result, it becomes a useful benchmark for carrying out simulations designed to ascertain the likely magnitudes of approximation errors. Consider the following example.

Let us suppose that consumer preferences are described by Houthakker's indirect addilog function (1960):

$$\nu = \sum a_i \left(\frac{Y}{p_i}\right)^{b_i} \qquad (3.74)$$

The first thing to note is that the money-metric associated with (3.74) cannot be expressed in terms of an elementary function except when all the b_i are equal. However, changes in the money-metric can be calculated via the numerical procedures just discussed. Application of Roy's identity yields the set of demand functions

$$X_i = \frac{a_i b_i Y^{b_i} p_i^{-(b_i+1)}}{\sum a_i b_i Y^{(b_i-1)} p_i^{-b_i}} \qquad (3.75)$$

Inspection of (3.75) reveals that it cannot be integrated in terms of an elementary function to obtain a consumer surplus measure. It should be emphasized that these two properties of the indirect addilog are not peculiar to it. Indeed, most preference functions will not admit to simple functional representations of either consumer surplus or the money-metric.

Let us now suppose that the parametric specification of (3.75) is as follows. The initial level of income is assumed to be 3,000, and this is spent on ten commodities whose initial prices all equal one. In addition,

$$
\begin{aligned}
a_i &= 1 & a_i &= 1, \ldots, 10 \\
b_1 &= 0.19 & b_6 &= 0.09 \\
b_2 &= 0.13 & b_7 &= 0.08 \\
b_3 &= 0.12 & b_8 &= 0.07 \\
b_4 &= 0.11 & b_9 &= 0.06 \\
b_5 &= 0.10 & b_{10} &= 0.05
\end{aligned}
$$

In Table 3.2 are shown the results for several examples using the two methods discussed in this chapter. In addition, a consumer surplus measure based on the indirect addilog is also calculated via Simpson's rule. The "path of calculation" is analogous to that used for the money-metric. [The path chosen is the same as that recently suggested by Willig (1979).] Cases 1 and 2 can be used as a rough indicator of the error bands associated with any range of variable change that is plus or minus 30 percent of the initial levels of expenditure and prices. In both instances the true change in money-metric utility is zero. The

Table 3.2

Case	Method 1		Method 2		Consumer surplus	
	E	$\dfrac{\text{Error}}{Y_0}$	E	$\dfrac{\text{Error}}{Y_0}$	CS	$\dfrac{\text{Error}}{Y_0}$
Case 1 $Y = 3,900$ $P_i = 1.3\ (i = 1,\ldots,n)$	9.83	—	0.15	—	−126.672	0.04
Case 2 $Y = 2,100$ $P_i = 0.7\ (i = 1,\ldots,n)$	7.25	—	2.12	—	−154.239	0.05
Case 3 $Y = 2,700$ $P_i = 1 + (-1)^i(0.3)$ $(i = 1,\ldots,n)$	73.35	—	65.45	—	41.13	0.01

errors associated with the second method are the smallest and indeed are virtually negligible as a proportion of initial expenditure. The errors associated with Method 1 are also small, but not as small as those for Method 2, since only information about a particular set of prices and expenditure is used in the Taylor series expansion. In contrast, Method 2 uses information over the whole range of the price variation. As we might expect, the errors associated with consumer surplus are definitely not close to zero, ranging between 4 and 5 percent of initial total expenditure.

A third test of the robustness of the proposed methods, a more complex price variation, was examined. This involved a 30 percent cut in p_1, a 30 percent rise in p_2, a 30 percent cut in p_3, and so forth. In addition, it was assumed that income fell from 3,000 to 2,700. As proportions of national income, the errors associated with all three are small, although here again that associated with consumer surplus is the largest. As a percentage of the true value of money-metric utility 65.45, however, Method 1 is in error by 12 percent, whereas the consumer surplus measure has an error of 37 percent. No appreciable error arises from using Method 2.

It should be emphasized that these examples are designed merely to illustrate the robustness of Method 2 and to a lesser extent the accuracy of the first method. Obviously, the nature of any calculations will depend on the complexity of the problem under consideration. In the past, most cost–benefit analysts have tended to evaluate projects within a partial equilibrium framework. The danger here is that secondary effects involving price and expenditure variations tend to be neglected. However, within the framework discussed in this book, these can be easily and accurately computed.

At a different level, consumer surplus techniques have been widely used in theoretical and applied studies involving two policy problems: (a) measurement of the social costs of monopoly and (b) measurement of the social costs of tariff protection. In each instance, elimination of the market imperfection can be expected to have important effects on relative prices and expenditure, and consumer surplus calculations are bound to generate significant errors. The money-metric approach, on the other hand, provides a consistent and accurate representation of the costs involved when monopoly, tariff protection or other restrictions, and market imperfections are important.

The same is also true if the procedures developed in this chapter are used to calculate the money-metric cost-of-living index and the Allen quantity index discussed in Chapter 6. Indeed, Case 1 provides a good representation of what might happen during periods of inflation. Both prices and income rise rapidly, but with no net effect on the standard of living. Although both Methods 1 and 2 have small errors, these will not be evident, because the appropriate index number will be unchanged up to the third digit.

Of course, for index-number calculations involving large numbers of price variables, it is quite likely that the magnitude of the error involved will be greater. If the error margins, as discussed earlier, appear unacceptable, then Methods 1 and 2 can be improved on by adopting more accurate numerical procedures. Where Taylor series expansions are involved, these can be extended to a higher order. With respect to Method 2, more accurate procedures than Simpson's rule (but similar to it) are available. However, discussion of these techniques is outside the scope of this volume; the interested reader is urged to consult appropriate sources (e.g., Courant, 1937; Householder, 1953; Apostol, 1967; Hildebrand, 1974).

3.9   Summary

The fact that the ordinal properties associated with any preference function are invariant under increasing, monotonic transformations provides us with an important degree of freedom. It means that we can choose any transformation such that the marginal utility of money and its higher-order derivatives with respect to expenditure take on any values that we wish at some given, arbitrarily chosen point. Thus, when a utility function is expressed in terms of a Taylor series expansion, all expressions involving the marginal utility of money can be replaced by other expressions involving only directly observable parameters and variables. One particular transformation involving

$$\lambda(p^0, Y) \equiv 1$$

and

$$\frac{\partial^i \lambda}{\partial Y^i}(p^0, Y) \equiv 0 \quad (i = 1, \ldots, \infty)$$

enables us to write any utility function as a money-metric equal to the equivalent variation.

The difficulty with a Taylor series formulation, however, is that it is computationally cumbersome. Hence, two alternative procedures are presented. Numerical examples indicate that they will provide superior results to the calculation of consumer surplus.

Appendix 3.1

The calculation of the money-metric by means of the modified Simpson's rule approach can be summarized by the following algorithm:

Algorithm

Input.

1. A set of n consumer demand functions and their derivatives with respect to prices and total expenditure (these functions must be consistent with the theory of consumer behavior).
2. A set of observations on n prices (p_i^0) and quantities demanded (X_i^0) for an arbitrarily chosen base period.
3. A set of observations on n prices (p_i^1) and quantities demanded (X_i^1) for a period different than the base period.
4. Initial values of the marginal utility of money and its derivatives up to the third order:

$$\lambda = 1$$

$$\frac{\partial^i \lambda}{\partial Y^i} = 0 \quad (i = 1, 2, 3)$$

Output. A monetary value representing the variation in the money-metric (i.e., the equivalent variation) associated with changes in prices and total expenditure from base levels to new levels.

Method.

1. Calculate λ for $p_i^m = p_i^0 + \Delta p_i/2$ and $p_i^1 = p_i^0 + \Delta p_i$ using the Taylor series method.
2. Calculate the change in the money-metric ΔM_i for commodity i by the Simpson's rule method.
3. Repeat steps 1 and 2 for all n commodities, using the value of $\lambda(p_i^1)$ as the starting point for the $i + 1$ iteration.
4. Sum all ΔM_i and $\Delta Y = \left(\sum_i p_i^1 X_i^1\right) - \left(\sum p_i^0 X_i^0\right)$ to obtain the total change in the money-metric.

On the basis of the discussion contained in this chapter and the preceding algorithm, it should be a fairly simple matter for readers to write computer programs to meet their needs. Because full programs will be different for different projects, only the basic calculation method will be shown. The following statements can provide the basis for a subroutine or can be incorporated directly into the user's main program. The sequence shown here must be repeated for each of the commodities whose price is varied.

Notation:

$$Y = \text{new value for total expenditure if this variable}$$
$$\text{has been altered in magnitude}$$
$$P(I) = \text{new price of commodity } i$$
$$H(I) = \text{old price of commodity } i$$
$$A1 = \text{the quantity demanded of } X_i$$
$$A2 = \partial X_i/\partial p_i$$
$$A3 = \partial^2 X_i/\partial p_i^2$$
$$A4 = \partial X_i/\partial Y$$
$$A5 = \partial^2 X_i/\partial Y^2$$
$$A6 = \partial^2 X_i/\partial Y \partial p_i$$
$$A7 = \partial^3 X_i/\partial p_i^3$$
$$A8 = \partial^3 X_i/\partial Y \partial p_i^2$$
$$A9 = \partial^3 X_i/\partial Y^3$$
$$L\emptyset = \text{the marginal utility of money } \lambda$$
$$L1 = \partial\lambda/\partial p_i$$
$$L2 = \partial^2\lambda/\partial p_i^2$$

Statements:

```
700        D(I) = (P(I) − H(I))/2
701          NØ = P(I)
702      FOR K = 1 TO 3
703          P(I) = NØ + (K − 1) * D(I)
```

```
801        A1 = ⎫
802        A2 = ⎪
803        A3 = ⎬
804        A4 = ⎪
805        A5 = ⎬       functions provided by user
806        A6 = ⎪
807        A7 = ⎬
808        A8 = ⎪
809        A9 = ⎭
```

810     $F(K) = -L\emptyset * A1$

901     $B1 = -L\emptyset * A4 - A1 * L1$

902     $B2 = -2 * L1 * A4 - L\emptyset * A5 - A1 * L2$

903     $B3 = -B2 * A1 - L1 * A2 - B1 * A4 - L\emptyset * A6$

904     $B4 = -3 * L2 * A4 - 3 * L1 * A5 - L\emptyset * A9 - A1 * L3$

905     $B5 = -B4 * A1 - 2 * B2 * A4 - L2 * A2 - 2 * L1 * A6 - B1 * A5 - L\emptyset * A9$

906     $B6 = -B5 * A1 - 2 * B2 * A2 - L1 * A3 - B3 * A4 - 2 * B1 * A6 - L\emptyset * A8$

910     $C = L\emptyset + B1 * D(I) + (B3/2) * (D(I) ** 2) + (B6/6) * (D(I) ** 3)$

911     $L\emptyset = C$

912     $C = L1 + B2 * D(I) + (B5/2) * (D(I) ** 2)$

913     $L1 = C$

914     $C = L2 + B4 * D(I)$

915     $L2 = C$

916   NEXT K

CHAPTER 4

The approach of Dupuit and Marshall

4.1   Introduction

In the preceding chapters we have shown that, in general, consumer preferences can be expressed in the form of a money-metric. In addition, provided that these preferences are "well behaved," the money-metric can be calculated from the parameters of ordinary demand functions. The question then arises: Why haven't economists, particularly those working in the areas of cost–benefit analysis and the theory of index numbers, appreciated these facts before? To properly answer this question, we really require a definitive theory concerning the evolution of scientific thinking. Alas, such an undertaking is not feasible. However, it is possible to offer one hypothesis in this respect, even though it may not be possible to to ascertain its validity. When a particular problem arises for the first time, initial attempts to solve it are inevitably simple, based as they are on a lack of prior experience. As time passes, the defects of any solution technique can be identified and gradually eliminated. However, in the process, paradigms or modes of thinking may develop. Although these may contain valuable insights into the nature of particular problems, their widespread adoption and use may blinker and limit scientific progress in a particular area. Such an explanation, I believe, goes a long way toward explaining the fact that consumer surplus techniques continue to play a central role in much of economic analysis.

Despite well-known defects, which we shall discuss in this and the next chapter, the pedagogic simplicity of consumer surplus made it difficult for previous generations of economists to achieve the progress that we have made in the preceding three chapters. To appreciate why this has been the case, it is necessary to examine the analytic underpinnings of the major contributions to the literature on consumer surplus: those of Dupuit, Marshall; and Hicks. The work of the first two authors will be the subject of this chapter. The work of Hicks will be discussed in Chapter 5. [For an alternative presentation of the various issues involved, the interested reader is referred to the survey article by Chipman and Moore (1980).]

4.2   The seminal work of Dupuit

In the early nineteenth century, economists and civil servants were becoming increasingly interested in establishing objective criteria that could be used to evaluate the net monetary benefits associated with a particular project or policy. The opportunities thrown open by the Industrial Revolution had created the requirement for a means to calculate the potential net gains (or losses) of an action in such a way that the results could be presented to the relevant financing body. The seminal paper in this area was by Jules Dupuit, not an economist, but an engineer serving as an inspector of bridges and highways in France. It is on his work that most of modern cost–benefit analysis is based.

Dupuit began his argument with a critique of J. B. Say's analysis of the relationship between price and utility. In particular, Say believed that "price is the measure of the value of things, and their value the measure of the utility imputed to them" (1880, p. 5). The implication of this approach is that total utility is obtained by multiplying the price of a commodity times the quantity purchased. According to Dupuit, however, the most that could be said of such a calculation is that it represents a lower bound on the level of satisfaction attained. His argument was that the price of a commodity does not represent the utility that a consumer enjoys from each unit of that commodity consumed. Rather, the price simply indicates the additional utility obtained from the last unit purchased. For other units, the consumer would have been willing to pay more than the market price. Hence, actual satisfaction obtained from a commodity will be in excess of actual expenditure. His argument can be paraphrased in the following way. Consider Figure 4.1. According to Dupuit, the first unit consumed will generate utility equal to p_1, because this is the price the consumer will be willing to pay for that first unit. The price p_2 is then the utility received from the second unit of consumption. And so forth. Thus, if the actual market price for the commodity is p_4, total satisfaction can be obtained, according to Dupuit, by adding up the areas of the four bars as drawn. If consumption is perfectly divisible, the demand curve shown in Figure 4.1 can be used to calculate the satisfaction enjoyed by consumers and will equal the "mixtilinear trapezium" $0ABD$. It is clear that this amount is greater than the area p_4BD0 that would be obtained by the application of Say's formula. This excess has come to be known as consumer surplus, defined as the amount that a consumer would be willing to pay for a given quantity of a commodity over the amount that actually is paid. In terms of Figure 4.1, the area ABp_4 represents this surplus.

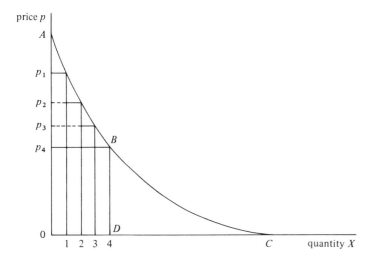

Figure 4.1

Dupuit, of course, was concerned with more than a theoretical formulation of consumer surplus. He was keen to apply this analytic tool
to practical problems. We shall examine here his analysis of the effect
of an imposition of a tax on some commodity that is "cheap and
consumed in large quantities." Consider Figure 4.2. If p is the given
free-market price of a commodity and pp^1 is a small tax, the loss of
consumer surplus equals the trapezoid pp^1n^1n. The gain in tax revenue is pp^1n^1q. Dupuit then added these together to obtain the "utility
lost both to the taxpayers and the fisc," the triangle n^1qn. If the tax is
doubled to the level pp^{11}, it is easily seen that the net loss of utility
becomes $n^{11}q^1n$, which is four times the loss associated with the tax pp^1.
Similarly, the tax pp^{111}, three times pp^1, yields a net loss nine times the
size of n^1qn. This led Dupuit to conclude that "the loss of utility
increases as the square of the tax" (1844, p. 281).

Dupuit's contribution to the historical development of applied welfare economics is twofold. First, his work represents the first serious
attempt to draw welfare conclusions from information about consumer demand curves, constructs that, in principle, are observable.
Second, he introduced the interpretation of willingness to pay or
compensation to the area beneath the demand schedule. Despite the
fact that Dupuit's analysis was formulated more than 135 years ago,
his interpretation remains the foundation stone around which much
of the theoretical and applied welfare economics literature has been

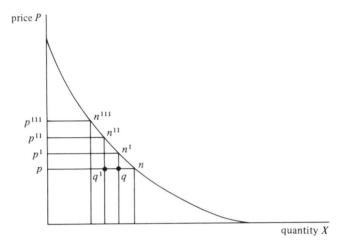

Figure 4.2

built. Indeed, the formula given earlier, whereby the net losses increase as the square of a tax, still plays a crucial role in the analysis of monopoly practices, measurement of the costs of protection, and other problems in the field of public policy. As we shall see, there have been arguments over interpretation, and, as a whole, the framework has become more refined and sophisticated with the application of mathematical techniques, particularly as the theory of consumer behavior has become better developed. However, in most modern texts, discussions of consumer surplus still trace their heritage to Dupuit.

4.3   Early criticisms of consumer surplus

Reservations about the foregoing approach did not begin to appear until the 1870s, when Jevons and Walras each raised a significant point. Let us consider them in turn.

Jevons's argument. In the following quotation from his *Theory of Political Economy*, Jevons used the notation

ΦX = the marginal utility of the commodity x (i.e., the "final degree of utility")

ΨC = the marginal utility of money

m = the price of x

Thus, he argued

We cannot really tell the effect of any change in trade or manufacture until we can with some approach to truth express the laws of the variation of utility numerically. To do this we need accurate statistics of the quantities of commodities purchased by the whole population at various prices. The price of a commodity is the only test we have of the utility of the commodity to the purchaser; and if we could tell exactly how much people reduce their consumption of each important article when the price rises, we could determine, at least approximately, the variation of the final degree of utility — the all important element in economics... For the first approximation we may assume that the general utility of a person's income is not affected by the changes of price of commodity; so that if in the equation $\Phi X = m \Psi C$ we may have many different corresponding values for x and m we may treat ΨC, the utility of money, as a constant, and determine the general character of the function ΨX, the final degree of utility. [p.175]

The foregoing reasoning would appear to imply that the consumer surplus measure will be proportional to total utility. Indeed, the two will be equal in the case where the price, denoted above as m, is one. However, Jevons was extremely reluctant to admit the generality of such an approach:

The method of determining the function of utility explained above will hardly apply, however, to the main elements of expenditure. The price of bread, for instance, cannot be properly brought under the equation in question, because, when the price of bread rises much, the resources of poor persons are strained, money becomes scarcer with them, and ΨC, the utility of money rises.

The implication of this statement is that the consumer surplus procedure suggested by Dupuit is likely to represent a poor approximation to the level of satisfaction, because it assumes away variations in the marginal utility of money.

Walras's argument.   Although Jevons did not refer to Dupuit's work at all, his argument is nonetheless relevant. Walras, on the other hand, was explicit in pointing out the significance of the French engineer's contribution, tempering his praise by pointing out an error in the analysis. Indeed, Walras did not believe that Dupuit's exposition was an improvement on Say's:

To be sure, the maximum pecuniary sacrifice which a consumer is willing to make in order to obtain a bottle of wine, for instance, depends, in part on the utility of this bottle of wine for this consumer; for according as this utility increases or decreases, the maximum sacrifice in question will increase or decrease. But Dupuit did not perceive that this maximum sacrifice depends, in part, also on the utility which bread, meat, clothes and furniture have for the consumer; for, as the utility he derives from other commodities increases or decreases, the maximum sacrifice that he will be willing to make for wine will decrease or increase...In general the maximum pecuniary sacrifice which a consumer is willing to make to obtain a unit of a product depends not only on the utility of the product in question, but also on the utility of all the other products in the market, and, finally on the consumer's means. [Walras, 1954, p. 445]

The upshot of these early criticisms of Dupuit's analysis is that in general it is not possible to carry out correct calculations of welfare changes via a partial equilibrium analysis by treating each commodity as if it were in some sense separate from all others. In the language of Chapter 3, we must make sure that the conditions for path independence hold. In general, this means that we must take into account variations in the marginal utility of money, which acts as an integrating factor in the construction of the desired measure.

4.4   The treatment of consumer surplus in Marshall's *Principles*

Both of the points raised earlier figure prominently in Alfred Marshall's discussion of consumer surplus in his *Principles* (1920). Because his analysis is more sophisticated in a number of respects, it is perhaps most appropriate to develop these issues in this context. Unfortunately, Marshall left his work open to a variety of competing interpretations. Basically, he failed to distinguish among

1. a measure of utility,
2. a measure relating to the area under a single demand curve, or set of demand curves, less total expenditure, and
3. "the excess of the price which he [i.e., a consumer] would be willing to pay rather than go without the thing, over that which he actually does pay." [1920, p. 124]

This latter concept figured prominently in John Hicks's attempt to rehabilitate consumer surplus in the 1940s. Thus, we shall postpone discussion of this particular measure until the next chapter, where we shall examine Hicks's work in some detail. Two other organizational points are in order at this stage. First, Marshall did not clearly distinguish between analysis of the marginal utility of money as an exact function whose value remains unchanged and analysis of situations in which changes in the marginal utility are small. In this chapter we shall confine ourselves to an examination of the first condition, postponing until Chapter 6 the implications of approximations. Second, in the various editions of the *Principles*, Marshall did not distinguish carefully between the singular *consumer's surplus* and the plural *consumers' surplus*. However, there are important technical and ethical problems to be dealt with before one can move from the former to the latter. For the moment we shall avoid these difficulties by continuing to proceed as if we are discussing only an individual or homogeneous group of individuals. This approach will be maintained until Chapter 8, where problems of aggregation and the construction of social welfare functions will be discussed.

Let us now focus our attention on Marshall's attempt to construct a measure of satisfaction based on demand functions. Unfortunately, even this narrowing down of the task to be pursued contains an important difficulty: The exact nature of Marshall's demand function is far from clear. Consider the following passage from the *Principles*:

> The larger the amount of a thing that a person has the less, other things being equal (i.e. the purchasing power of money, and the amount of money at his command being equal) will be the price which he will pay for a little more of it: or in other words his marginal demand price for it diminishes. [1920, p. 95]

If we interpret the purchasing power of money as synonymous with real income or the level of satisfaction, as Friedman (1949) has done, then we are led into a real dilemma. It is simply impossible to keep both the purchasing power of money and money income simultaneously constant, as it would appear that Marshall desired to do. The question then arises which approach should be adopted in this volume. I do not propose to undertake an exegesis on this point, partly because it would represent a diversion from the stated aims of this volume, and partly because a final resolution of any debate would really require a firsthand discussion with Marshall himself. Therefore, I propose to examine the concept of consumer surplus in the light of *both* competing interpretations. There are some compelling reasons for following this procedure.

First, Marshall's discussion itself is clearly dichotomous. The analysis of consumer surplus contained in the mathematical appendixes of the *Principles* tends to support the view that he was assuming money income constant and thus measuring the change in utility due to one or more price variations. In the text, however, he gave the distinct impression that he was holding the purchasing power of money constant in an attempt to measure, via consumer surplus, the compensation that a consumer would be willing to pay in order to maintain his level of satisfaction constant.

Second, the notion of a demand function derived on the basis of a constant level of satisfaction was not fully exploited until Hicks's famous attempt to rehabilitate consumer surplus in 1941 and the subsequent case put forward by Friedman in 1949. Prior to that, economists had been content to discuss consumer surplus in terms of demand curves derived on the basis of a constant income (e.g., Hotelling, 1938; Wilson, 1939).

Third, from an operational, practical point of view, the constant money income demand function is easier to derive and estimate. Indeed, this is the approach that applied econometric demand analysis has taken. In contrast, the constant utility demand curve is only indirectly observable. Not only do we need to know how the consumer is going to respond to a price variation; we also need to know how he will respond to variations in income, so that the latter can be undertaken to keep utility constant.

Thus, our plan of attack is as follows. In this chapter we shall concentrate our attention on the analysis contained in Marshall's mathematical appendixes, and in particular we shall evaluate it in light of the discussion contained in our preceding three chapters. Then, in the next chapter we shall examine the alternative constant utility interpretation, with particular reference to the work of Hicks.

4.5   Marshall's mathematical appendixes

In note VI of of his mathematical appendixes, Marshall developed the concept of consumer surplus along the following lines. First, he did not treat the quantity demanded as a function of price, but rather the converse. That is, the price of a commodity was written as a function of the quantity demanded. Then, he argued, "the total utility of a commodity is measured by $\int_0^a f(x)\,dx$, where a is the amount consumed." However, this formulation was immediately modified by the introduction of a parameter b that represented the minimum quantity of the commodity necessary for existence. This was necessary, Marshall believed, because "$f(x)$ will be infinite, or at least indefinitely great, for values of x less than b." Hence, for a single commodity, consumer surplus would be measured by

$$\int_b^a f(x)\,dx \tag{4.1}$$

In note VII, Marshall attempted to generalize equation (4.1) to the case of many commodities by writing total utility in a form equivalent to

$$\sum \int_b^a f(x_i)\,dx_i \tag{4.2}$$

However, he then concluded, "but we cannot do this: and therefore the formulae remains a mere general expression, having no practical application." At that stage he referred the reader back to a footnote on pp. 131–2 of the main text of the *Principles*. The note itself referred to the following passage:

It will be noted, however, that the demand prices of each commodity, on which our estimates of its total utility are and consumers' surplus are based, assume that *other things remain equal,* while its price rises to scarcity value: and when the total utilities of two commodities which contribute to the same purpose are calculated on this plan, we cannot say that the total utility of the two together is equal to the sum of the total utilities of each separately.

Then, in the note associated with that sentence, Marshall said:

Some ambiguous phrases in earlier editions appear to have suggested to some readers the opposite opinion. But the task of adding together the total utilities of all commodities, so as to obtain the aggregate of the total utility of all wealth, is beyond the range of any but the most elaborate mathematical formulae. An attempt to treat it by them some years ago convinced the present writer that even if the task be theoretically feasible, the result would be encumbered by so many hypotheses as to be practically useless.

This position was further reinforced at a later date in a letter Marshall wrote to one of his critics:

Some (American) writers have sought to aggregate consumer's surplus for all things. I never have. If the necessaries of life be taken for granted, and a number of arbitrary assumptions made, the surplus might conceivably be elaborated. But my own attempts (made twenty-five years ago) in this direction failed so completely that I never implied it could be done. [Nicholson, 1902, p. 65]

It is quite clear that Marshall was concerned with the same problem that concerned Walras: The interrelationship between commodities makes it impossible, in general, to add up consumer surpluses across goods. Unfortunately, Marshall did not provide us with any clear-cut indication as to the nature of his attempts or the properties of the mathematical formulas with which he experimented. We are left in the dark as to what he was actually thinking.

However, if we examine the concept of consumer surplus within the context of the modern theory of consumer behavior, we arrive at a number of conclusions that, remarkably, are consistent with what Marshall was saying. Let us begin as follows. In Chapter 2 we noted that it is possible to write any change in utility as

$$\Delta U = \sum \int_{a_i}^{b_i} \frac{\partial U}{\partial X_i} dX_i = -\sum \int_{a_i}^{b_i} \lambda p_i(X_1, \ldots, X_n, Y) dX_i \qquad (4.3)$$

We also showed that the marginal utility of money λ is not invariant under any arbitrary monotonic increasing transformation of the chosen utility function. However, all we need to do is find a particular formula for λ in order to obtain a utility index consistent with consumer behavior as revealed by the demand functions. Thus, in terms of this reasoning, Marshall's problem becomes one of finding a set of inverse demand functions $p_i(X_i, \ldots, X_n)$ such that, for a given transformation, λ is independent of all prices (but not total expenditure Y, which is given). In other words, we require that the inverse demand functions observe the following integrability condition:

$$\frac{\partial p_i}{\partial X_j} = \frac{\partial p_j}{\partial X_i} \tag{4.4}$$

This condition was first derived by Hotelling in 1938. However, its full meaning was not perceived at the time. The first thing to note is that the derivative $\partial p_i / \partial X_i$ must not be interpreted as the reciprocal of the ordinary price effect $\partial X_i / \partial p_i$. Inverse demand functions have their own properties. Although these constructs continue to play a prominent role in applications of surplus theory, the theory underlying them is rarely presented. One exception is I. F. Pearce's *Contribution to Demand Analysis*, on which the following discussion is based.

We know from the first-order conditions for maximization of a direct utility function that

$$\frac{\partial U}{\partial X_i} = \lambda p_i \quad (i = 1, \ldots, n) \tag{4.5}$$

If we substitute this condition into the budget constraint $Y = \Sigma p_i X_i$, we obtain an expression for λ, as follows:

$$\lambda = \frac{\Sigma (\partial U / \partial X_i) X_i}{Y} \tag{4.6}$$

Substitution of (4.6) into (4.5), followed by a rearrangement of terms, yields an expression for the inverse demand function:

$$p_i = Y \frac{U_i}{\Sigma U_k X_k} \tag{4.7}$$

This relationship is homogeneous of degree one in income. Then, for the integrability condition (4.4) to be fulfilled, the following two derivatives must be equal:

$$\frac{\partial p_i}{\partial X_j} = Y \left(\frac{U_{ij}}{\Sigma U_k X_k} - \frac{U_i U_j}{(\Sigma U_k X_k)^2} - \frac{U_i (\Sigma U_{kj} X_k)}{(\Sigma U_k X_k)^2} \right) \tag{4.8}$$

$$\frac{\partial p_j}{\partial X_i} = Y \left(\frac{U_{ji}}{\Sigma U_k X_k} - \frac{U_j U_i}{(\Sigma U_k X_k)^2} - \frac{U_j (\Sigma U_{ki} X_k)}{(\Sigma U_k X_k)^2} \right) \tag{4.9}$$

It is immediately apparent that the first two terms on the right-hand sides of (4.8) and (4.9) are equal. However, in general, the third terms of the two expressions will not be equal. The equality will hold if and only if there exists some factor $n(x)$ such that

$$\sum_{k} U_{kj}X_k = n(x)U_j \tag{4.10}$$

$$\sum_{k} U_{ki}X_k = n(x)U_i \tag{4.11}$$

conditions that imply that the utility index under examination is homothetic. (A proof of this proposition is contained in Appendix 4.1 at the end of this chapter.) That is, all income elasticities equal unity, a very strong restriction that has never been borne out by econometric demand analysis.

Marshall, of course, formulated his consumer surplus measure in terms that were even more restrictive than those we have just derived, for he assumed that the inverse demand functions were strictly independent of one another, except for the total expenditure variable Y. This restriction automatically guarantees that the integrability condition holds, because it implies that all inverse demand effects (e.g., $\partial p_i/\partial X_j$ and $\partial p_j/\partial X_i$) are equal to zero. To fully understand the implications of this condition, we shall rewrite the inverse demand function (4.7) as a general function of all commodities consumed:

$$p_i = Yh_i(X_1, \ldots, X_n) \quad (i = 1, \ldots, n) \tag{4.12}$$

If there is independence along the lines assumed by Marshall, then it must be the case that p_i depends only on its own quantity, that is,

$$p_i = Yg_i(X_i) \tag{4.13}$$

The adding-up condition implies that

$$\sum_{j} X_j g_j(X_j) = 1 \tag{4.14}$$

Hence, by differentiating (4.14) with respect to X_i, we obtain

$$g_i(X_i) + X_i \frac{\partial g_i}{\partial X_i} = 0 \quad (i = 1, \ldots, n) \tag{4.15}$$

If we then multiply (4.15) by X_i and sum over all commodities, we find

$$\sum X_j^2 \frac{\partial g_j}{\partial X_j} = -1 \tag{4.16}$$

which can be true only if

$$\frac{\partial g_i}{\partial X_i} = -\frac{b_i}{X_i^2} \tag{4.17}$$

or, equivalently, if

$$g_i = b_i/X_i \tag{4.18}$$

This means that the underlying

$$X_i = \frac{b_i}{p_i}Y \tag{4.19}$$

where b_i is the propensity to consume the ith commodity. However, (4.19) is simply a special case of the Klein-Rubin system discussed at length in Chapter 2. Hence, the utility index implied by Marshall's formulation can be rewritten as

$$U = \prod_i X_i^{b_i} \tag{4.20}$$

or, alternatively, as

$$V = \sum b_i \ln X_i \tag{4.21}$$

An interesting question is whether or not Marshall was aware of these issued. Earlier we noted that he explicitly rejected integration over a range from 0 to a on the grounds that $f(X)$ would be infinite. In 1942, Samuelson interpreted Marshall's consumer surplus as

$$\sum \int_0^{a_i} f(X)\, dX_i = \int_0^{a_i} \frac{b_i}{X_i} Y\, dX_i \tag{4.22}$$

and showed that it implied a utility function

$$U = \sum C_i \ln X_i \Big|_0^{a_i} \tag{4.23}$$

However, this implies that satisfaction is always minus infinity (see Samuelson, 1942). Marshall clearly avoided this difficulty by assuming a positive lower bound of integration equal to the subsistence level of consumption for the commodity in question. It should also be noted that the functional form (4.23), known generally as Bernoulli's hypothesis, was the subject of some discussion at the time and, indeed, figured prominently in Marshall's thoughts. Thus, although this specific relationship does not appear directly in his discussion of consumer surplus, he was certainly aware of it.

Another hint as to the degree to which Marshall appreciated the difficulties associated with consumer surplus arises in note VII of his mathematical appendix. He wrote that consumer surplus might be calculable "if we could find a plan for grouping together in one common demand curve all those things which satisfy the same wants, and are rivals; and also for every group of things of which the services are complementary." Since then, the precise mathematical conditions for "grouping" commodities together have been laid down. In 1958, Gorman showed that composite commodities could be constructed only if the income effects were equal for all goods making up the composite commodity. The condition of unitary income elasticities, noted earlier, is a sufficient condition, though admittedly not a necessary condition, for this to be the case. However, given the nature of Marshall's discussion, it is interesting to speculate as to his awareness of the problem and to see just how close he was to deriving such conditions himself.

4.6 Consumer surplus based on ordinary demand functions

Most writers have interpreted the term *Marshallian consumer surplus* in terms of ordinary demand functions rather than the inverse functions we have just been examining. However, this alternative approach generates results similar to those of Marshall, and because it is much simpler analytically, it warrants our attention. Let us now define the consumer surplus measure as

$$\text{CS} = \int \sum X_i(Y, p_1, \ldots, p_n)\, dp_i \tag{4.24}$$

The integrability condition implies the restriction that the matrix of ordinary uncompensated price effects be symmetric, that is,

$$\frac{\partial X_i}{\partial p_j} = \frac{\partial X_j}{\partial p_i} \tag{4.25}$$

If we substitute (4.25) back into the Slutsky equation,

$$\frac{\partial X_i}{\partial p_j} - X_i \frac{\partial X_j}{\partial Y} = \frac{\partial X_j}{\partial p_i} - X_j \frac{\partial X_i}{\partial Y} \tag{2.73}$$

we find that commodity demand must be proportional to the associated income effects:

$$\frac{X_i}{X_j} = \frac{\partial X_i / \partial Y}{\partial X_j / \partial Y} \tag{4.26}$$

It is easily determined from the budget constraint that if (4.26) holds for *all* pairs of commodities, then all income elasticities must equal unity.

However, if only a subset of prices is varying, then (4.25) and (4.26) imply a very special form of preference system, with those commodities whose prices do vary exhibiting identical income elasticities. To determine what is involved, however, let us first partition the vector of prices p into two parts, the first, p_m, containing all prices that vary, and the second, p_s, containing all prices that remain constant. If we express consumer preferences in indirect form, $v = v(Y, p)$, then from Roy's rule we obtain

$$X_i = -\frac{\partial v/\partial p_i}{\partial v/\partial Y} \quad (i = 1, \ldots, n) \tag{4.27}$$

For $i \in m$, symmetry of the matrix of ordinary, uncompensated price effects implies

$$\begin{aligned}
\frac{\partial X_i}{\partial p_j} &= -\frac{\partial^2 v/\partial p_i \partial p_j}{\partial v/\partial Y} + \frac{\partial v/\partial p_i}{(\partial v/\partial Y)^2}\frac{\partial^2 v}{\partial Y \partial p_j} \\
&= \frac{\partial^2 v/\partial p_j \partial p_i}{\partial v/\partial Y} + \frac{\partial v/\partial p_j}{(\partial v/\partial Y)^2}\frac{\partial^2 v}{\partial Y \partial p_i} \\
&= \frac{\partial X_j}{\partial p_i} \quad (i,j = 1, \ldots, m)
\end{aligned} \tag{4.28}$$

This equality, in turn, implies that

$$\frac{\partial v/\partial p_i}{\partial v/\partial p_j} = \frac{\partial^2 v/\partial Y \partial p_i}{\partial^2 v/\partial Y \partial p_j} \quad (i,j = 1, \ldots, m) \tag{4.29}$$

which is exactly equivalent to the condition that

$$\partial\left(\frac{\partial v/\partial p_i}{\partial v/\partial p_j}\right)\Big/\partial Y = 0 \tag{4.30}$$

That is, the ratio of marginal utilities in (4.30) is independent of the level of total expenditure. This peculiar form of indirect separability implies that consumer preferences must be of the form

$$v = v[\phi_1(p_m, p_s) + \phi_2(Y, p_s)] \tag{4.31}$$

where ϕ_1 and ϕ_2 must each be homogeneous of degree zero in their respective arguments. Equation (4.31) generates demand functions as follows:

$$X_i = -\frac{\partial \phi_1/\partial p_i}{\partial \phi_2/\partial Y} \quad (i \in m) \tag{4.32}$$

$$X_r = \frac{\partial \phi_1 / \partial p_r + \partial \phi_2 / \partial p_r}{\partial \phi_2 / \partial Y} \quad (r \in s) \tag{4.33}$$

It is easily calculated from (4.32) that for the class of commodities whose prices are changing, all income elasticities are identical:

$$\frac{\partial X_i / \partial Y}{\partial X_j / \partial Y} = \frac{X_i}{X_j} \tag{4.34}$$

However, the question is whether or not the conditions (4.34) are of sufficient "practical" interest, as Dixit and Weller (1979, p. 129) would claim. Whereas considerable research effort has gone into the estimation of systems of demand functions, little attention has been given to testing whether or not income elasticities are identical for groups of commodities. Indeed, as we have seen, this implies testing for the existence of a preference function that is separable in Y and p_m. All the most complex functional forms, such as the addilog, translog, and PIGL specifications that are popular in the current literature on applied demand analysis, adopt the maintained hypothesis that such separability does not exist. To pursue this line of empirical investigation, new classes of preference systems would have to be developed.

Nevertheless, even if it could reasonably be shown that the matrix of uncompensated price effects were symmetric with respect to certain commodity groupings, it is not clear that this would really be of much assistance in applied welfare economics. For one thing, consumer surplus techniques could only be used to evaluate policies affecting the prices of such commodities. Yet consumer surplus techniques have been widely applied to such general problems as measuring the social costs of monopoly and measuring the costs of tariff protection. The abolition of monopoly practices or the removal of tariffs would be bound to have widespread implications throughout the economy, with many prices being substantially affected. It would be only by chance that such a potentially large group of commodities would possess quantitatively identical income elasticities.

4.7   Bishop's interpretation of Marshall

In their survey of the consumer surplus literature, Currie, Murphy, and Schmitz (1971) showed a strong preference for the interpretation of Marshall's analysis offered by Robert Bishop (1943). In this formulation, Bishop drew a distinction between (a) the ordinary demand curve relating price and quantity, under the assumption that total expenditure and the prices of related commodities all remain constant, and (b) a marginal utility demand curve that involves assuming that the quantities as well as the prices of related goods remain constant. This latter situation is alleged to be achieved by varying total expenditure in such a way that the marginal utility of money remains exactly constant. To facilitate this result, Bishop assumed, as did Marshall, that preferences can be written in the form of an additive function. To see what is involved, let us suppose that the price of X_1 varies. We know that, in general, the marginal utility of money λ is equal to the ratio of the marginal utility of each commodity to its price:

$$\frac{\partial U_1/\partial X_1}{p_1} = \frac{\partial U_2/\partial X_2}{p_2} = \ldots = \frac{\partial U_n/\partial X_n}{p_n} = \lambda \tag{4.35}$$

Because preferences are assumed to be additive, and because income is varied so as to keep λ constant, it must be the case that for all commodities except X_1,

$$\frac{\partial^2 U}{\partial X_i^2}\left(\frac{\partial X_i}{\partial p_1}dp_1 + \frac{\partial X_i}{\partial Y}dY\right) = 0 \quad (i = 2,\ldots,n) \tag{4.36}$$

That is,

$$\frac{dY}{dp_1} = -\frac{\partial X_2/\partial p_1}{\partial X_2/\partial Y} = \ldots = -\frac{\partial X_n/\partial p_1}{\partial X_n/\partial Y} \tag{4.37}$$

a condition that is implied by a preference system that is written in additive form (see Houthakker, 1960). Hence, no additional restrictions are necessary to keep λ constant. Bishop then interpreted the income compensation necessary to preserve this constancy as the true consumer surplus.

However, there are two fundamental problems with this approach. First, fairly strong restrictions on the signs of the income and cross-price effects are required. An increase in p_1 will lead to a loss of welfare that according to Bishop should be measured by the change in income required to keep the marginal utility of money constant. However, for this to be the case, it must be true that the cross-price effects $\partial X_i/\partial p_1$ and the income effects $\partial X_i/\partial Y$, as in (4.37), should all have the same sign. In this sense, it would be convenient if all commodities possessed positive income effects and were gross substitutes (i.e., all $\partial X_i/\partial p_1$ greater than zero). However, this clearly rules out the plausible case of gross complementarity (i.e., negative $\partial X_i/\partial p_1$). In other words, Bishop's measure is not an increasing, monotonic transformation of a consumer preference system.

This conclusion can be made clearer by considering an example based on the Klein-Rubin linear expenditure system. We have already shown that this system can be derived from an additive preference system of the form

$$U = \sum b_i \ln(X_i - c_i) \tag{4.38}$$

Thus, Bishop's precondition is met, because

$$X_i - c_i = \frac{b_i}{p_i}(Y - \sum c_k p_k)$$

the function in (3.30) can be rewritten as

$$U = \sum b_i \ln\frac{b_i}{p_i} + \ln(Y - \sum c_k p_k) \tag{4.39}$$

As a result, we calculate directly the marginal utility of money associated with (4.38) and (4.39) as

$$\lambda = \frac{1}{Y - \sum c_k p_k} \tag{4.40}$$

This result can also be obtained by using (4.6). Thus, the change of income required to keep λ constant, given, say, an increase in p_i, will be

$$\Delta Y = c_i \Delta p_i$$

which may be either positive or negative, depending on the value taken by the parameter c_i. However, the change in satisfaction given by the function (4.39) will always be negative.

Appendix 4.1

We shall prove that symmetry of the matrix of inverse demand effects $|\partial p_i/\partial X_j|$ implies homotheticity.

Let us first differentiate the first-order conditions for utility maximization to obtain the following total differential expressions:

$$\sum_k U_{kj} dX_k - p_j d\lambda = \lambda dp_j \quad (j = 1,\ldots,n) \tag{A4.1}$$

$$\sum_k p_k dX_k = dY - \sum_k X_k dp_k \tag{A4.2}$$

Define the following bordered Hessian matrix:

$$
D = \begin{vmatrix}
U_{11} & U_{12} & \cdots & U_{1N} & P_1 \\
U_{21} & U_{22} & \cdots & U_{2N} & P_2 \\
\cdot & \cdot & & \cdot & \cdot \\
\cdot & \cdot & & \cdot & \cdot \\
\cdot & \cdot & & \cdot & \cdot \\
U_{N1} & U_{N2} & \cdots & U_{NN} & P_N \\
P_1 & P_2 & \cdots & P_N & 0
\end{vmatrix}
\tag{A4.3}
$$

It is well known that the income effect associated with the demand functions derived from the first-order conditions can be written as

$$
\frac{\partial X_j}{\partial Y} = \frac{|D_{N+1,j}|}{|D|}
\tag{A4.4}
$$

where $|D|$ is the determinant of D and $D_{N+1,j}$ is the co-factor associated with row $N + 1$ and column j of D. From (4.10) and (4.11) we know that symmetry of the inverse demand effects $|\partial p_i / \partial X_j|$ will occur if and only if

$$
\sum_k U_{kj} X_k = n(x) U_j \quad (j = 1, \ldots, n)
\tag{A4.5}
$$

or, equivalently, if

$$
p_j = \frac{1}{n \cdot \lambda} \sum_k U_{kj} X_k \quad (j = 1, \ldots, n)
\tag{A4.6}
$$

If we substitute (A4.6) into (A4.3) and then calculate (A4.4), we obtain

$$
\frac{\partial X_j}{\partial Y} = \frac{1}{\lambda \prod_{k \neq j} X_k} \frac{|D|}{|D|}
\tag{A4.7}
$$

If this condition holds for all n commodities, it must be the case that

$$
\frac{\partial X_j / \partial Y}{\partial X_i / \partial Y} = \frac{X_j}{X_i}
\tag{A4.8}
$$

which implies that all income elasticities must equal one.

CHAPTER 5

The Hicksian approach

5.1 Marshall's alternative definition of consumer surplus

Largely because of the objections that various economists had raised to the use of consumer surplus and Marshall's own apparent disenchantment with it as nothing more than a pedagogic device for introducing marginal analysis, interest in the concept remained dormant for most of the early twentieth century. This state of affairs changed dramatically in 1941 following the publication of J. R. Hicks's classic article "The Rehabilitation of Consumers' Surplus." This immediately generated considerable debate among economists as they attempted to understand the full implications of what Hicks was saying. Significant objections were again raised, particularly by Samuelson (1942) and Little (1960), with the result that interest in the subject among theoretical economists appeared to wane during the 1960s. Paradoxically, however, at this same time the concept of consumer surplus became one of the foundation stones of cost–benefit analysis. For this reason it is particularly important that we examine fully the thrust of Hicks's arguments.

Hicks's starting point was clearly the Marshallian definition as given in Section 4.4: "the excess of the price which he would be willing to pay rather than go without the thing, over that which he actually does pay" (Marshall, 1920, p. 124). In other words, Hicks was interested in answering this question: "What is the maximum amount which the consumer would be willing to pay for the particular quantity of the particular commodity if he were given the choice between having this quantity on such terms or not at all?" [Hicks, 1940; p. 108] The answer to this rhetorical question was that "consumer's surplus is the difference between the amount so defined and the amount of money actually paid." The key contribution that Hicks believed he was making was to point out that this concept was objective. As we shall see, it is invariant under monotonic, increasing transformations of any given utility function. Hence, it does not depend on subjective notions of utility. However, the reader should be forewarned that *this measure is not a representation of an ordinal preference function.*

5.2   Constancy of the marginal utility of money: an alternative approach

As Hicks claimed, the first step in his rehabilitation effort involved showing that "constancy of the marginal utility of money is an objective criterion, even though the marginal utility of money is not objective itself." In this regard he made use of a device that he and Allen (1934) had developed several years earlier. Let us suppose that we choose a commodity to serve as numeraire and normalize its price at one. Then the ratio

$$\frac{\partial U/\partial X_i}{\partial U/\partial X_n} = \frac{P_i}{P_n} \equiv P_i \qquad (5.1)$$

where X_n is the numeraire and, following Hicks, is called "money." As we showed in Chapter 2, such a ratio of marginal utilities is an objective concept. Hicks went one stage further so as to write the ratio as equal to the price of the commodity involved.

To gain initial insight into how Hicks made use of this device, let us consider Figure 5.1. On the vertical axis is plotted the numeraire commodity, "money." On the horizontal axis is plotted commodity X_1, whose price is given by the slope of the budget constraint CB. This is the case because $p_n = 1$. The actual pattern of consumption and money holding is indicated by the point E. Because $0C$ measures total money income, and $0K$ equals the amount of the numeraire held, the distance $FE = CK$ indicates the expenditure that the consumer is actually making on X_1. However, the amount of money the consumer would be willing to forgo rather than do without any consumption of X_1 at all is the amount CN. It can be seen from Figure 5.1 that the complete hoarding of one's income $0C$ generates the same level of satisfaction as consuming TL of X_1 and hoarding $0T$. In other words, as indicated by the indifference curve U_1, the consumer is indifferent between the consumption pattern at L and that at point C. The distance CN is, of course, the compensating variation as measured in units of the numeraire commodity. The foregoing analysis is reasonably general and can easily be extended to encompass several commodities. The only requirement on the nature of consumer preferences is that the indifference curves cross the axis along which the numeraire commodity is measured.

The foregoing interpretation, however, is somewhat different from what Hicks initially had in mind. From his definition of consumer surplus, quoted earlier, it is apparent that the magnitude he really desired to calculate was the amount of money the consumer would be

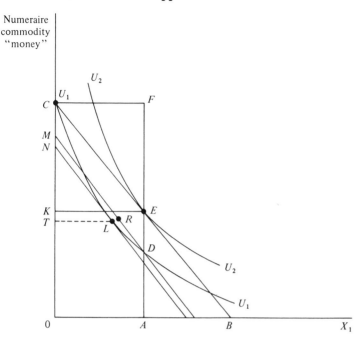

Figure 5.1

willing to forgo in order to maintain his consumption level at $0A$ rather than go without any X_1 at all. This is the amount $ED = CM$. Several properties of this measure are worth noting. First, the consumption pattern indicated by point D is not an equilibrium position for the consumer. Indeed, if the consumer did relinquish ED, he would not consume at D but would rearrange the expenditure to some point such as R that is tangent to an indifference curve.

Second, the amounts CM and CN will be equal if and only if the indifference curves are vertically parallel. This situation was discussed by Hicks in *Value and Capital* and is depicted in Figure 5.2. Here the compensation the consumer would be willing to pay (in order to return him to his initial level of satisfaction) and the amount he would be willing to pay for $0A$ rather than go without any X_1 at all are identical. The surplus is thus ED. It is at this juncture that Hicks's assumption of a constant marginal utility of the numeraire (or money) becomes important. Literally, such a condition implies that it is possible to find some transformation of any given utility function such that $\partial U / \partial X_n$ is independent of both X_1 and X_n, the numeraire. In other

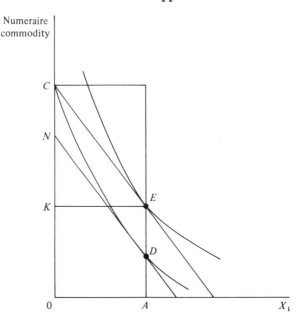

Figure 5.2

words, it is necessary that we be able to write consumer preferences in the form

$$U = \phi_1(X_1) + cX_n \tag{5.2}$$

where c is a positive constant. It is then a straightforward matter to find a linear transformation W of (5.2) such that

$$W = a + b(U) = a + b\phi_1(X_1) + X_n \tag{5.3}$$

where a and b are both positive and $b = 1/c$. For this representation, $\partial W/\partial X_n$ is a constant and, given the price of the numeraire, is always equal to one. In addition, this formulation is both necessary and sufficient for the marginal rate of substitution between X_1 and the numeraire to be independent of the latter. This result holds, of course, under any monotonic, increasing transformation H of W, namely,

$$\frac{\partial H/\partial X_1}{\partial H/\partial X_n} = \frac{(\partial H/\partial W)(\partial W/\partial X_1)}{(\partial H/\partial W)(\partial W/\partial X_n)} = P_1 \tag{5.4}$$

This is the requirement for drawing the parallel indifference curves as in Figure 5.2. As Hicks pointed out, this property implies that the demand schedule for X_1 is independent of the level of real income (and nominal income as well). Hence, the Marshallian consumer surplus and objective compensation measure are identical.

Subsequently, Hicks (1942) changed his view and argued that we are not necessarily interested in the all-or-none situation previously discussed. Rather, we should be interested in the change in income necessary to return the consumer to his initial level of satisfaction following a price variation. This *compensating variation* and the notion of consumer surplus are thus identifiably different. To make this apparent, Hicks (1946) labeled the measure based on the all-or-none situation the *compensating surplus*.

Despite this clarification, it is still necessary to distinguish between two entirely different formulations of the compensating variation. In one instance the numeraire commodity or "money" is an argument of the direct consumer preference function. The second formulation involves treating "money" simply as a constraint on consumer expenditure and hence not as an argument in the preference function. This parallels the approach we have been taking in the preceding chapters. Because many commentators have failed to distinguish between the compensating variation measures that derive from these alternative formulations, it is important that we examine them in some detail.

5.3 The compensating variation when "money" is an argument of the direct preference function

To determine what is involved in this case, we can extend the discussion of the preceding section by making use of the apparatus developed in Chapter 2. In general, the marginal rate of substitution between the ith commodity and the numeraire is a function of all n commodities:

$$\frac{\partial U/\partial X_i}{\partial U/\partial X_n} = \frac{p_i}{p_n} = f_i(X_1,\ldots,X_n) \quad (i = 1, n - 1) \tag{5.5}$$

This function is, of course, very similar to Marshall's inverse demand functions, with the main difference that the price of the numeraire is held constant. Consequently, it is possible to conceive of a consumer surplus measure based on these modified functions, namely,

$$\Delta X_n = -\int \sum f_i dX_i \tag{5.6}$$

In other words, we are asking this question: What change in the numeraire commodity is required to maintain a constant level of satisfaction in the face of given variations in the other quantities? In calculating (5.6) we could choose the strategy we adopted in previous chapters. For example, we can first evaluate the effects of a change in X_1, holding all other quantities constant. Then, with X_1 at its new level, we can evaluate the effects of varying X_2. And so forth. However, such calculations should be independent of the order in which the X_i are varied, and therefore we must inquire into the conditions under which the differential $\sum_{i=1}^{n-1} f_i \, dX_i$ is exact. Applying the results obtained earlier, we see that the necessary and sufficient condition for this to be the case is

$$\frac{\partial f_i}{\partial X_j} = \frac{\partial f_j}{\partial X_i} \quad (i \neq j) \tag{5.7}$$

If we substitute the ratio of marginal utilities (U_i/U_n) for f_i and then perform the differentiation indicated in (5.7), we obtain the interesting result

$$\frac{\partial U/\partial X_i}{\partial U/\partial X_j} = \frac{\partial^2 U/\partial X_n \partial X_i}{\partial^2 U/\partial X_n \partial X_j} \tag{5.8}$$

The empirical implications of this condition can be obtained by first noting that

$$\frac{\partial(U_i/U_j)}{\partial X_n} = \frac{U_{in}}{U_j} - \frac{U_i}{U_j^2} U_{jn} = \frac{U_{jn}}{U_j}\left(\frac{U_{in}}{U_{jn}} - \frac{U_i}{U_j}\right) \tag{5.9}$$

Thus, if (5.8) is to hold, it must be the case that the expression (5.9) equals zero. That is, the underlying preference function is additively separable in the form

$$U = U[\phi_1(X_1, \ldots, X_{n-1}) + \phi_2(X_n)] \tag{5.10}$$

The marginal rate of substitution between any two commodities (excluding the numeraire) must be independent of the numeraire.

The first-order condition associated with the numeraire

$$\phi_{2n} = \lambda p_n \tag{5.11}$$

can be differentiated with respect to total expenditure and any price p_k to yield

$$\phi_{2nn}\frac{\partial X_n}{\partial Y} = p_n\frac{\partial \lambda}{\partial Y} \tag{5.12}$$

$$\phi_{2nn}\frac{\partial X_n}{\partial p_k} = p_n\frac{\partial \lambda}{\partial p_k} \tag{5.13}$$

We know from the Slutsky equations that

$$\frac{\partial X_k}{\partial p_n} + X_n \frac{\partial X_k}{\partial Y} = \frac{\partial X_n}{\partial p_k} + X_k \frac{\partial X_n}{\partial Y} \tag{5.14}$$

Through substitution of (5.12) and (5.13) into (5.14) and the rearrangement of terms, we obtain

$$\frac{\partial X_k}{\partial p_n} = -\left(X_n + \lambda \frac{p_n}{\phi_{2nn}}\right)\frac{\partial X_k}{\partial Y} \tag{5.15}$$

If we now apply this condition to any pair of commodities, we obtain the ratio

$$\frac{\partial X_i / \partial p_n}{\partial X_j / \partial p_n} = \frac{\partial X_i / \partial Y}{\partial X_j / \partial Y} \tag{5.16}$$

That is, the ratio of the cross-price effects involving the price of the numeraire is equal to the ratio of the respective income effects. This empirical restriction is necessary and sufficient for compensation measured in terms of the numeraire to be calculable independent of the path of integration.

However, the relationship (5.16) does not guarantee that the compensation measure can also serve as an ordinal welfare indicator. For this latter condition to be met, we now require that the differential equation

$$dU = \sum_{i}^{n-1} f_i dX_i + dX_n = 0 \tag{5.17}$$

be exact. This implies that the compensation required to return the consumer to his initial level of satisfaction should always be the same irrespective of what pattern of consumption may have been taken up on a new indifference surface. Thus, in addition to the condition (5.8), we have

$$\frac{\partial f_i}{\partial X_n} = \frac{\partial (1.0)}{\partial X_i} = 0 \tag{5.18}$$

or, in terms of (5.9),

$$\frac{\partial (U_i / U_n)}{\partial X_n} = \frac{\partial (\phi_{1i} / \phi_{2n})}{\partial X_n} = \frac{\phi_{1in}}{\phi_{2n}} - \frac{\phi_{1i}}{(\phi_{2n})^2}\phi_{2nn} = 0 \tag{5.19}$$

However, ϕ_{1in} equals zero, so that ϕ_{2nn} must also equal zero. Thus, the underlying preference system emerges as a special case of (5.10):

$$U = U[\phi_1(X_1, \ldots, X_{n-1}) + CX_n] \tag{5.20}$$

The implications in terms of observable consumer behavior can easily be seen by rewriting (5.15) as

$$\frac{\partial X_K}{\partial Y} = -\frac{\partial X_k/\partial p_n}{X_n + \lambda P_n/\phi_{2nn}} = -\phi_{2nn}\frac{\partial X_k/\partial p_n}{\phi_{2nn}X_n + \lambda p_n} \tag{5.21}$$

which equals zero when ϕ_{2nn} is zero. This, of course, is a generalization of Hicks's discussion in which he examined the conditions under which the compensation measure and the Marshallian surplus measure were identical. All income effects except that associated with the numeraire are thus equal to zero (see Figure 4.2). Any additional income is hoarded. That is, such income is retained as a holding of the numeraire, money.

Despite the fact that any analysis based on these unrealistic assumptions is bound to be nonoperational, many economists have persisted in attempting to find some justification for assuming that income effects can, in general, be treated as zero. A most sophisticated but nevertheless erroneous argument relating to the Hicks formulation discussed here was contained in an article by Hause (1975, p. 1152):

> In almost all empirical applications, it is necessary to approximate the preference structure from demand information. The standard errors of the regression parameters of econometric demand functions are almost always large enough to swamp any differences in the CV (or CS) measure that could be attributed to income effects. If, relative to an initial bundle, X_1, a group of alternative bundles indicate approximately the same welfare gain or loss, even precise information on the preference structure is unlikely to create a compelling significant difference between the alternatives, and there is little purpose in assuming spurious precision in our estimates for distinguishing between the alternatives.

Two questions arise in this discussion. First, why should we be interested in the relationship between the compensating variation and compensating surplus when it is the equivalent variation that we really should be concerned about? Although it will be of some interest to calculate any compensation that losers might receive following the introduction of a policy, either of the two former measures is an ordinal metric. Indeed, the notion of the compensating surplus is of only historical interest as an idea that Hicks and others pursued in order to work out the logical foundations of an otherwise confused subject.

However, let us suppose for the sake of argument that the relationship between the compensating variation and the compensating surplus is crucial to an understanding of applied welfare economics.

Recall from Chapter 2 that the compensating variation associated with the Klein-Rubin utility function can be written as

$$
\text{CV} = (Y^0 - \sum c_i p_i^0) \prod_i \left(\frac{p_i}{p_i^0}\right)^{b_i} + \sum c_i p_i - Y \tag{5.22}
$$

where b_i is the marginal propensity to consume the ith commodity. If we assume that all income effects are zero, except that for the numeraire commodity, which is one, then we obtain a function such as Hause would suggest using:

$$
\text{CS} = \left(Y^0 - \sum c_i p_i^0\right) + \sum c_i p_i - Y \tag{5.23}
$$

From the analysis contained in Chapter 3 we are aware that the ability of one function such as (5.23) to approximate another depends basically on three factors: the initial conditions, the parameter values, and the magnitudes of the variable changes under consideration. If the information is stochastic (this is the point that Hause was making), then whether or not CS and CV are significantly different from a statistical point of view will also depend on the variances and covariances associated with the parameter estimates. Because most empirical work suggests that income effects are highly significant, it is reasonable to suppose that, in general, CS and CV will be significantly different. Hause's assumption of "spurious precision" in the available estimates implies that variances are always large. As a working hypothesis for applied welfare economics, this appears to be a questionable assumption.

5.4   A digression: the Antonelli integrability condition

Before continuing with our discussion of Hicks's approach to consumer surplus, it is important to contrast the analysis of the preceding section with the differing approaches taken by Marshall and Antonelli toward the construction of inverse demand functions. First, recall that Marshall's inverse demand function

$$
p_i = p_i(X_1, \ldots, X_n, Y) \quad (i = 1, \ldots, n) \tag{5.24}
$$

indicates the price that consumers will pay given the quantities X_i and total expenditure Y, under the assumption that satisfaction is maximized. In contrast, Hicks's consumer surplus formulation described in the preceding section and the inverse demand functions proposed by Antonelli in 1886 both assume that there is a numeraire commodity whose price remains constant. However, there the similarity ends. If we vary each of the n commodities by differing amounts, it is no longer possible for both p_n and total expenditure to remain constant. Total expenditure must vary so as to ensure that the available supplies of the n commodities are fully consumed. This is the approach adopted by Antonelli, and it stands in complete contrast to that used by Hicks, as discussed in the preceding section. There it was noted that although compensation is paid, it is paid in terms of a variable that is an argument in the consumer preference function and for the purpose of maintaining the level of satisfaction constant.

It is therefore of some interest to determine the conditions under which the matrix of cross-price effects associated with the Antonelli inverse demand functions is symmetric and to contrast these with the Marshallian and Hicksian results. Given a variation in the quantity of one of the commodities, the ultimate effect on any price will consist of two parts: (a) the direct effect arising through the inverse demand function (5.24) and (b) an indirect effect due to the variation in Y necessary to clear all markets. Thus, we can use (5.24) to construct an Antonelli inverse demand function

$$p_i = p_i[X_1, \ldots, X_n, Y(X_1, \ldots, X_n)] \quad (p_i = 1, \ldots, n - 1) \quad (5.25)$$

where $Y = Y(X_1, \ldots, X_n)$ indicates the total expenditure required to ensure market clearing, and p_n equal to a constant. From (5.25) we can derive the Antonelli substitution effects: First, let us modify the inverse demand function (5.24) to reflect the assumptions used by Antonelli.

$$A_{ij} = \frac{dp_i}{dX_j} = \frac{\partial p_i}{\partial X_j} + \frac{\partial p_i}{\partial Y}\frac{dY}{dX_j}\bigg|_{p_n=C} \quad (5.26)$$

and

$$A_{ji} = \frac{dp_j}{dX_i} = \frac{\partial p_j}{\partial X_i} + \frac{\partial p_j}{\partial Y}\frac{dY}{dX_i}\bigg|_{p_n=C} \quad (5.27)$$

From (4.7) we know that

$$p_i = Y\frac{U_i}{\sum U_k X_k} \quad (i = 1, \ldots, n)$$

Because p_i is homogeneous of degree one in income, it follows that

$$\frac{\partial p_i}{\partial Y} = \frac{p_i}{Y} \quad (i = 1, \ldots, n) \quad (5.28)$$

Further, because the price of the numeraire is held constant, by definition

$$\frac{dp_n}{dX_i} = 0 = \frac{\partial p_n}{\partial X_i} + \frac{\partial p_n}{\partial Y}\frac{dY}{dX_i}\bigg|_{dp_n=C} \qquad (i = 1,\ldots,n) \tag{5.29}$$

Substitution of (5.28) and (5.29) into (5.26) and (5.27) yields

$$A_{ij} = \frac{\partial p_i}{\partial X_j} - \frac{p_i}{p_n}\frac{\partial p_n}{\partial X_j} \tag{5.30}$$

$$A_{ji} = \frac{\partial p_j}{\partial X_i} - \frac{p_j}{p_n}\frac{\partial p_n}{\partial X_i} \tag{5.31}$$

If we are to be able to integrate the Antonelli inverse demand functions so as to obtain a utility indicator, then

$$A_{ij} = A_{ji} \quad \text{for all} \quad i,j = 1,\ldots,n-1 \tag{5.32}$$

Because

$$p_i = \frac{U_i}{\lambda}$$

it is the case that

$$\frac{\partial p_i}{\partial X_j} = \frac{1}{\lambda}\left(U_{ij} - \frac{U_i}{\lambda^2}\frac{\partial\lambda}{\partial X_j}\right) \quad (i,j = 1,\ldots,n) \tag{5.33}$$

Substitution of the appropriate equations from (5.33) into (5.30) and (5.31) yields the condition that

$$\frac{U_{ni}}{U_{nj}} = \frac{U_i}{U_j} \tag{5.34}$$

for the Antonelli symmetry condition to hold. However, this is exactly the condition (5.9) that was shown to be consistent with a preference function (5.10) that was additively separable into two groups of commodities: one consisting only of the numeraire X_n and the other consisting of the other $n-1$ commodities. This result stands in contrast to the somewhat more restrictive conditions associated with the symmetry of the inverse demand effects associated with the Marshallian and Hicksian formulations. Care must therefore be taken not to confuse these three alternative constructs.

5.5   The compensating variation when "money" is not an argument of the direct preference function

Subsequent to the first edition of Hicks's *Value and Capital,* Samuelson (1942) argued that the use of a numeraire commodity in defining the marginal utility of money was not consistent with Marshall's approach. Three points are involved. First, Samuelson argued that Marshall "rarely, if ever, employed the concept of a numeraire" (1942, p. 42). Second, Marshall stated that the marginal utility of money decreases with income. Applied to the function (5.20), this would imply that C is negative. But this is not possible. Third, Samuelson argued that Marshall "insists that the marginal utility of money is associated with a flow of income rather than a stock of commodity" (1942, p. 42). This reasoning then implies that compensation or willingness to pay should be measured in terms of total income or total expenditure, a variable that is not an argument in the consumer's direct utility function. This is the formulation of the compensating variation noted in Chapters 1 and 2. It has figured in a number of discussions by Hicks (e.g., 1946, pp. 329–33). And it is this approach that Friedman (1949) adopted in interpreting Marshall's demand curve. It is the relationship between such compensated demand schedules and the compensating variation that will provide the basis for our discussion in this section. To determine what is involved, we first calculate the compensation directly from the consumer preference function, as follows:

$$dU = \sum \frac{\partial U}{\partial X_j} \frac{\partial X_j}{\partial p_i} dp_i + \sum \frac{\partial U}{\partial X_j} \frac{\partial X_j}{\partial Y} dY = 0 \tag{5.35}$$

We can then make use of (2.35) and (2.36) to solve for

$$\frac{dY}{dp_i}\bigg|_{u=u^0} = \frac{\partial C}{\partial p_i} = -\sum p_j \frac{\partial X_j}{\partial p_i} = X_i^*(U_0, p_i, \ldots, p_n) \tag{5.36}$$

where X_i^* is the compensated demand function. These functions are not ordinary demand functions, however. Rather, they indicate that an income change has been implicitly carried out so as to maintain the level of consumer satisfaction constant at U_0, irrespective of commodity prices.

The relationship can be visualized by referring to Figure 5.3. The initial price/quantity situation is that indicated by point A. Suppose now that the price of X_1 is varied such that the new pattern of consumption occurs at B. The point B' in the lower diagram is thus a point on the ordinary, uncompensated consumer demand function LL. However, when compensation is paid so as to restore the initial

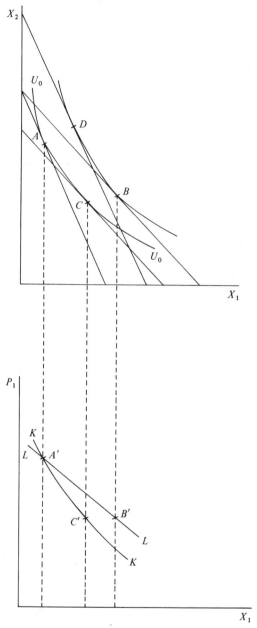

Figure 5.3

level of satisfaction U_0, the pattern of consumption becomes C, and this is represented by the point C' on the compensated demand curve shown as KK. It is thus clear that the two demand curves will not, in general, coincide.

It is now a straightforward matter to show that the area lying beneath the compensated demand curves can indeed be interpreted as the compensating variation. Consider the integral expression

$$\int \sum_i X_i^*(U_0, p_1, \ldots, p_n)\, dp_i \qquad (5.37)$$

Because $X_i^* = \partial C/\partial p_i$, it is immediately obvious that (5.37) is the compensation function and that

$$\frac{\partial^2 C}{\partial p_i \partial p_j} = \frac{\partial^2 C}{\partial p_j \partial p_i} \qquad (5.38)$$

This is just another way of saying that the matrix of Slutsky price effects is symmetric. Hence, it is a simple matter to reverse the exercise and retrieve the compensation function from the compensated demand functions. This is really a trivial result. However, from a technical point of view it must be contrasted with the problems we had in Chapter 2 when we attempted to derive a utility index from the ordinary demand functions. That exercise involved discovery of an integrating factor. None is required here. Further, this process does not imply the assumption of any restrictions about consumer behavior. The use of the ordinary demand functions to construct a utility indicator required unitary income elasticities. The result obtained here is perfectly general: The compensating variation can always be constructed from compensated demand functions irrespective of the structure of consumer preferences.

It is probably this fact that has led many economists to choose the compensating variation as the focal point for applied welfare economics. Another property that apparently acts in its favor is that it is perfectly analogous to the cost function of production theory. This relationship indicates the cost of producing a specified level of output on the basis of any set of factor prices. The compensation function enables the economist to calculate on the basis of any set of commodity prices. However, this similarity plus the fact that the compensated demand functions are integrable into the compensation function should not be allowed to delude us. As we determined in Section 2.9, the compensation function is capable of serving as an ordinal money-metric only in the case in which preferences are homothetic.

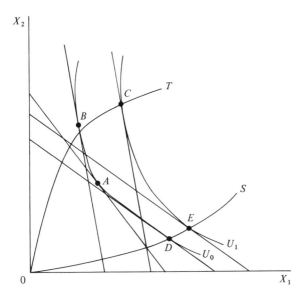

Figure 5.4

It is interesting to note here that the restrictions on consumer preferences necessary to justify the use of consumer surplus measures
based on ordinary or compensated demand functions are thus identical. This is not to say, however, that the two measures are themselves
identical. In the homothetic case the ordinary demand functions can
be written in the form

$$X_i = \frac{Y}{\theta(p_1,\ldots,p_n)} \frac{\partial \theta}{\partial p_i} \quad (i = 1,\ldots,n) \tag{5.38}$$

whereas the compensated demand functions will be

$$X_i^* = \frac{Y^0}{\theta(p_1^0,\ldots,p_n^0)} \frac{\partial \theta}{\partial p_i} \tag{5.39}$$

Thus, in general, it will be the case that

$$\int_c \sum X_i^* \, dp_i \neq \int_c \sum X_i \, dp_i \tag{5.40}$$

The required equality will occur if and only if all prices and total
expenditure vary by the same proportion.

5.6   Summary

The greatest modern stimulus to the development of consumer surplus techniques has come from the writings of John Hicks. Initially he attempted to work in terms of preference functions that contained money or numeraire commodity as an element. Whereas this would appear to free the analysis from discussion of an integrating factor, in point of fact the approach adopted imposed even more restrictive conditions on the forms of consumer behavior that could be considered. All income effects, except that associated with the numeraire, would have to equal zero. Subsequently, Hicks sought to develop the concept of the compensating variation and its relationship to a consumer surplus measure based on compensated demand functions. Unfortunately, such a measure can act as an ordinal welfare indicator if and only if preferences are homothetic.

CHAPTER 6

Approximations based on consumer surplus

6.1   Introduction

In Chapters 4 and 5 we examined the various restrictive assumptions that would be required if consumer surplus techniques were to satisfy the conditions of an ordinal welfare metric. The following question then arises. Suppose that preferences do not satisfy the required restrictions. Do consumer surplus procedures nevertheless provide "reasonably good" approximations to a true welfare indicator? Basically, two approaches to this approximation problem have emerged in the literature. The first assumes that we know only the prices and quantities that hold in alternative situations, but not information about the shape of preferences or the consumer demand functions. It is based on the use of the Paasche and Laspeyres index numbers, and as we shall see, it has a close affinity to a consumer surplus formulation discussed by Harberger (1971). The second approach assumes that we know the shape of consumer demand functions, and it attempts to formulate conditions under which the traditional Marshallian surplus measure can be used either to rank alternatives or to approximate the true compensating or equivalent variations. Given the procedures that we have fully discussed in previous chapters, this second approach is really superfluous, because we can obtain exact (not approximate) representations of the CV and EV measures only if we are armed with knowledge of the demand functions. Nevertheless, it is important that we have a perspective on the attempts to use the Marshallian surplus.

6.2   The Paasche and Laspeyres index numbers

An understanding of both of these approaches can easily be obtained if we examine a true welfare index expressed in terms of a differential. We have already noted that

$$dU = \sum \frac{\partial U}{\partial X_i} dX_i = \lambda \sum p_i \, dX_i \qquad (6.1)$$

and hence that for "small" changes,

$$dW = \sum p_i dX_i \qquad (6.2)$$

can be used as a welfare indicator, because it will always possess the same sign as dU. Using the budget constraint, we know that

$$\sum p_i dX_i = dY - \sum X_i dp_i \qquad (6.3)$$

and hence that (6.2) can be rewritten as

$$dW = dY - \sum X_i dp_i \qquad (6.4)$$

In these terms, all our problems would appear to be solved, primarily because for small changes in prices or quantities we need not worry about variations in λ, the marginal utility of money. Equation (6.2) can be interpreted as a quantity index, with the p_i serving as weights for the differential changes in quantities consumed. For small changes we need not worry whether the p_i are new or old prices. Similarly, $-\sum X_i dp_i$ in (6.3) can be interpreted as a price index, with the quantities consumed serving as the weights for the price variations. In addition, from (6.3), $dY = \sum p_i dX_i$ will indicate the equivalent change in income needed to achieve the same level of satisfaction as indicated by (6.2). Or, alternatively, $dY = \sum X_i dp_i$ will indicate the change in income necessary to compensate consumers such that $\sum p_i dX_i$ is equal to zero. Both the equivalent and compensating variations will equal the same amount. On top of this, $\sum p_i dX_i$ and $-\sum X_i dp_i$ can be interpreted as areas under a set of Marshallian demand curves and hence can be called consumer surplus. Again, we need not worry about variations in the marginal utility of money, because our calculations are assumed to be of the first order.

However, if we now attempt to redefine the differential variations discussed earlier in discrete terms, then it is no longer safe to assume that λ will remain constant, a result that follows from the analysis of previous chapters. However, it is possible to identify certain restrictions on price/commodity configurations that will enable us to use index numbers based on discrete data. The basic problem revolves around whether to use, as weights for the quantity index, the prices holding in the initial situation (written as p_i) or the prices holding in the new or alternative situation (written as p_i^*). In the first instance, the index

$$\sum p_i \Delta X_i \qquad (6.5)$$

is the Laspeyres quantity variation (LQV), whereas in the second case, the index

$$\sum p_i^* \Delta X_i \tag{6.6}$$

is the Paasche quantity variation (PQV). It is possible to think of these two indicators as representing first-order approximations to the change in any underlying utility indicator, that is,

$$\Delta U \approx \lambda \sum p_i \Delta X_i = \lambda \cdot \text{LQV} \tag{6.7}$$

and

$$\Delta U \approx \lambda^* \sum p_i^* \Delta X_i = \lambda^* \cdot \text{PQV} \tag{6.8}$$

where λ and λ^* are evaluated at p_i and p_i^*, respectively. Although λ and λ^* will both be positive, this interpretation does not provide us with any additional information. As we showed in Chapter 3, an exact representation of ΔU is possible if we know the form of consumer demand functions. This will then enable us to add the necessary higher-order terms to (6.7) and (6.8) in order to obtain an exact indicator. However, because we are assuming in this section that we do not know the required demand function, we must seek an alternative approach in interpreting PQV and LQV.

The key to understanding this problem is the so-called region of ignorance that delineates the boundaries within which the foregoing quantity variations can be used effectively. Although the analysis involved is well known and straightforward, it is worthwhile to present a full discussion, because it provides significant insights into an important consumer surplus approximation.

Let us examine the two quantity variations in terms of the situations depicted in Figures 6.1A and 6.1B. In both cases the initial pattern of consumption is indicated by the point I associated with relative prices indicated by the slope of GC. This is to be compared with the new situation II involving relative prices equal to the slope of EA. If we use initial prices as the basis for our calculation, then we obtain a Laspeyres quantity variation equal to the value of HG that is positive. However, if we use new prices, we find that moving from I to II generates a negative Paasche index. This well-known ambiguity can be highlighted further by examining the nature of consumer preferences that would be consistent with this situation. Thus, we see in Figure 6.1A that moving from I to II could be associated with an

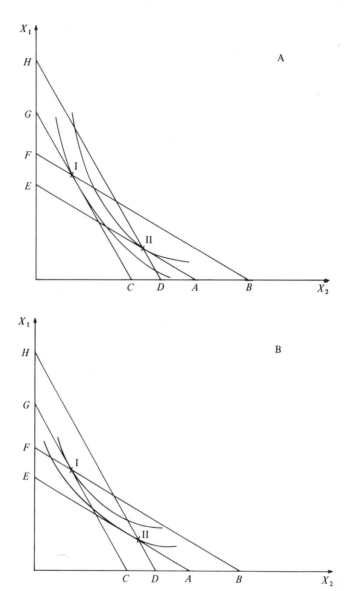

Figure 6.1

improvement in welfare, because we are moving to a higher level of satisfaction. However, such a move could just as well be consistent with a deterioration in welfare, as shown in Figure 6.1B.

All is not lost, because it is possible to identify situations in which the two quantity variations will be of the same sign. The basic argument can be traced back to Hicks (1940). If the Paasche variation is zero or positive (i.e., if it is nonnegative), then we know that in the new situation consumers can afford to purchase either the new commodity bundle or the old commodity bundle. However, because they have chosen to consume the new bundle of goods, they must be better off. In other words, a nonnegative PQV is a sufficient condition for an improvement in satisfaction.

This result was subsequently used by Samuelson (1947) to delineate a region of ignorance in which the ambiguities shown in Figure 6.1 will arise, but outside of which index-number calculations can be used in a straightforward manner. Consider Figure 6.2. As before, we begin with the price/quantity situation indicated by I. However, now we examine alternative patterns of consumption that arise from rotating the budget constraint using point I as the axis. In the process, a locus of consumption patterns can be identified. Two possible consumption patterns on this locus are identified by points III and IV in Figure 6.2. The significance of this locus is as follows. Everywhere along ZZ the Paasche variation is zero. Hence, we know that every such consumption pattern must represent an improvement over that holding in the original situation. Because every pattern of consumption to the northeast of ZZ generates a positive Paasche quantity variation, these will also be consistent with an improvement in satisfaction. It should be noted that we are not confined to examination of situations where more units of all commodities are consumed (i.e., points in the northeast quadrant). For example, point IV involves the consumption of fewer units of X_2. Yet we are able to say that it is unambiguously better than I.

The foregoing discussion establishes an upper boundary for the region of ignorance. The lower boundary is simply the budget line associated with point I. If we calculate a negative Laspeyres variation, we know that the new situation must lie within the triangle $0GC$. Hence, it must be inferior to I. Thus, any consumption pattern lying within the region bounded by the budget constraint and the locus ZZ will be in the region of ignorance. Comparisons between such points and point I will be impossible, because they would generate a positive LQV and negative PQV in the same manner as in the example shown in Figure 6.1.

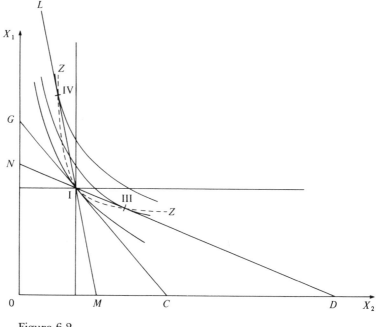

Figure 6.2

6.3   Pearce's iterative technique

Unfortunately, as stated, the foregoing procedure suffers from a rather serious drawback. Although it enables us to determine whether or not alternatives are superior to the status quo or initial situation, it does not enable us to identify which of the alternative situations is to be preferred. For example, in Figure 6.2, both III and IV generate a zero Paasche index, and yet IV is to be preferred to III.

A solution to this problem has been suggested by I. F. Pearce in the context of finding an optimum tariff t to be placed on importable commodities. Because at the optimum, dU/dt equals zero, Pearce suggested the following procedure:

If then $\sum p_i \Delta X_i$ is positive but there exists some level of policy at which the estimate $\sum p_i \Delta X_i$ turns negative, a good first step might well be to choose that level of application of the policy which puts $\sum p_i^* \Delta X_i$ at zero. [1970, p. 372]

The implications of applying this rule in the case of tariff policy can be seen from Figure 6.3. Here we have constructed the conventional Edgeworth box diagram on the assumption that each of two countries

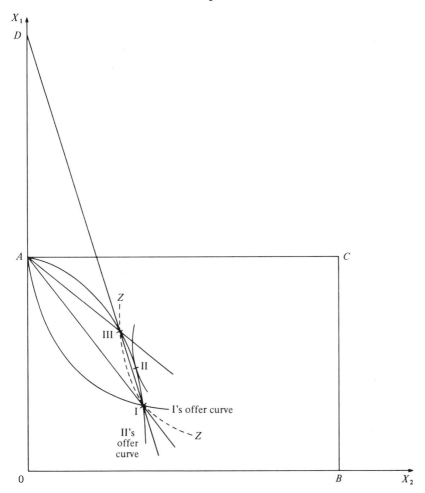

Figure 6.3

specializes in the production of one commodity. Thus, X_1 represents the home country's product, of which $0A$ is produced at full employment, and X_2 represents the foreign country's product, of which $0B$ is produced at full employment. Each country's offer curve is then derived in the usual way, with the result that under free trade the consumption pattern indicated by point I is the only one that simultaneously clears commodity markets in both countries and also produces an overall trade balance (see McKenzie, 1974, especially pp. 27–8).

That is, the value of imports equals the value of exports for both countries.

Now let us trace out the upper boundary of the region of ignorance facing the home country, the locus ZZ. We know that anywhere along or above this curve the home country can improve its situation. If we follow Pearce's procedure, this will lead us to the consumption pattern III, because it is the only point on the locus ZZ that is also on the foreign country's offer curve. This is achieved by imposing a tariff on the foreign country's exportable such that the slope of A-III indicates the foreign terms of trade and the slope of D-III the domestic terms of trade. The tariff proceeds DA have been assumed to be redistributed to consumers.

The approximate nature of Pearce's approach can now be seen. The true optimal tariff would yield the pattern of consumption indicated by II, because this represents the highest level of satisfaction the home country can achieve given the foreign country's offer curve. However, because we do not know the demand functions possessed by either the home country or the foreign country, we do not know this solution. Rather, we are led into a solution that forces us to overshoot our desired objective. Nevertheless, we can improve on this situation, because the calculation can be repeated until the true optimum is finally reached. Consider Figure 6.3 again. The budget line can be rotated using III as an axis until a new locus is created defining a new region of ignorance. Pearce's procedure is then repeated, enabling us to reach a new consumption pattern such as IV, which is closer to the optimum. The approach is formally similar to Newton's iterative method for solving equations.

The question now arises how practicable such a procedure can be. On the one hand, certain types of governmental actions are taken on a continuous basis, and this raises the possibility that revision can easily be introduced. Income and excise taxes are raised or lowered according to the aims of the authorities. The same applies to tariffs and other restrictions. Thus, there is no reason that such alterations cannot be put on a rational footing by adopting the foregoing procedures, gradually altering a policy so as to bring prices closer to the optimum. In a dynamic world, the optimum will, of course, always be moving. But this need cause no difficulty, for the authorities should be gathering data on a continuous basis and making forecasts that should enable them to redesign their policies in such a fashion as to bring the economy nearer to the chosen objectives.

However, certain types of policies, such as those involving the building of roads and airports, are not so easily modified. Yet even here there is some leeway. For example, a roadway has many characteristics: durability, comfort to the driver, speed restrictions, safety, and so forth. By varying the cost of the road, the authorities can vary the quality of the services that it generates and hence its value to the public. These services can then be compared with the services generated by existing facilities, and the relevant Paasche and Laspeyres variations can be calculated. The first step of the Pearce criterion can then be applied.

The difficulty in evaluating the costs and benefits of a road or dam is not that it is a "lumpy" or indivisible commodity but that once it is built and in operation the services that it generates are not easily varied. The situation is not impossible, however. If a road is ascertained to be more durable than is really desired, maintenance can be postponed until a suitable time. Or if the road is unsafe, various features can be added on a marginal basis. If the road directs too much traffic into a congested city area, then this can be partially corrected by levying tolls and other means. Thus, even the iterative stages of Pearce's decision process are relevant.

In principle, of course, great care must be taken not to over-emphasize narrow efficiency aspects of policy formulation. In the example given earlier, the imposition of an optimum tariff leads to a higher level of satisfaction for the imposed country, but of course a lower level for the country whose imports are being discriminated against. All policies and projects inevitably involve such distributional considerations, and therefore great care must be used in identifying them (see Chapter 8).

6.4   Harberger's approximate consumer surplus measure

Samuelson (1947, p. 149) pointed out that it is impossible to improve on the region of ignorance discussed earlier without additional information about preferences. Nevertheless, it is instructive to show explicitly that consumer surplus does not add any additional insights, especially because many of its advocates claim that it does (e.g., Harberger, 1971).

Let us assume that the underlying utility function is quadratic. This means that we can express the change in satisfaction exactly as a second-order Taylor series expansion:

$$\Delta U = \sum U_i \Delta X_i + \frac{1}{2} \sum_i \sum_j U_{ij} \Delta X_i \Delta X_j \tag{6.9}$$

where U_{ij} represents $\partial^2 U / \partial X_i \partial X_j$. We have two reasons for writing ΔU in this fashion. First, Harberger (1971, p. 791) claimed that a quadratic such as (6.9) unambiguously enables us to use consumer surplus without "any errors of approximation." We shall prove that this contention is false. Second, whether we assume that the utility function is quadratic or any other form, it is possible to use the Pearce approach, as discussed earlier, to set limits on those errors of approximation.

All expansions of the first-order condition $\partial U/\partial X_i = \lambda p_i$ yield

$$\sum_j U_{ij}\Delta X_j = p_i\Delta\lambda + \lambda\Delta p_i + \Delta p_i\Delta\lambda \tag{6.10}$$

In addition, a change in the budget constraint ΔY can be written exactly as

$$\Delta Y \equiv \sum_i p_i\Delta X_i + \sum_i X_i\Delta p_i + \sum_i \Delta p_i\Delta X_i \tag{6.11}$$

For simplicity, we shall assume that ΔY equals zero. That is, there is no change in total expenditure. Substituting (6.10) into (6.9), we obtain

$$\begin{aligned}
\Delta U &= \left(\lambda + \frac{1}{2}\Delta\lambda\right)\left(\sum_i p_i\Delta X_i\right) + \frac{1}{2}(\lambda + \Delta\lambda)\left(\sum_i \Delta p_i\Delta X_i\right) \\
&= \left(\lambda + \frac{1}{2}\Delta\lambda\right)\left[\sum_i p_i\Delta X_i + \frac{(\lambda + \Delta\lambda)}{(2\lambda + \Delta\lambda)}\left(\sum_i \Delta p_i\Delta X_i\right)\right]
\end{aligned} \tag{6.12}$$

As noted earlier, the change in the marginal utility of expenditure, $\Delta\lambda$, depends on the variations in all prices and expenditure resulting from the policy shift. In addition, as we have already taken great pains to emphasize, $\Delta\lambda$ is not invariant given any monotonic transformation of the preference function. *To say that the change in the marginal utility of expenditure resulting from a policy is small implies that there is a particular transformation of the utility function that will bring this about.* Although changes in prices and total expenditure can have a minor effect on the λ associated with that particular function, a suitable transformation can be found to make the effect arbitrarily large or small.

Nevertheless, we can determine the range within which $\Delta\lambda$ can lie. If we write $\Delta\lambda = \alpha\lambda$, we know

$$-1 < \alpha < \infty \tag{6.13}$$

Let

$$r = \frac{\lambda + \Delta\lambda}{2\lambda + \Delta\lambda} = \frac{(1 + \alpha)}{(2 + \alpha)}$$

Then

$$0 < r < 1$$

If r were zero, the change in utility described by equation (6.12) would have the same sign as the Laspeyres variation $\sum p_i \Delta X_i$. If r were one, ΔU would have the same sign as the Paasche variation. Because we do not know whether r is close to one or close to zero or somewhere in between, we are forced to rely on the rationale of the preceding section. If the Paasche variation is nonnegative, the Laspeyres variation will be positive, and we know there has been an improvement. If the Paasche variation is negative and the Laspeyres variation is positive, we are in the region of ignorance. The addition of the second-order terms has not increased our knowledge at all.

The foregoing analysis stands in contrast to the claims of consumer surplus advocates, even though the procedures followed are formally similar to those of Hotelling and, more recently, Harberger (1971). Why, then, do the results conflict? Let us rewrite equation (6.12) in the form presented by Harberger:

$$\frac{\Delta U}{\left(\lambda + \frac{1}{2}\Delta\lambda\right)} = \sum p_i \Delta X_i + \frac{1}{2}\sum \Delta p_i \Delta X_i + \frac{1}{4}\frac{\Delta\lambda \sum \Delta p_i X_i}{\left(\lambda + \frac{1}{2}\Delta\lambda\right)}$$

(6.14)

The last term can be neglected, he claimed, because it is a third-order term (Harberger, 1971, p. 788). As a result, (6.14) becomes

$$\frac{\Delta U}{\left(\lambda + \frac{1}{2}\Delta\lambda\right)} = \sum p_i \Delta X_i + \frac{1}{2}\sum \Delta p_i \Delta X_i$$

(6.15)

or by using (6.11) as the familiar consumer surplus measure,

$$-\sum X_i \Delta p_i - \frac{1}{2}\sum \Delta X_i \Delta p_i$$

(6.16)

Because $\lambda + \frac{1}{2}\Delta\lambda$ is always positive, it is claimed that (6.16) and ΔU will always be of the same sign (provided U is a quadratic function). But we cannot neglect the last term of (6.14)! As we emphasized earlier, $\Delta\lambda$ is not invariant under a monotonic transformation: It can be as large or as small as we wish to make it. As a result, the neglected third-order term in (6.14) can be of the same magnitude as the included terms.

This result can be shown another way. Let us suppose that preferences can be described by the following quadratic form:

$$U = \theta\left[\sum a_i X_i + \frac{1}{2}\sum\sum a_{ij} X_i X_j\right]$$

(6.17)

$$\frac{\partial^2 U}{\partial X_i \partial X_j} = \theta a_{ij} \tag{6.18}$$

It is thus apparent that (6.9) is simply another way of writing (6.16). As we saw in Chapter 5, it is, in general, possible to write the marginal utility of money as

$$\lambda = \frac{\Sigma_i (\partial U / \partial X_i) X_i}{Y}$$

which in the case of (6.17) becomes

$$\lambda = \frac{\theta[\Sigma_i a_i X_i + \Sigma_i (\Sigma_j a_{ij} X_j) X_i]}{Y} \tag{6.19}$$

Changes in λ can be expressed exactly as a second-order Taylor series expansion in the X_i. First, we determine that

$$\frac{\partial \lambda}{\partial X_i} = \theta \left(a_i + 2 \sum a_{ij} X_j \right) Y \tag{6.20}$$

$$\frac{\partial^2 \lambda}{\partial X_i \partial X_j} = \theta 2 a_{ij} Y \tag{6.21}$$

Therefore,

$$\Delta \lambda = \left(\sum \frac{\partial \lambda}{\partial X_i} \Delta X_i + \frac{1}{2} \sum_i \sum_j \frac{\partial^2 X}{\partial X_i \partial X_j} \Delta X_i \Delta X_j \right) Y$$

$$= \theta \left[\sum_i \left(a_i + 2 \sum a_{ij} X_j \right) \Delta X_i + \sum_i \sum_j a_{ij} \Delta X_i \Delta X_j \right] Y \tag{6.22}$$

Given any changes in the quantities demanded, $\Delta \lambda$ can be made as large or as small as one wishes simply by changing the (positive) value of θ. Not only does this have no effect on the properties of the underlying demand functions; it is also the case that the quadratic nature of the underlying preference function is perfectly preserved.

The inherent weakness of the Harberger consumer surplus (HCS) measure can be best appreciated by showing its relationship to the Paasche and Laspeyres quantity variations discussed earlier in this chapter. Stated quite simply, the Harberger measure is the average of these two variations. This is easily seen:

$$\text{HCS} = \sum p_i \Delta X_i + \frac{1}{2} \sum \Delta p_i \Delta X_i$$

$$= \frac{1}{2} \left[\sum p_i \Delta X_i + \sum (p_i + \Delta p_i) \Delta X_i \right]$$

$$= \frac{1}{2} (\text{LQV} + \text{PQV}) \tag{6.23}$$

In other words, like the two quantity variations, Harberger's measure also suffers from the region of ignorance. If a positive LQV is greater than a negative PQV in absolute value, then HCS will be positive. Conversely, if a positive LQV is less than a negative PQV in absolute value, then HCS will be negative. But in both instances the underlying change in satisfaction can be positive or negative. The HCS therefore provides us with no additional useful information. To ascertain whether or not there has indeed been an improvement, we will have to calculate the Paasche quantity variation in any case. The fact that Harberger's measure appears to have second-order terms is superfluous.

6.5   Diewert's special case

In 1976, Diewert showed that in one particular case the Harberger consumer surplus measure will yield an exact welfare indicator. On the basis of our analysis in previous chapters, it should not come as too much of a surprise to learn that the required function is homothetic, in this case the homothetic quadratic

$$U = \frac{\theta}{2} \sum a_{ij} X_j X_i \tag{6.24}$$

Following Diewert, we normalize prices by total expenditure Y such that the first-order conditions for utility maximization become

$$\frac{\partial U}{\partial X_i} = \theta \sum_j a_{ij} X_j = \lambda p_i = Y \lambda \hat{p}_i \tag{6.25}$$

where $\hat{p}_i = p_i / Y$ is the normalized price variable. From (6.19) and (6.24) we obtain

$$\lambda = \frac{\theta \sum_i (\sum_j a_{ij} X_j) X_i}{Y} = \frac{2U}{Y} \tag{6.26}$$

Then we can rewrite (6.10) on the basis of (6.24) through (6.26) as follows:

$$\theta \sum a_{ij} \Delta X_j = 2[\hat{p}_i \Delta U + U \Delta \hat{p}_i + \Delta \hat{p}_i \Delta U] \tag{6.27}$$

An exact expression for the change in satisfaction can now be obtained from (6.24):

$$\Delta U = \theta \sum_i \sum_j \alpha_{ij} X_j \Delta X_i + \frac{\theta}{2} \sum_i \sum_j \alpha_{ij} \Delta X_j \Delta X_i \tag{6.28}$$

which can be rewritten as

$$\Delta U = Y\lambda\left(\sum_i \hat{p}_i \Delta X_i + \frac{1}{2}\sum_i \Delta\hat{p}_i \Delta X_i\right)$$
$$+ \Delta U\left[\sum_i (\hat{p}_i + \Delta\hat{p}_i)\Delta X_i\right] \tag{6.29}$$

on substitution of (6.25) through (6.27). Finally, on rearranging terms, we obtain

$$\frac{1 - \sum_i (\hat{p}_i + \Delta\hat{p}_i)\Delta X_i}{\lambda Y}\Delta U = \sum_i \hat{p}_i \Delta X_i + \frac{1}{2}\sum_i \Delta\hat{p}_i \Delta X_i \tag{6.30}$$

The left-hand-side expression

$$\frac{1 - \sum_i (\hat{p}_i + \Delta\hat{p}_i)\Delta X_i}{\lambda Y}$$

must always be positive, because $\lambda > 0$ and

$$Y + \Delta Y - \sum(\hat{p}_i + \Delta\hat{p}_i)\Delta X_i > 0$$

Hence, the change in satisfaction ΔU and the Harberger measure, as normalized by Diewert, must always possess the same sign, provided, of course, that preferences are (a) quadratic and (b) homothetic.

6.6   Hicks's approximations to the compensating and equivalent variations

Another approach to the use of consumer surplus as an approximate welfare indicator involves the establishment of bounds within which it can be said to be a good approximation to the equivalent variation and/or the compensating variation. Recent articles by Willig (1976), Seade (1978), and Dixit and Weller (1979) all represent attempts in this direction. However, Hicks was the first to make inquiries in this direction, and thus it is logical to examine his results initially.

Hicks chose to work with second-order Taylor series approximations to both the equivalent and compensating variations:

$$\text{EV} = \sum_i \frac{\partial M}{\partial p_i}\Delta p_i + \frac{1}{2}\sum\sum\frac{\partial^2 M}{\partial p_i \partial p_j}\Delta p_i \Delta p_j \tag{6.31}$$

$$\text{CV} = \sum_i \frac{\partial H}{\partial p_i}\Delta p_i + \frac{1}{2}\sum\sum\frac{\partial^2 H}{\partial p_i \partial p_j}\Delta p_i \Delta p_j \tag{6.32}$$

where, as in Chapter 2, $M = C[U(Y, p); p^0]$ and $H = C[U(Y^0, p^0); p]$, and all derivatives in the expansions are evaluated at base prices and expenditure. We have already done the calculations necessary to express (6.31) in terms of observables when we expanded the money metric earlier:

$$\text{EV} = -\sum X_i \Delta p_i - \frac{1}{2} \sum \sum \left(\frac{\partial X_i}{\partial p_j} - X_i \frac{\partial X_j}{\partial Y} \right) \Delta p_i \Delta p_j \qquad (6.33)$$

Because the compensating variation is the equivalent variation evaluated at the new prices rather than base prices, it would be possible to write (6.32) in a form analogous to (6.33), where all derivatives would then evaluated at the new prices. However, this would make a direct comparison between EV and CV a bit difficult. A much more straightforward approach is to make use of the properties of the compensation function, as discussed in Section 2.09.

$$\frac{\partial C}{\partial p_i} = X_i^{u=c} \qquad (6.34)$$

and

$$\frac{\partial^2 C}{\partial p_i \partial p_j} = \frac{\partial X_i^{u=c}}{\partial p_j} \qquad (6.35)$$

where $X_i^{u=c}$ and $(\partial X_i / \partial p_j)^{u=c}$ are constructed in such a way that utility is held constant at the base level. Evaluated at base prices and income, $X_i^{u=c} = X_i$, and the Slutsky substitution term $(\partial X_i / \partial p_j)^{u=c} = \partial X_i / \partial p_j + X_j(\partial X_i / \partial Y)$. Hence,

$$\text{CV} = \sum X_i \Delta p_i + \frac{1}{2} \sum \sum \left(\frac{\partial X_i}{\partial p_j} + X_j \frac{\partial X_i}{\partial Y} \right) \Delta p_i \Delta p_j \qquad (6.36)$$

It is easy to see that both (6.33) and (6.36) involve second-order approximations to a consumer surplus indicator, namely,

$$\text{MCS}_2 = -\sum X_i \Delta p_i - \frac{1}{2} \sum \sum \frac{\partial X_i}{\partial p_j} \Delta p_i \Delta p_j \qquad (6.37)$$

Hence,

$$\text{EV} = \text{MCS}_2 + \frac{1}{2} \sum \sum X_i \frac{\partial X_j}{\partial Y} \Delta p_i \Delta p_j \qquad (6.38)$$

and

$$\text{CV} = -\text{MCS}_2 + \frac{1}{2} \sum \sum X_j \frac{\partial X_i}{\partial Y} \Delta p_i \Delta p_j \qquad (6.39)$$

The two relationships led Hicks and subsequent writers (notably Mishan, 1976) to conjecture that if the income effects (associated with those goods whose prices are changing) are small (i.e., close to zero), then consumer surplus will be a reasonable approximation to both the equivalent and compensating variations. However, there are several problems. First, even though $\partial X_i / \partial Y$ may be small, it is multiplied through by a quantity, and this latter figure may be large. Second, even though the term involving the income effect in both (6.38) and (6.39) may be small relative to the level of income, it may be quite large relative to the consumer surplus measure. In other words, the relative or percentage error involved in using consumer surplus to approximate either the equivalent variation or compensating variation can be quite substantial. Of course, there is no way of determining any hard and fast rules for delimiting the possible errors, because these will depend not only on the magnitudes of the quantities and income effects but also on the sizes of the price changes whose effects are being evaluated. In addition, Hicks's entire analysis would seem to depend on the ability of a second-order Taylor series approximation to accurately measure the indicators involved.

6.7   Willig's error bounds

Recent attempts to justify the use of consumer surplus have focused on the integral version as an approximation to the equivalent and compensating variations. The procedures used are alleged to be more "exact" than those adopted by Hicks. However, the standard problems remain: Unless we know exactly the function that we are attempting to approximate, it is impossible to establish convincing error bounds or regions of ignorance. Inevitably, special assumptions are required, as is evident from procedures suggested by Willig (1976) and Seade (1978). We shall examine these two approaches in turn. Concerning Willig's error bounds, let us denote n_{iu} and n_{il} as the upper and lower bounds for the income elasticity of demand for commodity i over a defined range of price and income variations. Then it is a straightforward matter to show that

$$\left[\frac{Y^*}{Y^0}\right]^{n_{il}} \leq \frac{X_i(p, Y^*)}{X_i(p, Y^0)} \leq \left[\frac{Y^*}{Y^0}\right]^{n_{iu}} \tag{6.40}$$

Let $Y^* = C(U', p)$, the cost of achieving the level of satisfaction U'. Then (6.31) can be rewritten as

$$\left[\frac{C(U', p)}{Y^0}\right]^{n_{il}} \leq \frac{X_i[p, C(U', p)]}{X(p, Y^0)} \leq \left[\frac{C(U', p)}{Y^0}\right]^{n_{iu}} \tag{6.41}$$

From Shephard's lemma [see equation (2.90)] we recall that

$$X_i[p, C(U', p)] = \frac{\partial C(U', p)}{\partial p_i}$$

Hence, we obtain, on rearranging (6.40),

$$X_i(p, Y^0)(Y^0)^{-n_{il}} \leq \frac{\partial C(U', p)}{\partial p_i}[C(U', p)]^{-n_{il}} \tag{6.42}$$

and

$$\frac{\partial C(U', p)}{\partial p_i}[C(U', p)]^{-n_{iu}} \leq X_i(p, Y^0)(Y^0)^{-n_{iu}} \tag{6.43}$$

Integration of (6.42) and (6.43) enables us to construct the following bounds:

$$Y^0\left[\frac{A}{Y^0}(1 - n_{il}) + 1\right]^{1/(1-n_{il})} \geq C(U', p_0)$$

$$\geq Y^0\left[\frac{A}{Y^0}(1 - n_{iu}) + 1\right]^{1/(1-n_{iu})}$$

$$\tag{6.44}$$

where A is the surplus integral:

$$A = -\int X_i \, dp_i$$

Recalling our definition of the equivalent variation as

$$EV = C(U', p_0) - Y^0$$

we can rewrite (6.37) as

$$\frac{[(A/Y^0)(1 - n_{il}) + 1]^{1/(1-n_{il})} - 1 - A/Y^0}{|A|/Y^0} \geq \frac{EV - A}{|A|}$$

$$\geq \frac{[(A/Y^0)(1 - n_{iu}) + 1]^{1/(1-n_{iu})} - 1 - A/Y^0}{|A|/Y^0} \tag{6.45}$$

Then, according to Willig (1976, p. 594), the equivalent variation can be "tightly estimated" provided that

$$1 + (1 - n_l)A/Y^0 > 0$$
$$1 + (1 - n_u)A/Y^0 > 0$$

and that n_l and n_u are sufficiently close in value. Willig (1976, p. 590) claimed that "measured income elasticities of demand tend to cluster closely about 1.0, with only rare outliers." However, there really is little empirical evidence to suggest that this is the case. A more important criticism, however, is the fact that, in general, the magnitude of the income elasticity is not independent of the own-price. Thus, if n_l and n_u are assumed to be close in value, it must also be the case that the range of price variation under consideration is not very great. Consequently, it will be true that the magnitude of the consumer surplus integral will be small.

A simple example will illustrate this proposition. The income elasticity associated with the Klein-Rubin linear expenditure system is

$$n_i = \frac{b_i Y^0}{p_i X_i} = \frac{b_i Y^0}{b_i \left(Y - \Sigma_{j \neq i} c_j p_j\right) + (1 - b_i) c_i p_i} \tag{6.46}$$

Obviously, any variations in n_i will depend on the magnitudes of the parameter values, and hence, as usual, no general rules can be applied. However, suppose that

$$b_i = 0.1 \qquad\qquad Y^0 = 100$$
$$c_i = -10 \qquad\qquad p_i^0 = 1$$
$$c_j = 0 \quad (j \neq i)$$

and that we allow $n_{iu} - n_{il}$ a range of variation of 0.2. Then, solving out (6.46), the maximum allowable range of price variation is -0.002! The value of the consumer surplus integral in this case is also 0.002.

Other examples could be calculated. Nevertheless, the general principle remains: If price variations are small, then the consumer surplus integral will be a good approximation to the equivalent variation. This is not a particularly useful result, however, because most policies that are of interest will involve rather large discrete price variations.

Finally, it is worthwhile noting that in most cases the consumer surplus integral cannot be expressed in terms of elementary functions [e.g., equation (3.14)]. Numerical methods will have to be used. For this reason, it is preferable to use the procedures discussed in Chapter 3, because these have firmer theoretical underpinning.

6.8   Seade's approximation procedure

Like Willig, Seade (1978) was motivated by a desire to maintain the consumer surplus measure as a focal point for applied welfare analysis. However, he was not concerned with identifying conditions under which the surplus measure could be used as a direct approximation for the equivalent variation (or compensating variation). Rather, he devised an alternative formula that does incorporate the surplus measure, although it is designed to be relevant only for systems exhibiting linear Engel curves. In such a world, consumer preferences can be written in the following general form:

$$v = \frac{Y - a(p)}{b(p)} \tag{6.47}$$

where $a(p)$ and $b(p)$ are functions that are homogeneous of degree one in prices. The money-metric associated with (6.47) is easily seen to be

$$M = v \cdot b(p^0) + a(p^0)$$
$$= \frac{Y - a(p)}{b(p)} b(p^0) + a(p^0) \tag{6.48}$$

From Roy's identity, the demand functions associated with (6.40) or (6.48) are seen to be

$$X_i = \frac{\partial a}{\partial p_i} + \frac{Y - a(p)}{b(p)} \frac{\partial b}{\partial p_i} \quad (i = 1, \dots, n) \tag{6.49}$$

A check shows that the income effect,

$$\frac{\partial X_i}{\partial Y} = \frac{\partial b}{\partial p_i} \frac{1}{b(p)} \tag{6.50}$$

is itself independent of income, and hence the Engel curves are linear. Let us suppose that we start off with complete information about the functional forms of the n demand equations (6.49) and are interested in calculating the change in satisfaction due to variations in one or more prices.

As we have done throughout this volume, Seade placed great emphasis on the relationship of the integrating factor or marginal utility of money to the set of observable demand functions. In the case of a system exhibiting linear Engel curves, this turns out to be a particularly straightforward exercise. From (6.48), we obtain

$$\lambda(p) = \frac{\partial M}{\partial Y} = \frac{b(p^0)}{b(p)} \tag{6.51}$$

From a comparison of (6.44) and (6.43), we can easily establish, as did Seade (1978), that in the case of the preference system (6.47) the marginal utility of expenditure depends only on the income effects $\partial X_i/\partial Y$, as follows:

$$\lambda(p) = \exp\left(- \int_c \sum \frac{\partial X_i}{\partial Y} dp_i\right) \tag{6.52}$$

$$= \exp\left[- \int_c \sum \left(\frac{\partial b}{\partial p_i} \frac{b(p^0)}{b(p)}\right) dp_i\right]$$

$$= \exp\{-\ln[b(p)/b(p^0)]\} = b(p^0)/b(p) \tag{6.53}$$

Thus, provided we know the demand functions and hence the income effects and provided that the integration indicated in (6.52) can be undertaken in terms of elementary functions, then we are able to form an expression for the integrating factor. In addition, we are then able to combine (6.53) with the known demand functions (6.48) to form the basis for the following calculation:

$$M = - \int_c \sum \lambda X_i dp_i \tag{6.54}$$

$$= - \int \sum \left[\frac{b(p^0)}{b(p)} \frac{\partial a}{\partial p_i} + \frac{b(p^0)(Y - a(p))}{[b(p)]^2}\right] dp_i$$

$$= \frac{Y - a(p)}{b(p)} b(p^0) + a(p^0) \tag{6.55}$$

It is then a straightforward matter to compute the money-metric. In other words, under the stated conditions, both U and the money-metric can be computed exactly.

Curiously, however, Seade did not appear to fully appreciate this fact, for he proceeded to develop an approximation to (6.54). In this respect, his overriding aim was that of Willig: to maintain the consumer surplus integral as the focal point for applied welfare analysis. To achieve this objective, he first used the mean-value theorem of the integral calculus to rewrite (6.52) as

$$\lambda(p) = \exp\left(- \int_c \frac{1}{Y} n_i X_i dp_i\right)$$

$$= \exp\left(- \frac{\tilde{n}_i}{Y} \int_c X_i dp_i\right)$$

$$= \exp\left(\frac{\tilde{n}_i}{Y} \text{MCS}\right) \tag{6.56}$$

where it is assumed that (a) only the price of commodity i is being varied and (b) the income elasticity $\tilde{n}_i$ is evaluated at $\tilde{p}_i : p_i^1 > \tilde{p}_i > p_i^0$. If we now recall that the equivalent variation EV is simply $M - Y^0$, then we can combine (6.54) and (6.56) to obtain Seade's approximation:

$$\text{EV} \approx \frac{Y}{\tilde{n}_i}\left[\exp\left(\frac{\tilde{n}_i\,\text{MCS}}{Y}\right) - 1\right] \qquad (6.57)$$

Although in practice, equation (6.57) generates highly accurate approximations when only one price varies, in the more realistic case in which several price changes are involved this is not the case (see Chapter 9). And, as we have already noted, it is superfluous, because as much information is required to calculate (6.57) as to calculate the exact version (6.55). And, as we have already noted in the preceding section, there are many instances in which the consumer surplus integral cannot be expressed in terms of elementary functions. Consequently, we must resort to the more general approximation methods discussed in Chapter 3.

Finally, a few comments are in order concerning a misleading conclusion drawn by Seade. In his study he compared a second-order approximation to the money-metric (erroneously calling this the McKenzie-Pearce approach) with his own approximation to the compensating variation. Not surprisingly, this calculation produces a substantial error. In the first instance, changes in the money-metric are equal to the equivalent variation, not the compensating variation. Second, as Pearce and I explained in our 1976 article, truncating the Taylor series expansion after the second-order terms is likely to incur a significant error of approximation. Hence, Seade's own calculations do not represent an acceptable test of his method.

6.9   A major problem

As we have shown in previous chapters, if more than one price varies, the calculation of the consumer surplus measure is not independent of the path over which it is calculated, unless preferences are homothetic. This problem was recognized explicitly by Seade, who argued that his approximation procedure could be generalized to several commodities only if income elasticities were locally equal to one. Unfortunately, he did not appreciate the fact that when Engel curves are linear, the equivalent variation can easily and exactly be calculated for many price changes from observable information without resort to consumer surplus procedures.

On the other hand, Willig claimed that in normal circumstances the path over which the surplus measure is calculated does not really matter very much. We have already discussed in Chapter 3 the com-

putationally simple "rectangular" path of calculation, which is the one
that he proposed. As in the example discussed in that chapter, let us
suppose that variations in the prices of three commodities are being
evaluated. Then the surplus integral will be calculated for the variation in p_1, holding p_2 and p_3 at their initial values. Next, the integral
will be calculated for the variation in p_2, with p_1 at its new level but p_3
at its initial level. However, this procedure is valid for consumer surplus calculations if and only if the relevant integrating factor is independent of the three prices being varied. As we have already indicated
in Chapter 4, this implies very strong restrictions. And as we showed
in the example in Chapter 3, in more general cases the extent of the
numerical error is bound to be substantial (see the numerical results
derived in Chapter 8).

If Willig's article and his subsequent reply to my critique (Willig,
1979) are studied, it becomes apparent that he did offer a number of
caveats to the use of consumer surplus. He argued that it can be used
without apology if (a) the price variations under study have a relatively
small impact on welfare, (b) all prices variations are in the same direction, (c) the income effects associated with the commodities under
study are small, or (d) preferences are homothetic. Specifically ex-
cluded are cases in which some prices rise and some fall and where the
particular project or policy has a substantive impact on a particular
group of people. However, these are precisely the circumstances that
are of greatest interest in applied economics.

6.10   The additive and multiplicative errors associated with consumer surplus approximations

In Sections 6.8 and 6.9 we alluded to the fact that the consumer
surplus integral frequently will have to be approximated by numerical
methods. Another look at equation (3.66) suggests what would be
involved. In the case of a change in the price of commodity one, we
have

$$\Delta M_1 \approx -\frac{p_1^1 - p_1^0}{6}[\hat{\lambda}(p_1^0)X_1(p_1^0) + 4\hat{\lambda}(p_1^m)X_1(p_1^m)$$
$$+ \hat{\lambda}(p_1^1)X_1(p_1^1)] \tag{3.66}$$

If we introduce the assumption that $\lambda(p)$ remains unchanged as p_1
varies, we obtain an approximation to the change in the consumer
surplus integral

$$\Delta CS_1 \approx -\frac{p_1^1 - p_1^0}{6}[X_1(p_1^0) + 4X_1(p_1^m) + X_1(p_1^1)] \tag{6.58}$$

In general, however, $\lambda(p)$ will not be independent of p_1 or other prices, and hence (6.58) will contain a "conceptual" approximation error over and above the "numerical" approximation error inherent in (3.66) (see Section 3.9). A comparison of the two formulas reveals that the consumer surplus approximation (6.58) contains both additive and multiplicative error components. Let

$$\frac{\hat{\lambda}(p_1^m)}{\hat{\lambda}(p_1^0)} = 1 + a_1 \tag{6.59}$$

$$\frac{\hat{\lambda}(p_1^1)}{\hat{\lambda}(p_1^0)} = 1 + b_1 \tag{6.60}$$

and

$$h_1 = [4a_1 X_1(p_1^m) + b_1 X_1(p_1^1)] \tag{6.61}$$

Then, from (3.66) and (6.58), we have

$$\Delta M_1 = \hat{\lambda}(p_1^0)\Delta CS + \hat{\lambda}(p_1^0) \cdot h_1 \tag{6.62}$$

where $\hat{\lambda}(p_0^1)$ can be thought of as a *multiplicative correction factor* to consumer surplus and $\hat{\lambda}(p_0^1) \cdot h_1$ the *additive correction factor*. In the case of only one price variation, $\hat{\lambda}(p_1^0)$ will equal one, and the additive factor will be the relevant concern. However, for the case of more than one price variation, λ will vary as we follow the stepwise path of integration suggested by Willig. Thus, as λ deviates from the value of one, the multiplicative factor will become increasingly important.

6.11   Summary

The objective of this chapter has been to examine the nature of the assumptions implicit in attempts to use consumer surplus as an approximation to some true ordinal welfare indicator or metric. The prime difficulty is that we have no operational criteria that can be used to judge whether or not a particular procedure will be reasonably accurate in any given situation. First of all, we do not know the form that consumer preferences take. If we did, we would not need to resort to approximations at all. Second, the accuracy of any particular procedure depends on the initial conditions and the magnitude of the variable changes under consideration, as well as the underlying parameter values. About the only thing that we can say with "reasonable" certainty is that if there is only one price variation and it is small, then consumer surplus can reasonably be used as a welfare indicator. For other situations, there is no definitive answer. However, a rough idea of the magnitude of the problems involved can be gained from the numerical example discussed in detail in Chapter 9.

CHAPTER 7

A reconsideration of the theory of index numbers

7.1 Introduction

The theoretical heritage of cost-of-living indices derives from two related lines of thought. On the one hand, Irving Fisher, in 1911, and again in 1922, proposed a number of criteria that such indices should meet in order to be considered "ideal." The approach adopted can be characterized as being mechanistic and only very indirectly based on any consistent theory of consumer behavior [Frisch (1936) called it "atomistic"]. In contrast, the Russian economist Konüs wrote in 1924 that when computing the true cost of living we should compare "the monetary cost of two different combinations of goods which are connected by the condition that during consumption of these two combinations, the general status of want-satisfaction (the standard of living) is the same" (1939, p. 10). This definition has subsequently been adopted by most of the leading writers in this area of investigation, such as Bowley (1928), Frisch (1936), Schultz (1939), Klein and Rubin (1947–8), and Malmquist (1953), and more recently Afriat (1972), Pollak (1971), Samuelson and Swamy (1974), Diewert (1980), and Sen (1979).

It is immediately apparent that the Konüs index is based on the concept of the compensating variation, which we have shown in previous chapters to be unsatisfactory as a welfare indicator. Indeed, many economists have long been aware that something was amiss. Beginning in the 1930s, several investigators began to focus their attention on whether or not the Konüs definition fulfilled the various Fisher test criteria. Unfortunately, the results have not been entirely satisfactory. First, it has generally been agreed that the Fisher criteria are inconsistent (Frisch, 1936; Swamy, 1965; Eichhorn, 1976). Second, it has been shown that the Konüs cost-of-living index is an ordinal welfare indicator only under the restrictive condition that consumer preferences are homothetic (Malmquist, 1953; Samuelson and Swamy, 1974; Diewert, 1980).

Some writers have suggested that nothing can be done about this unfortunate situation. For example, Samuelson and Swamy (1974,

p. 592) concluded that we should not shoot "the honest theorist who points out to us the unavoidable truth that in non-homothetic cases of realistic life, one must not expect to be able to make the naive measurements that untutored common sense always longs for; we must accept the sad facts of life, and be grateful for the more complicated procedure economic theory devises."

Fortunately, there is an alternative. In the first instance, this involves a reconsideration of the standards by which price and quantity index numbers have traditionally been evaluated. Thus, in Section 7.2, two specific criteria derived from the theory of consumer behavior are proposed as a basis for index-number theory. In Section 7.3, a new approach to index-number construction, proposed by Pearce and myself (1976), is discussed in light of these criteria. Then, in Section 7.4, it is shown that the traditional approach does not satisfy the points involved. Next, Irving Fisher's test criteria are reexamined in light of the suggested revisions. Various alternative index-number relationships, including Debreu's coefficient of resource utilization, are examined. The general conclusion reached is that the criteria that economists have previously adopted are overrestrictive and that this has prevented them from formulating a truly operational theory of index numbers. In contrast, the approach presented in this chapter is operational, with the proposed indices being easily calculated by means of the algorithm presented in Chapter 3.

7.2   The two fundamental criteria

Index numbers are summary statistics designed to characterize the effects (which may be fairly complex) that arise from changes in the underlying variables. Because more often than not such summary statistics are designed for public consumption, it is desirable that they be amenable to interpretations that are reasonably intuitive. Thus, a quantity index, from the consumer point of view, should reflect changes in real standards of living. The more we consume, in some very general sense, the better off we are. In contrast, a price index has a more limited objective. Changes in living standards arise from variations in the levels of both prices and total expenditure. A price index is designed to isolate the effects on living standards arising solely from some variation in individual commodity prices. Given some level of total expenditure, the price index should reflect whether the current situation is more or less expensive, in some general sense, than the situation holding in the base period.

We shall now turn our attention to formalizing these basic ideas. Let q be a vector of commodities consumed, p be a vector of prices, and $Y = p'q$ be total expenditure. Following the analysis of previous chapters, we assume that consumer preferences can be expressed in terms of an indirect utility function:

$$v = v(Y, p) \tag{7.1}$$

The superscripts k and 0 will be used to refer to the current and base-period vectors, respectively. We shall postpone until Chapter 8 considerations that arise from changes in the distribution of income. For the time being, we assume that our theory is designed to characterize the behavior of a homogeneous group of consumers.

The following general criterion can now be stated:

The transitivity criterion. For Q and P to be economically meaningful quantity and price indices, respectively, they should be formulated as follows:

$$Q = G[v(Y^k, p^k); \; v(Y^0, p^0)] \tag{7.2}$$

and

$$P = F[v(\hat{Y}, p^k); \; v(\hat{Y}, p^0)] \tag{7.3}$$

where G is a monotonic, increasing function of $v(Y^k, p^k)$ and F is a monotonic, decreasing function of $v(\hat{Y}, p^k)$ given $\hat{Y}$.

The first part of this criterion indicates that the quantity index Q should act as a welfare indicator. It is designed to answer this question: Has the "real income" of consumers increased or decreased? In contrast, equation (7.3) indicates that for any arbitrary level of expenditure $\hat{Y}$, an increase (decrease) in the value of the price index should be synonymous with a decrease (increase) in satisfaction. That is, the level of expenditure $\hat{Y}$ is able to purchase more (less) as the cost-of-living index or price index falls (rises). The aim of (7.3) is to distinguish between (a) those changes in satisfaction that are due solely to price variations and (b) those due also to variations in disposable or real income.

To appreciate how this might work, consider the following two simple examples. In the first case, suppose that commodity prices remain constant and that income doubles. The transitivity criterion requires that the chosen price index P remain constant, even though consumers are better off. However, the latter implication should be reflected in the quantity index. For the second case, assume that all prices and incomes double. The index P should also increase (preferably doubling), even though there has been no change in the level of satisfaction (Q does not vary).

The transitivity criterion also reflects the principle that the ordering capability of the price and quantity indices should not depend on the choice of base situation. That is, any arbitrary price/quantity situation can be chosen as the reference point. The indices constructed thus permit all alternative situations to be directly compared with this reference point, and because the index is in a metric form, all alternatives can be directly compared with each other. Whenever the reference point is varied, a different increasing, monotonic transformation of the underlying utility function is constructed. Thus, according to this criterion, it would be inconsistent to compare index numbers based on different reference situations. To make such comparisons would be analogous to comparing various temperatures on the assumption that there is a one-to-one correspondence between the Fahrenheit and centigrade scales.

In addition, the transitivity criterion calls attention to the fact that we are interested in more than simply making binary comparisons. If we desire to rank n alternative price/quantity situations (e.g., each representing different years), it is technically most efficient to be able to calculate an $n \times 1$ vector of numbers that, on examination, will enable us to see immediately how each situation lies relative to the others. This criterion requires that we do this by choosing some monotonic transformation (again depending on the chosen base situation) that permits a cardinal representation of consumer preferences in terms of an index number.

The weak factor reversal criterion. For P and Q to be economically meaningful price and quantity indices,

$$P \cdot Q = \frac{Y^k}{Y^0} \qquad (7.4)$$

This standard is due to Samuelson and Swamy (1974), and it represents a modification of Fisher's 1922 factor reversal test. It simply requires that for the sake of consistency, the product of the price and quantity indices should equal the expenditure index Y^k/Y^0. Fisher's original test required that any index-number formula "permit interchanging the prices and quantities without giving inconsistent results — i.e., the two results multiplied together should give the true value ratio" (1922, p. 72). Thus, suppose that we are given a particular functional form for a quantity index. According to Fisher, the complementary price index would be created by substituting price for quantity variables in the chosen function. There is no particular economic rationale for this procedure. As Samuelson and Swamy pointed out (1974, p. 572), most cost-of-utility functions do not possess the property of self-duality. Hence, the original test as stated by Fisher has limited appeal.

Over the years, many index-number formulations have been proposed. In the next section, a particular pairing of price and quantity indices derived from the money-metric approach will be shown to satisfy the two criteria. This result will then be contrasted with several other formulations proposed in the literature. It will be shown that these do not satisfy the criteria.

7.3   The money-metric approach to index-number theory

We know from the analysis of Chapter 2 that corresponding to any continuously differentiable utility function, such as (7.1), there exists a cost-of-utility function:

$$C = C(\nu, p) \tag{7.5}$$

This relationship is derived by asking this question: What is the minimum cost or level of expenditure required to achieve a given level of satisfaction [e.g., $\nu^0 = \nu(Y^0, p^0)$] for any set of prices? From this we derive the money-metric

$$M(k, 0) = C[\nu(Y^k, p^k); p^0] \tag{7.6}$$

which represents the minimum amount of expenditure required to achieve any given level of satisfaction ν, given base prices p^0.

As we have already established, M is thus a monotonic, increasing function of ν and hence is a welfare indicator in its own right. The difference between M and base expenditure Y^0 is equal to the equivalent variation associated with a movement from the initial point to any other price/quantity situation.

We are now in a position to define an economically meaningful cost-of-living index. $M(k, 0)$ is the minimum cost of achieving the utility level defined by (Y^k, p^k), but at the initial price vector p^0, $M(k, k)$ equal to Y^k is, of course, the actual cost of achieving that level of satisfaction. Therefore, we can write the actual cost of living relative to the level of (money-metric) utility as

$$P_M(k, 0) = \frac{M(k, k)}{M(k, 0)} = \frac{C[\nu(Y^k, p^k); p^k]}{C[\nu(Y^k, p^k); p^0]}$$

$$= \frac{Y^k}{C[(Y^k, p^k); p^0]} \tag{7.7}$$

This index was first proposed by Pearce and myself in 1976. It is immediately obvious that given Y^k, P_M is a monotonically decreasing function of utility and hence satisfies the transitivity criterion. Therefore, to construct a true cost-of-living index, we should compare the monetary cost actually required to achieve a particular level of satisfaction with the monetary cost associated with this same level, but given initial prices.

Corresponding to this cost-of-living index we shall need a complementary quantity index. One possible candidate is the index suggested by Allen (1949):

$$Q_M(k, 0) = \frac{M(k, 0)}{M(0, 0)} = \frac{C[\nu(Y^k, p^k); p^0]}{C[\nu(Y^0, p^0); p^0]} \tag{7.8}$$

This indicates the monetary cost of achieving a particular level of satisfaction, but given initial prices, relative to the actual minimum cost of the base situation. It is immediately obvious that $Q_M(k, 0)$ is an increasing, monotonic transformation of $\nu(Y^k, p^k)$ and hence satisfies the transitivity criterion. In addition, it and $P_M(k, 0)$ also satisfy the weak factor reversal test, as is easily seen from the following:

$$P_M \cdot Q_M = \frac{Y^k}{C[\nu(Y^k, p^k); p^0]} \frac{C[\nu(Y^k, p^k); p^0]}{C[\nu(Y^0, p^0); p^0]} = \frac{Y^k}{Y^0} \tag{7.9}$$

In light of these properties of the money-metric/Allen quantity index, it is interesting to note Deaton's (1979, p. 400) curious procedure of chain-linking this index and thereby completely destroying its metric ordinal properties. That is, in his approach the base of the money-metric is continually updated. It is true that such an index permits a binary comparison of the current period with the previous period. However, if we were interested in ranking n price/quantity situations according to whether "real income" has increased or decreased, then $\sum_i^n (i - 1)$ such binary comparisons would have to be undertaken. In other words, we would have to present our index-number calculations in triangular form (i.e., as elements on one side of the diagonal of a symmetric matrix) rather than in time-series (vector) form if we followed Deaton's procedure to its logical conclusion. Thus, the fixed base cost-of-living and quantity indices (7.7) and (7.8) are both more economical and simpler to interpret.

7.4   The traditional approach to the theory of index numbers

Allen (1949) and many others, including Samuelson and Swamy, have paired Q_M with the Konüs cost-of-living index. The latter can be written in terms of the cost-of-utility function as follows:

$$P_K(k, 0) = \frac{C(\nu^0; p^k)}{C(\nu^0; p^0)} = \frac{C(\nu^0; p^k)}{Y^0} \tag{7.10}$$

That is, this index refers to the cost of achieving ν^0 given the set of prices p^k relative to the cost of the base situation.

At first glance, it may be tempting to conclude that (7.10) and the McKenzie-Pearce price index (7.7) are the same thing; both appear to be defined with respect to some level of satisfaction ν. However, this similarity is deceptive, as can be seen from Table 7.1. The Konüs index at every time period is defined with respect to the base or initial level of satisfaction. The question is asked: What is the cost of achieving $\nu(Y^0, p^0)$ given some alternative vector of prices? In contrast, the index defined by (7.7) is defined with respect to the current level (not the base level) of satisfaction: Current expenditure is deflated by the cost of achieving the current level of satisfaction on the basis of prices existing in the base period. In other words, the denominator is the money-metric.

For the transitivity criterion to be fulfilled, the price index must remain constant for any movement along a particular indifference surface, given base prices and any arbitrary level of expenditure. It is immediately apparent that the money-metric price index P_M satisfies this condition, because

$$P_M = \frac{Y^k}{C(\nu^k, p^0)} \tag{7.11}$$

It does not matter what vector of prices is generating the level of satisfaction ν^k given Y^k; the index P_M remains invariant. In general, this is not true for the Konüs index. For it to satisfy the transitivity criterion, it must be the case that

$$\frac{C(\nu^0; p^2)}{C(\nu^0; p^0)} = \frac{C(\nu^0, p^1)}{C(\nu^0, p^0)} \tag{7.12}$$

However, as was shown in Section 5.4, this equality will only hold if preferences are homothetic. Hence, the Konüs approach provides a meaningful cost-of-living index if and only if all income elasticities equal unity.

The implications of this difficulty become more apparent when we inquire whether or not the Konüs and Allen indices satisfy the weak factor reversal criterion. Let us multiply these two indices:

$$P_K \cdot Q_M = \frac{C(\nu^0; p)}{C(\nu^0; p^0)} \cdot \frac{C(\nu; p^0)}{C(\nu^0; p^0)} \tag{7.13}$$

Table 7.1

Time period	McKenzie-Pearce index	Konüs index
0 (base period)	1	1
1	$\dfrac{C[\nu(Y^1,p^1),p^1]}{C[\nu(Y^1,p^1),p^0]}$	$\dfrac{C[\nu(Y^0,p^0),p^1]}{C[\nu(Y^0,p^0),p^0]}$
2	$\dfrac{C[\nu(Y^2,p^2),p^2]}{C[\nu(Y^2,p^2),p^0]}$	$\dfrac{C[\nu(Y^0,p^0),p^2]}{C[\nu(Y^0,p^0),p^0]}$
3	$\dfrac{C[\nu(Y^3,p^3),p^3]}{C[\nu(Y^3,p^3),p^0]}$	$\dfrac{C[\nu(Y^0,p^0),p^3]}{C[\nu(Y^0,p^0),p^0]}$
$\vdots$	$\vdots$	$\vdots$
n	$\dfrac{C[\nu(Y^n,p^n),p^n]}{C[\nu(Y^n,p^n),p^0]}$	$\dfrac{C[\nu(Y^0,p^0),p^n]}{C[\nu(Y^0,p^0),p^0]}$

We multiply the denominator and numerator of (7.13) by $C(\nu; p)$ and rearrange terms so as to obtain

$$P_K \cdot Q_M = \frac{Y^k}{Y^0} \cdot \frac{C(\nu^0,p)}{C(\nu,p)} \cdot \frac{C(\nu,p^0)}{C(\nu^0,p^0)} \tag{7.14}$$

The product of the two indices will equal the value ratio if and only if

$$\frac{C(\nu; p)}{C(\nu; p^0)} = \frac{C(\nu^0; p)}{C(\nu^0; p^0)} \tag{7.15}$$

which, once again, implies homotheticity, a result we derived in Section 2.9.

These particular results concerning the Konüs index are well known and were fully summarized in the survey article by Diewert (1980). Their restrictive nature stands in marked contrast to the positive (but not widely appreciated) results involving the money-metric approach derived in Section 7.3.

That the Konüs and Allen indices satisfy the two criteria in the case where preferences are homothetic can easily be seen as follows. From (2.87) we know that any such preference function can be written in the form $\nu = Y/P(p)$. Hence, it is straightforward to calculate

$$P_K = \frac{\nu(Y^0,p^0) \cdot P(p)}{\nu(Y^0,p^0) \cdot P(p^0)} = \frac{P(p)}{P(p^0)} \tag{7.16}$$

Given expenditure, $P(p)$ is an inversely monotonic function of U, and hence P_K satisfies the transitivity criterion in this special case. In addition, we are able to write the Allen quantity index as

$$Q_M = \frac{\nu(Y,p) \cdot P(p^0)}{\nu(Y^0,p^0) \cdot P(p^0)} = \frac{\nu(Y,p)}{\nu(Y^0,p^0)} \tag{7.17}$$

Hence

$$P_K \cdot Q_M = \frac{P(p) \cdot \nu(Y,p)}{P(p^0) \cdot \nu(Y^0,p^0)} = \frac{Y}{Y^0} \tag{7.18}$$

The weak factor reversal criterion is fulfilled as well.

However, does the pairing of the Konüs and Allen indices make sense in the first place, even if the world were homothetic? The answer must be no. Multiplication of P_K and Q_M is analogous to multiplying the price of apples times the quantity of peanuts. The entities involved are entirely different. On the other hand, calculation of P_K, involving the compensating variation, assumes that compensation is paid after a price change so as to maintain the consumer at the initial level of satisfaction. In contrast, calculation of the equivalent variation takes initial prices as given and examines the change in income required to achieve the new level of satisfaction after prices have varied. In terms of economic interpretation, the two concepts are completely asymmetric.

7.5   A reconsideration of Fisher's test criteria

Successful performance of the money-metric cost-of-living and quantity indices obviously depends very heavily on the nature of the criteria by which they are judged. This consideration is also important in explaining the unsatisfactory state of traditional index-number discussions. In very large measure the culprit is Fisher's "circular test," a criterion that, according to Samuelson and Swamy, "is as required as is the property of transitivity itself. And this regardless of homotheticity or non-homotheticity" (1974, p. 576). In this section we shall argue that the circular test, although sufficient for transitivity, is by no means necessary.

To appreciate what is involved, let us begin with Fisher's own description of the circular test:

By the so-called "circular test," taking New York as base (=100) and finding Philadelphia 110, then taking Philadelphia as base (=100) and finding Chicago (115), we ought, when we complete the circuit and take Chicago as base (=115), to find, by direct comparison, New York 100 again. Or again, if Chicago is found to be 115 via Philadelphia, it ought consistently to be 115 when calculated directly. [1922, p. 270]

In terms of the Allen quantity indices, this test requires that

$$Q_M(2, 1) \cdot Q_M(1, 0) = Q_M(2, 0) \tag{7.19}.$$

or, equivalently, that

$$\frac{C(v^2; p^1)}{C(v^1; p^1)} \cdot \frac{C(v^1; p^0)}{C(v^0; p^0)} = \frac{C(v^2; p^0)}{C(v^0; p^0)} \tag{7.20}$$

For this to be the case, however,

$$\frac{C(v^2; p^1)}{C(v^2; p^0)} = \frac{C(v^1; p^1)}{C(v^1; p^0)} \tag{7.21}$$

which implies homothetic preferences, again from Section 2.9.

The modern version of the circularity test takes a somewhat different form. For most index-number theorists it is important that the value of the index under consideration be independent of the reference situation chosen. That is,

$$\frac{C(v^2; p^j)}{C(v^1; p^j)} = \frac{C(v^2; p^i)}{C(v^1; p^i)} \tag{7.22}$$

which, of course, is simply (7.21) rearranged.

By 1922 Fisher had abandoned this criterion on the grounds that "a *perfect* fulfillment of this so-called circular test should really be taken as proof that the formula which fulfills it is erroneous" (1922, p. 271). Samuelson and Swamy reproached him for this comment, but Fisher's conclusion is not as "obscure" as Samuelson and Swamy would make out. Most, if not all, policies and projects are evaluated with respect to the current (or base-period) environment. There is no need to compare the absolute magnitude of an index using p^2 as a base with another index based on p^1. The sort of calculation involved in the circular test is not unlike that in the following analogy. Suppose that the temperature rises from 100 degrees to 212 degrees Fahrenheit. Then the scale is changed to degrees centigrade just before there is a further rise from 100 degrees centigrade to 110 centigrade. Clearly, the circular test does not hold:

$$\frac{230}{100} \neq \frac{110}{100} \cdot \frac{212}{100} = \frac{233.2}{100}$$

Yet both Fahrenheit and centigrade scales or indices are themselves ordinal indicators of temperature. There is no reason that we should want to change the scale of measurement every time we move from one situation to another.

The foregoing analogy is similar to one given in Fisher's 1922 discussion of the circular test. His example was based on a price index-number comparison among the state of Georgia (U.S.), Egypt, and Norway. He argued that if we are interested in comparing prices in Norway (p^3) with those in Egypt (p^1), as in the circular test criterion, "we shall not go to Georgia for our weights" (1922, p. 272). But this is exactly what the circular test requires.

The circular test should therefore be abandoned and replaced by the weaker transitivity requirement proposed earlier in this chapter. If, for a given level of expenditure, consumers are worse off following some price change, then the price or cost-of-living index should indicate an increase. Similarly, if a change in total expenditure more than offsets the foregoing price variation, such that consumers are actually better off, then the quantity index should show an improvement. But these statements need be true only for a given base situation. The only meaningful economic objective of index-number construction is to rank alternatives, and this can be achieved by the choice of any arbitrary reference point (analogous to the zero points on the centigrade and Fahrenheit temperature scales).

7.6 Alternative index-number formulas

In this section we shall examine three alternative formulations that have received attention in the literature dealing with index numbers.

1. Pollak (1971, p. 64) suggested that a quantity index can be defined from the Konüs cost-of-living index and the weak factor reversal criterion. That is, Q_P can be defined from

$$P_K \cdot Q_P = \frac{C(\nu^0; p)}{C(\nu^0; p^0)} \cdot Q_P = \frac{Y}{Y^0} \qquad (7.23)$$

Hence

$$Q_P = \frac{Y}{C(\nu^0; p)} = \frac{C(\nu; p)}{C(\nu^0; p)} \qquad (7.24)$$

As Pollak showed, and as is immediately apparent from our preceding discussion in this chapter, Q_P will be an ordinal welfare indicator if and only if preferences are homothetic. It should be noted that Deaton (1979, p. 397) labeled the index (7.24) the money-metric. This, of course, is incorrect, because the money-metric/Allen quantity index is defined with respect to a set of reference prices, whereas the Pollak quantity index is defined with respect to a reference level of satisfaction.

2. In 1953, Malmquist proposed a quantity index that involves constructing an equivalence scale on the basis of a reference vector of commodities. This, he suggested, should be paired with the Konüs index. Let q^0 and q^k represent the consumption patterns associated with the base situation and kth situation, respectively. Then consider an alternative consumption pattern, proportional to q^k by a factor $1/\alpha$, that generates the same level of satisfaction as $U(q^0)$. That is,

$$U(q^k/\alpha) = U(q^0) \tag{7.25}$$

Malmquist then defined

$$\alpha = \alpha[U(q^0), q^k] \tag{7.26}$$

as a quantity index. More recently it has been labeled the *distance function*. However, it does not satisfy the transitivity criterion. This can easily be determined by substituting the appropriate demand functions, thereby creating an indirect version of the distance function:

$$\alpha = \alpha[U(Y^0, p^0); q(Y^k, p^k)] \tag{7.27}$$

It is immediately apparent that (7.27) will satisfy the transitivity criterion only if preferences are homothetic.

3. Deaton (1979) proposed a variant of the Malmquist index discussed in the preceding section. Consider the consumption pattern $\beta \cdot q^0$, which generates the same level of satisfaction as derived from q^k. That is,

$$U(\beta \cdot q^0) = U(q^k) \tag{7.28}$$

Then

$$\beta = \beta[U(q^k); q^0] \tag{7.29}$$

can also be called a quantity index. It is easily determined that β is an increasing, monotonic transformation of $U(q^k)$ that satisfies the transitivity criterion. Deaton suggested that (7.29) is the dual of the Allen index. It is, of course, true that the two are complements in a sense. The Allen index is defined with respect to a vector of prices, whereas the β index is defined with respect to a vector of quantities. But both are quantity indices. Neither is capable of indicating changes in the cost of living, given the level of expenditure, and hence the pairing must be rejected as incapable of achieving the objectives set out in the transitivity criterion.

7.7   Debreu's coefficient of resource allocation

In the early 1950s, Debreu (1951, 1954) proposed that an index could be constructed so as to measure the distance by which the economy deviates from the optimal situation. Unfortunately, several interpretations of his analysis are possible. Let us examine these in turn. In 1954, Debreu suggested that a coefficient of resource utilization could be calculated as follows:

> We multiply, for each commodity, the difference between the available quantity and the optimal quantity by the price derived from the intrinsic price system whose existence has been previously proved. We take the sum of all such expressions for all commodities, and we divide by a price index in order to eliminate the arbitrary multiplicative factor affecting all the prices. [p. 274]

The prices derived from the "intrinsic price system" are those associated with the optimal situation. If we label these as p^*, the first part of Debreu's calculation can be written as

$$p^*q^* - p^*q \tag{7.30}$$

where q^* and q are the quantity vectors associated with the optimal and suboptimal situations. Dividing through by p^*q^*, we obtain

$$1 - \frac{p^*q}{p^*q^*} = 1 - \rho \tag{7.31}$$

where ρ is the coefficient of resource allocation. However, in this case it is nothing more than a Laspeyres quantity index, with the vector p^* providing the base weights. If we are concerned solely with binary comparisons, such an index will indeed indicate that a particular price/quantity situation is inferior to the optimum. However, for the reasons discussed in Chapter 6, it cannot be used as a metric for ordering all suboptimal situations.

Debreu also referred to the "dead loss" associated with the suboptimal situation and suggested that the inefficiency of the economy can be described by "a certain number of dollars representing the value of the physical resources which could be thrown away without preventing the achievement of the prescribed levels of satisfaction" (1954, p. 275). If we use this concept as a basis for an alternative definition of the coefficient of resource utilization, we will obtain the money-metric/Allen index.

The value of physical resources that can be "thrown away" is equal to

$$C[\nu(Y^*, p^*), p^*] - C[\nu(Y, p), p^*] \qquad (7.32)$$

Divide through by $C[\nu(Y^*, p^*), p^*]$ and we obtain

$$1 - \frac{C[\nu(Y, p); p^*]}{C[\nu(Y^*, p^*); p^*]} = 1 - \eta \qquad (7.33)$$

where η can be defined as the money-metric or Allen coefficient of resource utilization. It is clearly an ordinal metric. Because $C[\nu(Y, p); p^*] \leq C[\nu(Y^*, p^*); p^*]$, according to how far away from the optimum the economy is operating, the index will tend toward zero the more efficiently the given stock of resources is used.

Subsequently, Debreu (1954) suggested yet another possible interpretation that completely parallels the Deaton interpretation of the Malmquist index. Debreu wrote:

Given a set of values $(s_1, \ldots, s_i, \ldots, s_m)$ of the individual satisfactions, the economic efficiency of this situation is defined as follows: the quantities of all the available resources are multiplied by a number such that using these new resources and the same technological knowledge as before it is still possible to achieve for the ith individual ($i = 1, \ldots, m$) a satisfaction at least equal to s_i. The smallest of the numbers satisfying this condition is p, the coefficient of resource utilization of the economy. [1954, p. 14]

7.8   Summary

The objective of this chapter has been to free the orthodox theory of index numbers from a straightjacket that has been highly restrictive in terms of behavioral requirements. By reconsidering traditional criteria and by providing an alternative formula for the cost-of-living index, we are led to the conclusion that the restrictive assumption of homotheticity is no longer required. The orthodox approach, based on the work of Konüs, should be abandoned and replaced by the modern money-metric approach that provides the basis for the analysis of this volume. If these steps are taken, then the economics profession will possess an economically meaningful and operational means for consistently ranking alternative price/quantity situations.

CHAPTER 8

The money-metric as a basis for calculation of social welfare functions

8.1 Introduction

In the first chapter of this book we emphasized that two basic steps must be taken if attempts to calculate a measure of economic welfare are to be successful. First, the measure must be capable of characterizing the preferences of an individual or homogeneous group. Second, the value judgments involved in aggregating the individual welfare functions must be made explicit. So far, however, we have said very little about the latter principle. The justification for proceeding in this dichotomous fashion is a purely pedagogic one. Our prime objective in previous chapters has been to develop in detail the theory and technical apparatus necessary for constructing an applied welfare indicator. Having now accomplished this aim, we are in a position to deal with real-world situations involving heterogeneous groups of individuals possessing different preferences and enjoying different income levels.

8.2 Social welfare functions based on the money-metric

As before, let us denote consumer preferences by an indirect preference function

$$v_i = U_i[F_i(Y_i, p_1, \ldots, p_n)] = v_i(Y_i, p) \quad (i = 1, \ldots, n) \tag{8.1}$$

where U_i is an increasing, monotonic transformation of the function F_i and the subscript indicates that the relevant variable or function refers to the ith individual. Then it is possible to construct a *Bergson-Samuelson social welfare function*:

$$W = W(U_1, \ldots, U_n) \tag{8.2}$$

In the analysis that follows, we shall assume that the relationship that exists between W and its arguments is basically the same as that existing between consumer satisfaction and the quantities of goods consumed. This statement involves our making the following assumptions:

Assumption 1. The social welfare function is capable of ordering all possible combinations of individual satisfaction levels $S = S(U_1, \ldots, U_n)$. Thus, for every possible pair of combinations, denoted S_i and S_j, one of the following relationships must hold:

1. S_i is preferred to S_j
2. S_j is preferred to S_i
3. The consumer is indifferent between S_i and S_j

Assumption 2. For all possible combinations S, if S_i is preferred to S_j and S_j is preferred to S_k, then S_i is preferred to S_k.

Assumption 3. The social welfare function W, which orders the various combinations S, is continuous. Recall that we have also assumed the individual preference functions U_i to be continuous.

Assumption 4. The social welfare function W is increasing over the various individual preference orderings. More is always preferred to less.

Assumption 5. For any pair of individual satisfaction levels U_i and U_j, the satisfaction levels of all other individuals remaining constant, the rate at which U_i is substituted for U_j along any social welfare indifference surface increases or remains constant as U_i increases. This assumption involves a very important value judgment, for it indicates that as welfare is redistributed from individual j to individual i, U_i receives a smaller (or constant) weight. As we shall determine, this assumption need not imply complete equality of satisfaction or income. However, it does rule out situations in which U_i receives lesser weight and U_j greater weight as satisfaction is redistributed from j to i along any social welfare indifference surface.

Assumption 6. We also rule out circumstances in which an individual or group of individuals is somehow "eliminated" from society. Of course, history abounds with examples in which particular societies have violated this assumption. Wars and genocide have been widespread. Somewhat less harsh was the policy of transportation that enforced the resettlement of many Britons in North America and Australia during the nineteenth century.

As it stands, there still remains an important ambiguity implicit in the social welfare function (8.2). In general, this function reflects the trade-off that society is willing to make in the underlying satisfaction levels of its individual members. Thus, by assumption 5, some high value of U_1 and a low value of U_2 could generate the same value of W as some low value of U_1 and a high value of U_2. But, as we noted in

Chapter 2, consumer behavior is unaffected by any increasing, monotonic transformation of the individual's utility function. The ordering of the alternative individual consumption levels is preserved. However, this fact introduces a problem for the interpretation of social welfare. Suppose that we specify a particular functional form for (8.2). Then any increasing, monotonic transformation of, say, individual j's preference function will appear to give greater weight to that person than to other individuals in the calculation of social welfare. Of course, one could reformulate the social welfare function in such a way that this is taken into account and the original social ordering is preserved. Obviously, great care is required in setting up any discussion of social welfare so that we can keep separate (a) the issue of characterizing the preference ordering of each individual and (b) the function used to aggregate these individual preference relationships so as to form a meaningful aggregate indicator.

In the first instance, we require that individual preferences be expressed on the same scale in such a way that it is possible to infer that some policy variation has caused individual 1 to gain (or lose) x times the amount that 2 has gained (or lost). The ideal candidate to fulfill this role is the money-metric:

$$M_i = M_i[\nu_i(Y_i, p); p_0] \quad (i = 1, \ldots, n) \tag{8.3}$$

Although the money-metric is a welfare indicator, as we have emphasized in earlier chapters, it has an economic interpretation in its own right. To repeat, it indicates the cost of achieving any level of satisfaction $\nu(Y, p)$, given base prices, and hence it is a measure that can be used to make direct comparisons between individuals. Further, use of this concept enables us to make explicit that any evaluation of alternative social states will depend solely on the structure of the social welfare function. For example, a particular policy might yield a gain to individual 1 that is equivalent to 200 dollars but a loss to individual 2 that is equivalent to 100 dollars. This result is completely invariant when the consumer preference function is subject to increasing, monotonic transformations. Whether or not an income redistribution represents a net gain or net loss to society depends entirely on the structure of the social welfare function.

To motivate subsequent discussion, it will be useful to examine two special forms that the social welfare function can take.

Case 1. Harberger (1971) has argued that the gains and losses arising out of the implementation of a particular project or policy should be added together, irrespective of who gains and who loses. This is his "third postulate" for applied welfare economics. In this instance, (8.2) will take the form of a simple additive relationship:

$$W = M_1 + M_2 + \ldots + M_n \tag{8.4}$$

In the simple case in which only two individuals are involved, the social welfare indifference surfaces W_0, W_1, and W_2 will appear as straight lines, as in Figure 8.1A. Along any social indifference surface, society appears to be indifferent between any distributions of the level of aggregate income. Thus, in the example given earlier, the sum of individual 1's gain of 200 dollars and individual 2's loss of 100 dollars will represent a net increase in social welfare.

Case 2. The foregoing result contrasts with the case depicted in Figure 8.1B, where it is the minimum level of money-metric utility enjoyed by any individual that determines the level of social welfare. Thus, the level of utility $0A$ enjoyed by individual 2 determines that society is located on the indifference surface W_1. That level remains unchanged whether individual 1 enjoys the same level of money-metric utility as individual 2 (i.e., $0B$), or whether individual 1's level is greater (e.g., $0C$). If the starting point for both individuals is the same, then the redistribution that was used in the preceding case will generate a decline in social welfare if the function is of the type described.

Let us now put the social welfare function to work. The individual money-metric functions are based on the assumption that each individual is maximizing his satisfaction, given prices and income level. The objective of using a social welfare function W is to determine the distribution of nominal income that will maximize that function. To facilitate this, let us form the Lagrangian expression

$$\mathcal{L} = W(M_1, \ldots, M_n) + \theta\left(Y - \sum_{}^{n} Y_i\right) \tag{8.5}$$

which on maximization with respect to each Y_i yields the following first-order conditions:

$$\frac{\partial \mathcal{L}}{\partial Y_i} = \frac{\partial W}{\partial M_i} \frac{\partial M_i}{\partial Y_i} - \theta = 0 \quad (i = 1, \ldots, n) \tag{8.6}$$

subject to

$$Y - \sum_{}^{n} Y_i = 0 \tag{8.7}$$

Because aggregate income Y is given, (8.6) and (8.7) represent $n + 1$ equations in $n + 1$ unknowns, the individual income levels Y_i and θ.

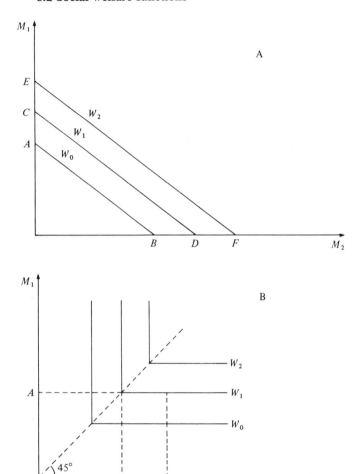

Figure 8.1

Hence, in principle, we can solve this system to obtain n income distribution functions explaining each individual income level in terms of aggregate income and prices,

$$Y_i = f_i(Y, p) \quad (i = 1, \dots, n) \tag{8.8}$$

The basic rule involved in this exercise, as can be seen from (8.6), is that the marginal social welfare that derives from an individual's income should be identical for all individuals. This is a well-known result, but its underpinnings are frequently misinterpreted. The problem arises from the need to distinguish again between the social values implicit in a particular welfare function and the properties of the individual consumer preference function. This distinction has already been mentioned in this section. However, we can now clarify the issue further by noting that the marginal social utility of money income consists of two parts. The first, $\partial M_i/\partial Y_i$, is the marginal utility of income that characterizes individual i's situation. The second part, $\partial W/\partial M_i$, indicates the weight to be given to $\partial M_i/\partial Y_i$ when computing the marginal contribution of an additional unit of money to social welfare. Unless all such weights are identical, it will be the case that the marginal utility of money for each individual will be different at the point where W is maximized. It should be emphasized that, in general, the "weighting" term $\partial W/\partial M_i$ will be a function of both prices and the individual income levels.

8.3   Frisch's approach

Now let us contrast the preceding analysis with statements frequently made by many economists. It is often argued that income should be equalized between consumers on the grounds that the marginal utility of money declines as income increases. This supposedly objective notion has found strong support among the followers of Ragnar Frisch. If we call ω the income elasticity of the marginal utility of money, then Frisch (1959, p. 189) believed that this variable would exhibit the following range of values:

We may, perhaps, assume that in most cases the money flexibility has values of the order of magnitude given below:

$\omega = -10$ for an extremely poor and apathetic part of the population

$\omega = -4$ for the slightly better off but still poor part of the population with a fairly pronounced desire to become better off

$\omega = -2$ for the middle income bracket, "the median part" of the population

$\omega = -0.7$ for the better-off part of the population

$\omega = -0.1$ for the rich part of the population with ambitions towards "conspicuous consumption."

It would be a very promising research project to determine ω for different countries and for different types of populations; a universal "atlas" of the values of ω should be constructed. It would serve an extremely useful purpose in demand analysis.

Provided that prices are always equal to their base values, it must be the case that $\partial M_i / \partial Y_i$ will remain unchanged. In order that the equalities implied by (8.6) can hold, it will have to be the "weights" $\partial W / \partial M_i$ that vary. Thus, if the welfare function consists of only two arguments M_1 and M_2 and it is the case that $\partial W / \partial M_1 > \partial W / \partial M_2$, then income will need to be redistributed. The question is: In which direction? The answer depends on the properties of the social welfare function and in particular on assumption 5 noted earlier. As income is redistributed from individual 2 to individual 1, the ratio $(\partial W / \partial M_1)/(\partial W / \partial M_2)$ will fall until the required first-order conditions are achieved. Thus, as income is redistributed, the "weights" themselves are altered. This situation stands in marked contrast to that generated by the social welfare function implied by Harberger's rule. In that instance, $\partial W / \partial M_i$ is constant at a value equal to one, and hence the marginal rate of substitution between M_1 and M_2 also equals one. The implication is that any distribution of income is equally acceptable.

For the purposes of constructing social welfare functions, this formulation suggests the following sort of analysis. Suppose that we adopt an additive, utilitarian approach and we are considering a redistribution of income away from individual 1 toward individual 2 on the basis of the fact that

$$\frac{\partial U_1}{\partial Y_1} < \frac{\partial U_2}{\partial Y} \tag{8.9}$$

There are two fundamental difficulties with this plan, however. First, as we have taken great pains to emphasize in this chapter, the marginal utility of money is not invariant, given increasing, monotonic transformations of the consumer preference function; indeed, it can increase or decrease as income increases without having any effect on the pattern of consumer demand. Second, the foregoing approach does not make explicit the real social welfare function involved. It may be true that it is additive. But it is also true that most of the work is being done by the supposed objective property of diminishing marginal utility of money. By simply taking an increasing, monotonic transformation of the consumer preference functions, we could have reversed the preceding result and had income being redistributed from individual 1 to individual 2. In essence, the choice of transformation involves a value judgment.

Since this is the case, why not make the values explicit? This is exactly what the procedure proposed in the preceding section achieves. By using the money-metric, we are able to make relevant interpersonal comparisons. If the social welfare function puts great weight on equality of income, then the necessary redistribution can be undertaken according to the philosophical values made explicit by that function. It is an entirely erroneous matter that the argument for income equality derives from an alleged objective property of consumer preferences, the diminishing marginal utility of money.

8.4   The aggregate money-metric indicator

We now come to a crucial question insofar as this chapter is concerned: Is it possible to express the social welfare function as a money-metric? We have already noted Harberger's suggestion that monetary gains and losses should simply be added up, irrespective of to whom they accrue. But this effectively neglects the income distribution problem. We require a more general social welfare function that not only enables trade-offs to be made more explicit, in the manner discussed previously, but also possesses a monetary interpretation. To achieve this objective, we define the *optimally distributed base-price equivalent aggregate income*. This is the aggregate amount of money that when optimally distributed on the basis of the initial or reference price vector yields the same level of social welfare as that generated by some alternative price vector and distribution of income. This definition can be restated more formally as follows. Let us suppose that we are given some vector of commodity prices p' and the level of income Y_i' obtained by every individual. Then, on the basis of some social welfare function, we can undertake the following calculation:

$$W = W\{M_1[\nu_1(Y_1',p'); p^0], \ldots, M_n[\nu_n(Y_n',p'); p^0]\} \qquad (8.10)$$

where aggregate income Y' equals $\Sigma Y_i'$.

Now consider an alternative level of aggregate income Y^* that is optimally distributed, given some alternative vector of prices $\hat{p}$, so as to achieve the same level of social welfare as indicated by (8.10). In this instance, individual income levels are given by equation (8.8), namely,

$$Y_i^* = f_i(Y^*, \hat{p}) \qquad (8.11)$$

Thus, we obtain

$$W = W\Big(M_1\{\nu_1[f_1(Y^*, \hat{p}); p^0]\}, \ldots, M_n\{\nu_n[f_n(Y^*, \hat{p}); p^0]\}\Big)$$

$$= W[\eta(Y^*, \hat{p}); p^0] \qquad (8.12)$$

where η is a function of (a) the weighting factors that define the particular social welfare function and (b) the individual money-metric functions.

We are now in a position to identify the aggregate cost-of-social-welfare, money-metric, and compensation functions, all of which have interpretations analogous to those relationships associated with individual preference orderings. If we invert (8.12) to solve for Y^*, we obtain, in the first instance, a cost-of-social-welfare function:

$$C_{sw} = C_{sw}(W; \hat{p})$$
(8.13)

which indicates the aggregate optimally distributed cost of achieving the level of social welfare W given some price vector $\hat{p}$. If that vector contains the base or reference prices p^0, then we obtain an aggregate, optimally distributed money-metric function:

$$M_{sw} = C_{sw}\{W[\eta(Y', p'), p^0]; p^0\}$$
$$= C_{sw}(W; p^0)$$
(8.14)

This measure indicates *the optimally distributed base-price equivalent aggregate income.*

It is now easily seen that M_{sw} is an increasing, monotonic transformation of W. All we need to do is to establish that the derivative $\partial W / \partial Y$ is positive. Thus, from (8.6),

$$\frac{\partial W}{\partial Y} = \sum \frac{\partial W}{\partial M_i} \frac{\partial M_i}{\partial Y} \frac{\partial Y_i}{\partial Y}$$

$$= \theta \sum \frac{\partial Y_i}{\partial Y} = \theta > 0$$
(8.15)

Hence, the aggregate, optimally distributed money-metric is a social welfare indicator in its own right. Further, we can construct a socially optimal equivalent variation

$$EV_{sw} = M_{sw} - Y^0 = C_{sw}\{W[\eta(Y', p'), p^0]; p^0\} - Y^0$$
(8.16)

This indicates the change in the optimally distributed aggregate income required to generate the same variation in social welfare as some alternative vector of prices and total expenditure. It should be emphasized again that because the individual preferences that compose the social welfare function are expressed in money-metric terms, both M_{sw} and EV_{sw} are invariant when consumer preferences are subjected to increasing, monotonic transformations.

On the basis of the cost-of-social-welfare function (8.13), it is also possible to formulate an aggregate optimally distributed compensation function:

$$H_{sw} = C_{sw}(W^0; p)$$
(8.17)

which indicates the level of optimally distributed aggregate income required to generate the level of social welfare W^0 given any vector of prices p. The aggregate socially optimal compensating variation can then be calculated as

$$\text{CV}_{sw} = H_{sw} - Y^0 \tag{8.18}$$

However, the function H_{sw} or CV_{sw} is not an ordinal welfare metric. The reasoning behind this conclusion parallels that for the individual's compensation function and hence will not be repeated (see Section 2.9).

The difference between the optimally distributed base-price equivalent aggregate income M_{sw} and the optimally distributed compensation is illustrated in Figures 8.2A and 8.2B. We shall assume that the economy consists of two individuals, labeled 1 and 2. Aggregate income $0A$ can be distributed in any proportion along the line AB. The optimal distribution would occur at R, because this would generate the maximum feasible level of social welfare W_1. However, the actual distribution of income is at Z. It is easy to see from Figure 8.2A that this is equivalent to an optimally distributed aggregate income M_{sw} equal to $0C$. Hence, the suboptimal distribution is equivalent to a loss equal to AC. Now contrast this measure with that shown in Figure 8.2B. If we choose the actual distribution, as opposed to the optimal distribution, as the reference point, then we will ask this question: What level of aggregate income, given the actual distribution, is required to generate the same level of social welfare as the optimal distribution W_1. This measure H_{sw} is equal to the distance $0E$, since the distribution at Q generates W_1. In other words, compensation equal to AE would have to be paid to cancel out the effects of the suboptimal income distribution. In general, the distances AC and AE will never equal each other. However, in the case in which the social welfare function is homothetic, then the ratios $0A/0C$ and $0E/0A$ will be identical.

8.5   An example

For simplicity, let us suppose that our economy consists of only two individuals (or homogeneous groups), each possessing preferences of the Klein-Rubin form, but with different parameter values, namely,

$$p_i X_{ij} = b_{ij} Y_j + c_{ij} - b_{ij} \sum_k c_{kj} p_k \quad (i = 1, \ldots, n; j = 1, 2) \tag{8.19}$$

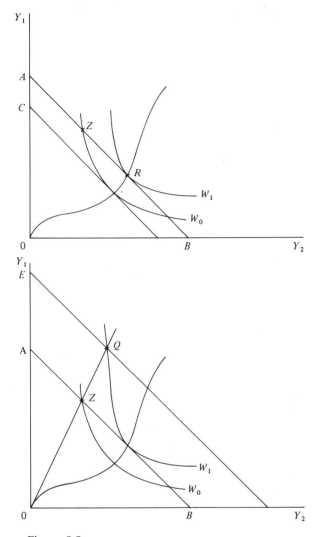

Figure 8.2

where X_{ij} is the amount of the ith commodity consumed by the jth individual and b_{ij} and c_{ij} are the parameters associated with the jth individual's demand functions. Thus, from (2.48), the money-metric function will be

$$M_j = \left(Y_j - \sum c_{kj} p_k\right) \prod_i \left(\frac{p_i^0}{p_i}\right)^{b_{ij}} + \sum c_{kj} p_k^0 \qquad (8.20)$$

Suppose also that an appropriate social welfare function can be written as

$$W = (a_1 M_1^\sigma + a_2 M_2^\sigma)^{1/\sigma} \tag{8.21}$$

where $a_1 + a_2 = 1$. The following calculations are necessary before we can proceed:

$$\frac{\partial W}{\partial M_i} = (a_1 M_1^\sigma + a_2 M_2^\sigma)^{(1-\sigma)/\sigma} a_i M_i^{\sigma-1} \tag{8.22}$$

and

$$\frac{\partial M_i}{\partial Y_i} = \prod_k \left(\frac{p_k^0}{p_k}\right)^{b_{ki}} \tag{8.23}$$

From (8.6) we determine that social welfare maximization requires that

$$\frac{\partial W}{\partial M_i}\frac{\partial M_i}{\partial Y_i} = [(a_1 M_1^\sigma + a_2 M_2^\sigma)^{(1-\sigma)/\sigma} a_i M_i] \prod_k \left(\frac{p_k^0}{p_i}\right)^{b_{ki}} \quad (i = 1,2) \tag{8.24}$$

must be identical for all individuals in the society. For the two-person society of our example, (8.24) implies

$$\frac{M_1}{M_2} = \left[\frac{a_2}{a_1} \prod_k \left(\frac{p_k^0}{p_k}\right)^{b_{k2}-b_{k1}}\right]^{1/(\sigma-1)} = Z(p) \tag{8.25}$$

In the context of this example, it is crucial whether or not the propensities to consume, b_{ki}, each of the k commodities are identical for the two individuals. If they are not, then the optimal distribution of income will change as prices vary. However, for the moment, we shall be concerned with calculation of the optimally distributed base-price equivalent aggregate income. In this situation, (8.25) becomes independent of commodity prices, namely,

$$\frac{M_1^*}{M_2^*} = \left[\frac{a_2}{a_1}\right]^{1/(\sigma-1)} \tag{8.26}$$

Because $M_1^* + M_2^* = Y^*$, we can solve for M_1^* and M_2^* as follows:

$$M_1^* = \frac{(a_2/a_1)^{1/(\sigma-1)}}{1 + (a_2/a_1)^{1/(\sigma-1)}} Y^* \tag{8.27}$$

$$M_2^* = \frac{Y^*}{1 + (a_2/a_1)^{1/(\sigma-1)}} \tag{8.28}$$

Equations (8.27) and (8.28) can then be substituted back into the social welfare function (8.21) to obtain

$$
W = Y^* \left[a_1 \left(\frac{(a_2/a_1)^{1/(\sigma-1)}}{1 + (a_2/a_1)^{1/(\sigma-1)}} \right)^\sigma + a_2 \left(\frac{1}{1 + (a_2/a_1)^{1/(\sigma-1)}} \right)^\sigma \right]^{1/\sigma}
$$

$$
= \frac{Y^*}{1 + (a_2/a_1)^{1/(\sigma-1)}} \left[a_1 \left(\frac{a_2}{a_1} \right)^{\sigma/(\sigma-1)} + a_2 \right]^{1/\sigma} \tag{8.29}
$$

If the actual individual money-metrics generated by the price vector p' and total incomes Y_1' and Y_2' are indicated by M_1' and M_2', then

$$
W = [a_1(M_1')^\sigma + a_2(M_2')^\sigma]^{1/\sigma} \tag{8.30}
$$

By combining (8.29) and (8.30), we can solve for the value of Y^* associated with any distribution of M_2' and M_2', namely,

$$
Y^* = \frac{[1 + (a_2/a_1)^{1/(\sigma-1)}][a_1(M_1')^\sigma + a_2(M_2')^\sigma]^{1/\sigma}}{[a_1(a_2/a_1)^{\sigma/(\sigma-1)} + a_2]^{1/\sigma}} \tag{8.31}
$$

This formula for the optimally distributed aggregate level of income can easily be generalized to encompass a larger population of individuals.

The social welfare function (8.21) is fairly simple. Yet, as we shall see, it is one that is frequently used in both applied and theoretical work. Hence, it is of some interest to examine its properties. Here we shall examine the factors that determine the distribution of Y^*.

In general, the elasticity of substitution along the surface of the social welfare function is defined as

$$
\rho = \frac{\partial \ln(M_1/M_2)}{\partial \ln[(\partial W/\partial M_1)/(\partial W/\partial M_2)]} \tag{8.32}
$$

which, in the case of (8.21), equals

$$
\frac{1}{\sigma - 1} < 0 \tag{8.33}
$$

The sign condition on ρ follows directly from assumption 5 stated in Section 8.2. Thus, σ can take on values in the range of one to minus infinity.

If we return to the distribution equation (8.24), we see that the value of ρ (i.e., σ) and the parameters a_1 and a_2 are crucial in the determination of the proportion of aggregate income Y^* accruing to each individual. Thus, given any value of ρ, which must be negative, we see that the proportion M_1^*/M_2^* will be greater the larger the parameter a_1

is relative to a_2, and conversely. The distribution of income will also depend on the value that the elasticity of substitution takes on. If the ratio a_1/a_2 is less than one, then the larger in absolute value is ρ, the greater will be the proportion of aggregate income received by individual 2. If a_1 and a_2 are equal, then the optimal distribution of aggregate income will also be equal. And if a_1 is greater than a_2, then the larger is ρ in absolute value, the greater will be the proportion of Y^* received by individual 1. It should also be noted that the closer is ρ to zero, the closer will incomes approach equality.

8.6   The social welfare loss function

The discussion in the preceding two sections suggests that we should be able to construct an index that indicates the degree to which any suboptimal distribution of income deviates from the optimal. First, as before, we calculate the optimally distributed base-price equivalent aggregate income

$$M_{sw} = C_{sw}(W\{M_1[\nu_1(Y_1',p');p^0],\dots,M_n[\nu_n(Y_n',p');p^0]\};p^0)$$

(8.34)

associated with the individual money-metric functions M_i, generated by the suboptimal income levels Y_i'. Then we calculate the levels of Y_i^* that will maximize the social welfare function W on the assumption that aggregate income Y' and the vector of commodity prices p' remain unchanged. In general, this latter condition will hold only if we are considering a small open economy. In other circumstances, any redistribution can generate a new set of prices, and these will need to be taken into account. However, because no points of principle are involved at this stage, we shall maintain the assumption that commodity prices remain constant.

Having calculated the optimal distribution of income, we now calculate the optimally distributed base-price equivalent aggregate income associated with this new situation:

$$M_{sw}^* = C_{sw}(W\{M_1[\nu_1(Y_1^*,p');p^0],\dots,M_n[\nu_n(Y_n^*,p');p^0]\};p^0)$$

(8.35)

Then we can define the index

$$I_L = 1 - \frac{M_{sw}}{M_{sw}^*}$$

(8.36)

as representing the degree to which society deviates from the optimum as reflected in the social welfare function W. Because $M_{sw} \leq M^*_{sw}$ by definition, the index will lie between zero and one. The zero value indicates that the actual and optimum distributions of income coincide. An important property of (8.36) is that it can be used to indicate how any deviation from the social optimum is widening or narrowing over time. The foregoing exercise can simply be repeated for any alternative price vector and distribution of income. First, the individual money-metrics are calculated, and then these values are used to calculate the new optimally distributed base-price equivalent income. Then this "aggregate" equivalent income is calculated for the optimal distribution at current prices. Finally, (8.36) is recomputed. If the index is tending more toward zero, then society is moving closer to the optimum, as defined by W. If it is moving toward one, the situation is deteriorating.

A special case of the index (8.34) has been proposed as an index of inequality by Atkinson (1970) and Sen (1973). The basis of this index is the concept of an *equally distributed equivalent level of income:* "the level of income per head which if equally distributed would give the same level of social welfare as the present distribution" (Atkinson, 1970, p. 250). In this formulation, all individual satisfaction levels are treated symmetrically. Hence, the optimum or norm against which the actual income distribution is compared is one of income equality. To illustrate this, we make use of the social welfare function discussed by Atkinson:

$$W = \left(\sum \frac{1}{n} Y_i^\sigma\right)^{1/\sigma} \tag{8.37}$$

which is seen to be a special case of (8.21). That is, all the weighting parameters a_i equal $1/n$, where n is the population size. Then there exists an equally distributed equivalent level of per capita income $\hat{Y}$ that generates W as well:

$$W = \left(\frac{1}{n}\sum \hat{Y}^\sigma\right)^{1/\sigma} = \hat{Y} \tag{8.38}$$

Thus, $\hat{Y}$ is a welfare indicator that can be set equal to (8.37). The Atkinson-Sen index of inequality is then defined as

$$I_{AS} = 1 - \frac{\hat{Y}}{\bar{Y}} = 1 - \frac{[(1/n)\sum^n Y_i^\sigma]^{1/\sigma}}{\bar{Y}} \tag{8.39}$$

$$= 1 - \left[\frac{1}{n}\sum^n_i \left(\frac{Y_i}{\bar{Y}}\right)^\sigma\right]^{1/\sigma} \tag{8.40}$$

where $\overline{Y}$ is the average level of individual income, $(1/n)\sum Y_i$. As we have noted before, the parameter σ falls in the range $-\infty \leqslant \sigma \leqslant 1$. Thus, the smaller is σ for any actual distribution of income, the more weight will be given to those incomes that are less than the average, and consequently $\hat{Y}$ will become smaller and smaller. Thus, the Atkinson index tends to one the smaller is σ. In the case in which σ equals one, the index equals zero. In this case, the social welfare function is of the Harberger type, and any income distribution appears to be equally acceptable.

It is now easy to determine how the Atkinson-Sen index relates to the more general formula (8.36). If the income distribution is optimally distributed according to (8.38), then everyone will receive the same (or average) level of income. Hence, M_{sw}^* equals $n\overline{Y}$. The optimally distributed base-price equivalent aggregate income M_{sw} associated with any suboptimal situation is $n\hat{Y}$. Hence, the index (8.34) becomes

$$I = 1 - \frac{n\hat{Y}}{n\overline{Y}} = 1 - \frac{\hat{Y}}{\overline{Y}}$$

which is exactly identical with the Atkinson-Sen inequality indicator.

By comparison, the social welfare loss (SWL) index (8.36) is considerably more general than (8.39). First, the SWL index does not depend on the optimal situation being one one of complete income equality. This is only one of an infinity of conceivable social optima that might be compared with any given actual distribution of income. As we have taken pains to emphasize, the concept of a socially optimal distribution of income depends on the particular set of political values that manifest themselves in the guise of the parameters of the social welfare function. This is not to deny that the exercise undertaken by Atkinson is useful. Income equality has been a social objective advocated by many persons for centuries. Thus, it is important to determine, in some objective fashion, the degree to which society deviates from this norm. However, it is also important to examine other norms as well in order to determine whether the existing distribution of income is consistent or inconsistent with these. Such comparisons are possible with the SWL function.

A second deficiency of the Atkinson index is that it does not allow intertemporal comparisons. If relative commodity prices change over time, the level of nominal income is no longer a meaningful index of the level of individual satisfaction. However, this situation is easily remedied by substitution of the money-metric indicators M_i in place of the individual income levels Y_i. Thus, if we use the Atkinson-Sen social welfare function,

$$W = \left(\frac{1}{n}\sum M_i^\sigma\right)^{1/\sigma}$$

$$= \left(\frac{1}{n}\sum \hat{M}^\sigma\right)^{1/\sigma} = \hat{M} = \hat{Y} \tag{8.41}$$

The interpretation of this is as follows: Given base prices, the cost of any individual utility level will be indicated by the M_i. This generates a level of social welfare W that is equivalent to that generated by the equally distributed income level $\hat{Y}$ at given base prices. If we know the money-metric indicators for all individuals, it is a simple matter to calculate $\hat{Y}$ from (8.41) and then to form the index

$$I_M = 1 - \frac{\hat{Y}}{(1/n)\sum M_i} \tag{8.42}$$

It must be emphasized that unless prices remain at their base levels, $\sum M_i$ will not equal $\sum Y_i$. The index described by (8.42) will thus enable a meaningful time series to be computed. If all incomes increase proportionally, the index will remain unchanged. However, if individual incomes vary in different proportions and relative price changes have different impacts on the individuals affected, then the index will, of course, vary according to whether the distribution of satisfaction as measured by the individual money-metric functions are more or less equally distributed.

Predating the work of both Atkinson and Sen, Champernowne suggested in 1952 that it would be useful to calculate "the proportion of total income that is absorbed in compensating for the loss of aggregate income due to inequality." This provides the basis for the following approach. If we use the social welfare function (8.38), then the average level of income $\overline{Y}$, equally distributed, will be the level that maximizes social welfare, given aggregate income. However, the actual level of social welfare is that generated by

$$W = \left(\frac{1}{n}\sum Y_i^\sigma\right)^{1/\sigma} \tag{8.43}$$

To compensate for the loss of welfare due to this suboptimal distribution, let us suppose that all individual incomes are increased by a proportion ϕ such that the level of satisfaction is that generated by the equally distributed $\overline{Y}$. Thus, an index of inequality

$$I_c = 1 - \frac{\phi\overline{Y}}{\overline{Y}} = 1 - \phi \tag{8.44}$$

can be constructed. Equation (8.44) is clearly based on the compensation function (8.17) As we have already noted, if the social welfare function is homothetic, as (8.38) is, then it will be the case that the Atkinson and Champernowne indices will be equal. This is in spite of the fact their logical underpinnings are different.

8.7   Calculation of the aggregate money-metric from observable data

We have now established that it is possible to construct a social welfare function that possesses a meaningful money-metric interpretation in the aggregate. However, this analysis has been based on the assumption that it is possible to calculate the individual money-metrics that form the basis of the optimally distributed base-price equivalent aggregate income. From a practical point of view, however, there will be many circumstances in which sufficient data on individual preferences simply do not exist. For example, in the construction of price and quantity indices, such as those discussed in the preceding chapter, it is likely that only price and aggregate expenditure data will be available. The question then arises: Is it possible to calculate the optimally distributed base-price equivalent aggregate income? The answer is affirmative provided that we are prepared to assume that society acts according to some social welfare function that is invariant over time. This is obviously a very strong and questionable assumption. Yet it is one that is implicit in the actual calculation of index numbers. Hence, it is important to examine the logical underpinnings of this procedure.

In Chapter 3 we showed that the money-metric for an individual can be written in terms of the parameters of the demand functions characterizing that individual's behavior. We shall now examine whether or not it is possible to express the *aggregate money-metric* in terms of the parameters of *aggregate demand functions*. In particular, it will be important to determine whether or not Roy's identity is applicable to this problem.

Explicit in this formulation of the aggregate money-metric is the assumption that society always acts in such a way as to optimally redistribute income following the introduction of any project or policy.

That is, individual income is determined by equation (8.8), and therefore the individual preference function can be rewritten as

$$v_i = v_i[f_i(Y, p), p] \tag{8.45}$$

where, as before, f_i indicates the optimally distributed income level for individual i, given aggregate income Y and prices. This fact must now be taken into account when formulating the individual demand functions. Consider the demand by individual i for commodity k. First, we calculate that

$$\frac{\partial v_i}{\partial p_k} = \frac{\partial v_i}{\partial Y_i}\left(\frac{\partial f_i}{\partial p_k} - X_{ik}\right) \tag{8.46}$$

where X_{ik} represents the demand by i for commodity k. Next,

$$\frac{\partial v_i}{\partial Y} = \sum_j \frac{\partial U_i}{\partial X_{ij}} \frac{\partial X_{ij}}{\partial Y_i} \frac{\partial f_i}{\partial Y}$$

$$= \lambda_i \sum_j p_j \frac{\partial X_{ij}}{\partial Y_i} \frac{\partial f_i}{\partial Y}$$

$$= \lambda_i \frac{\partial f_i}{\partial Y} \tag{8.47}$$

where λ_i is i's marginal utility of money. By taking the ratio of (8.46) and (8.47) and rearranging terms, we obtain

$$X_{ik} = \frac{\partial f_i}{\partial p_k} - \frac{\partial f_i}{\partial Y}\frac{\partial E_i/\partial p_k}{\partial U_i/\partial Y} \tag{8.48}$$

Now let us sum this expression across all individuals, as follows:

$$X_k = \sum_i X_{iu} = \sum \frac{\partial f_i}{\partial p_k} - \sum \frac{\partial f_i}{\partial Y}\frac{\partial E_i/\partial p_k}{\partial E_i/\partial Y}$$

$$= -\sum \frac{\partial f_i}{\partial Y}\frac{\partial E_i/\partial p_k}{\partial E_i/\partial Y}$$

$$= -\sum \frac{\partial E_i/\partial p_k}{\partial E_i/\partial Y_i} \tag{8.49}$$

since $\sum \partial f_i/\partial p_k$ equals zero, from (8.12), and $\partial U_i/\partial Y = \partial U_i/\partial f_i \cdot \partial f_i/\partial Y$. It can now be easily determined that (8.49) can be rewritten in the form of an aggregate version of Roy's identity:

$$X_k = -\frac{\partial W/\partial p_k}{\partial W/\partial Y} \tag{8.50}$$

The denominator of (8.50) equals

$$\frac{\partial W}{\partial p_k} = \sum \frac{\partial W}{\partial E_i}\left(\frac{\partial E_i}{\partial f_i}\frac{\partial f_i}{\partial p_k} + \frac{\partial E_i}{\partial p_k}\right)$$

$$= \sum \frac{\partial W}{\partial E_i}\frac{\partial E_i}{\partial f_i}\frac{\partial f_i}{\partial p_k} + \frac{\partial E_i/\partial p_k}{\partial E_i/\partial F_i}$$

$$= \theta \sum \frac{\partial f_i}{\partial p_k} + \frac{\partial E_i/\partial p_k}{\partial E_i/\partial f_i}$$

$$= \theta \sum \frac{\partial E_i/\partial p_k}{\partial E_i/\partial f_i} \qquad (8.51)$$

It is easily seen that the numerator of (8.50) is

$$\frac{\partial W}{\partial Y} = \sum \frac{\partial W}{\partial E_i}\frac{\partial E_i}{\partial f_i}\frac{\partial f_i}{\partial Y}$$

$$= \theta \sum \frac{\partial f_i}{\partial Y}$$

$$= \theta \qquad (8.52)$$

Hence, (8.49) and (8.50) are identical. This means that we can retrieve the aggregate money-metric or optimally distributed base-price equivalent aggregate income directly from the parameters of the aggregate demand functions.

It should be emphasized that such an aggregate indicator must be interpreted on a strictly conditional basis. This procedure assumes that society does act as if a social welfare function existed. However, it says nothing about its form or, indeed, about the value implicit in the function.

8.8   The compensation principle

The previous sections of this chapter have really involved no more than placing fine trimmings on a cake that someone else has baked. The social welfare foundation of the discussion has been explicitly based on the work of Samuelson (1956), whereas that concerning inequality indicators has been derived most directly from the analysis of Atkinson and Sen. The only difference has been that the social welfare function approach has been recast in terms of the money-metric. However, the approach that most cost−benefit analysts have adopted is considerably different. Indeed, it is often claimed that one of the two foundation stones of cost−benefit theory is the *compensation principle* (the other is consumer surplus).

Unfortunately, there are two versions of this principle that are widely used in the literature. However, as we shall see, they are equally defective.

Version 1. If those who gain following the introduction of a project or policy can compensate the losers, then there is a gain in economic welfare, and conversely.

Version 2. If those who gain following the introduction of a project or policy can compensate the losers, then there is a gain in efficiency, and conversely.

The fact that the principle is open to two such divergent philosophical and economic interpretations is characteristic of the ambiguity that continues to cloud its use. Nevertheless, in order that the case for the money-metric can be considered to be complete, it is necessary that we submit the compensation principle to a full examination.

The objections to the use of the compensation principle as a welfare indicator follow immediately from two fundamental points discussed previously. First, the principle effectively involves adding up compensating variations across individuals. However, the compensating variation is not a welfare indicator in its own right. Hence, it is illogical to expect that the aggregate version could be used to measure social welfare. Second, even if the compensating variation were capable of ordering social states for individuals (as when preferences are homothetic), the utilitarian social welfare function involved in the calculation would imply a particular set of ethical judgments that might not be widely acceptable. A superior approach is to make explicit a social welfare function in the manner proposed in this chapter. In this way the ethical judgments involved can be made explicit through the distribution and substitution parameters.

The compensation principle has in the past been subject to one major criticism. In 1941, Scitovsky pointed out that the principle is subject to embarrassing inconsistency. Suppose that following a move from one price/quantity situation to another it is determined that the sum of all individual compensating variations is positive. That is, the gainers can more than compensate the losers. However, once having moved to the new situation, it is possible to calculate that a move to the old situation would also generate a positive sum for the compensating variations. An example generating this result is depicted in Figure 8.3. Let us first contemplate a move from situation 1 to situation 2, where both are located on the contract curve. The levels of satisfaction enjoyed by the two individuals change from U_1^1 and U_2^1 to U_1^2 and U_2^2, respectively. It is easily seen that the level of compensation that individual 1 will be willing to pay is greater than the amount of money individual 2 will need to receive in order to achieve his original level

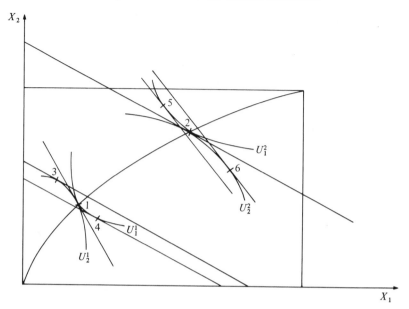

Figure 8.3

of satisfaction. According to the compensation principle, there has been a gain. Now let us reverse the calculation by starting at situation 2. Here we find that the amount that individual 2 will be willing to pay is greater than the amount individual 1 will require in compensation. We have the paradoxical result that the original situation is now to be preferred. Why is this so? Steeped in the analysis of the previous chapters, it might be tempting to conclude that this result arises simply because the compensating variation is not an ordinal welfare metric. However, this line of reasoning is not particularly helpful. Indeed, we would find that use of a proper ordinal money-metric, the equivalent variation, would produce a similar paradoxical result. This result can easily be seen by recalling that the compensating variation associated with the move from 2 to 1 is also the equivalent variation associated with the move from 1 to 2, and conversely. Does this imply that the equivalent variation is equally defective, despite all the work contained in previous chapters? Fortunately, the answer to this question is no.

This conclusion follows in part from our discussion of index numbers in Chapter 7. Let us construct a utilitarian social welfare function based on the individual equivalent variations. To require that the gains from moving from 1 to 2 should equal the losses associated with moving from 2 to 1 requires that the utilitarian social welfare function satisfy the circularity test discussed in Chapter 7. However, because we are simply adding up individual utility indicators, it must therefore be the case that each and every individual measure satisfies the circularity test. However, as we determined, this will be true if and only if all individual preferences are homothetic.

Just as we argued that there was no particular reason why we should want all individual preference functions to satisfy this rigid requirement, so there is no reason why we should want the social welfare function to do so. When we construct a social welfare function, we explicitly choose a particular cardinal representation for individual preferences. It could be the money-metric, the equivalent variation, or some other transformation. In the case of the first two measures, the cardinalizations clearly depend on the initial levels of prices and income. These are then aggregated according to some explicit weighting scheme. All alternative social states can then be ordered. This is all that is required.

If we now choose to construct the social welfare function starting from an additional set of initial conditions, we are choosing a different cardinal representation of individual utilities, and hence we are really constructing a different social welfare function. To require that the same result be generated by all cardinalizations is simply too restrictive. It is oversufficient and not necessary for the social evaluation of alternative price/quantity situations.

8.9   Summary

In previous chapters we have been concerned with the technical and theoretical issues involved in the construction of an operational welfare measure that can be used to characterize the preferences of an individual or a homogeneous group of consumers. In this chapter we have taken a further step forward by showing how the money-metric can be formulated in the aggregate, provided that the values implied by the social welfare function used as the aggregator are made explicit. Further, we have shown that the money-metric formulation makes possible (a) an important extension of the Atkinson-Sen inequality index and (b) an alternative to the compensation principle that has dominated cost-benefit analysis.

CHAPTER 9

Measurement of the social costs of monopoly

9.1 Introduction

In preceding chapters we have examined in detail a measure that, in principle, is superior to the various other indicators that form the basis of conventional applied welfare analysis. For the theorist, that examination should be sufficient. However, those concerned with actual use of operational procedures are bound to raise additional questions. Are the numerical procedures being proposed of sufficiently greater accuracy to warrant the scrapping of the traditional tools of analysis? Are the new procedures more complex? If so, does their greater accuracy outweigh their additional complexity and warrant abandonment of the somewhat less accurate measures currently in use?

In regard to the first question, it is impossible to establish any meaningful general criteria to determine whether or not the errors of approximation inherent in traditional approaches are likely to be small for the new procedures. Such errors inevitably depend on a variety of factors: (a) the initial price/quantity situation, (b) the magnitude of the variable change being evaluated, and (c) the characteristics of the approximation procedure being used. Thus, depending on the situation, it is likely that one particular method will work well in some circumstances but not in others and that performance will vary from situation to situation. This proposition must also inevitably hold for the approximation procedures based on the money-metric discussed in Chapter 3. There it was suggested that accurate measures can be constructed from information about the derivatives of the demand function up to the third order. Consideration of fourth-order derivatives would have permitted even greater accuracy. Nevertheless, extensive simulations have indicated that the proposed methods are consistently more precise than those alternatives that many economists have preferred in the past. The theoretical reasons for this are not surprising, and they clearly reveal that the proposed measure will be superior to all other methods in all circumstances of interest in the applied economics. The basic argument bears repeating. Orthodox applied welfare measures are not path-independent. The implication of this characteristic has been one of the major underlying themes of this volume. In contrast, the procedures proposed here permit the integrating factor to be incorporated into the calculation procedure in a very precise manner. Consequently, a path-independent approximation to the money-metric is achieved.

Despite this statement of principle, it is useful to examine the performances of the various alternative applied welfare measures in a particular context, although this does not, in principle, enable us to draw any general conclusions. However, such analysis does provide us with examples to counter those who would argue that consumer surplus procedures are "likely" to be highly accurate for most practical problems. As a basis for these comparisons, we have chosen the problem of measuring the social costs of monopoly. There are three reasons for concentrating on this particular area: (a) There is already a substantial body of literature on this topic, and new contributions are continually being made. (b) The measure most frequently used to calculate the welfare loss due to monopoly is consumer surplus. (c) Previous research in this area has provided good illustrations of the numerous difficulties that arise in applied welfare economics.

9.2   The traditional approach to measurement of the social costs of monopoly

The basis of modern-day attempts to measure the cost of monopoly power resides in the theory of imperfect competition as developed in the 1930s. In particular, Lerner's (1934) index of monopoly power is relevant. This is defined as the percentage divergence between price and marginal cost:

$$Z = \frac{p - mc}{p} \tag{9.1}$$

where Z is the index, p is the price chosen by the monopolist, and mc is marginal cost. Let us consider the problem as depicted in Figure 9.1. Suppose that all firms in an industry possess identical marginal and average cost schedules and that costs are constant irrespective of the level of output. Within this partial equilibrium *ceteris paribus* framework, the perfectly competitive equilibrium price will be p^0, and output will be X^0. However, if one firm were able to obtain control of the entire industry, *ceteris paribus,* it would be able to raise the price of output to the level p^m. By assumption, marginal costs remain unchanged at p^0. Average profits are $p^m - p^0$. The Lerner index can be written as $AB/0A$. Total monopoly profits are calculated as the area of the box $ABCD$. According to this mode of analysis, the loss of con-

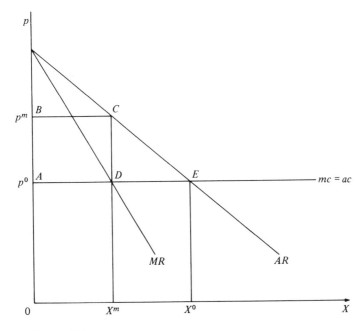

Figure 9.1

sumer surplus due to the monopoly is equal to the area of the shape *ABCE*. The sum of the gain in the form of monopoly profits and the loss in consumer surplus equals the area of the triangle *CDE*. Alternatively, this net loss can be written as

$$-\frac{1}{2}\Delta X \cdot \Delta p \tag{9.2}$$

where $\Delta p = p^m - p^0$ and $\Delta X = X^m - X^0$. This is designated the *deadweight loss* due to the existence of monopoly.

For the most part, calculations of the deadweight loss have followed the basic method contained in Harberger's seminal 1954 article. This involves assuming that the difference between the monopoly and competitive output levels can be approximated by the expression

$$\Delta X = X^m \eta \frac{\Delta p}{p^m} \tag{9.3}$$

where

$$\eta = \frac{p}{X} \frac{\partial X}{\partial p}$$

is the own-price elasticity of the commodity under examination. All expressions are evaluated at the monopoly price level. Consequently, the deadweight loss can be approximated by the formula

$$-\frac{1}{2}p^{m}X^{m}\eta Z^{2} \qquad (9.4)$$

To calculate the total social cost of monopoly practices, the losses obtained for each industry by application of (9.4) are then summed together.

Harberger initially assumed an own-price elasticity equal to minus one. However, such an elasticity value is not consistent with profit maximization. With own-price elasticities everywhere equal to minus one, it will pay each industry to continue to raise the price of its output, because total revenue will remain constant irrespective of the level of sales. Total costs will fall, and hence profits will increase, the higher the price.

This approach was subsequently modified by Kamerschen (1966), who sought to make use of the result that, *ceteris paribus*, each industry will maximize its profits when

$$Z = \frac{p^{m} - p^{0}}{p^{m}} = -\frac{1}{\eta} \qquad (9.5)$$

If both the numerator and denominator of the left-hand side of (9.5) are multiplied by the quantity demanded and then the terms are rearranged, we obtain an expression for the elasticity of demand:

$$\eta = -\frac{p^{m}X^{m}}{(p^{m} - p^{0})X^{m}} = -\frac{R}{\pi} \qquad (9.6)$$

where R represents the total receipts of the industry or firm under study and π equals the excess, monopoly profits. Kamerschen proposed that the elasticity of demand can then be estimated from profits and revenue data and then substituted into equation (9.3) to obtain an approximation to the deadweight loss (DWL). This procedure involves the strong assumption that firms (or industries, if aggregated data are used) actually do maximize their profits.

A variant on the foregoing theme has been provided by Cowling and Mueller (1978). If we write monopoly profits as

$$\pi = p^{m}X^{m}\frac{(p^{m} - p^{0})}{p^{m}} \qquad (9.7)$$

then this expression can be substituted along with (9.6) into (9.4) to yield the computationally simple result

$$\text{DWL} = \frac{1}{2} p_m^m X_m^m \eta Z^2 = \frac{1}{2} \pi \qquad (9.8)$$

This result can be appreciated a bit more fully if we examine the special case depicted in Figure 9.1. On the assumption that the demand curve is linear, the marginal revenue schedule must intersect the line AE. Consequently, it is easy to see that the deadweight loss triangle CDE is equal to one-half of profits (i.e., the rectangle $ABCD$).

Within the foregoing methodological framework, various technical modifications have been implemented or suggested. Some have concerned the methods by which "normal" profits are constructed (e.g., Worcester, 1973; Cowling and Mueller, 1978). Leibenstein (1966) argued that the calculations must be modified to take into account the loss from X-efficiency, (i.e., the failure of monopolies to minimize costs). At a more general level, Bergson (1973) criticized the literature in this area on the grounds that it is "partial equilibrium" in nature and thus completely neglects the complex interactions of various sectors of the economy. Pearce (1975) questioned whether or not it is logically possible to consider a general model in which all firms appear to maximize profits.

None of these studies, however, questioned whether or not the concept of consumer surplus is a reasonable measure to use in the calculation of the social costs of monopoly. There are several aspects to this problem. Does the Harberger method outlined in this section afford a reasonable approximation? Provided sufficient information about consumer demand functions is available, do the measures proposed by Willig and Seade (see Chapter 7) afford reasonable approximations to the money-metric? Or does the modified Simpson's rule procedure advocated in this volume provide a superior result? Let us deal with these issues in turn.

9.3   A second-order comparison

As we have already seen in the preceding section, the method followed by Harberger and others assumed that a second-order consumer surplus approximation permits a reasonably accurate calculation of the social cost of monopoly. It is therefore of some interest to compare this approach with a second-order approximation to the money-metric. In doing so, we shall consider the general case involving several monopolies. A number of preliminary results are required. First, because costs are constant, it is the case that along the production-possibility frontier,

$$\sum p_i^c (X_i^c - X_i^m) = 0 \tag{9.9}$$

Second, we shall assume that aggregate expenditure remains unchanged. That is, monopoly profits arise solely from a redistribution of income away from the basic factors of production. Third, we note that a first-order expansion of the consumer demand functions is written

$$(X_i^c - X_i^m) = \sum_j \frac{\partial X_i}{\partial p_j} (p_j^c - p_j^m) \tag{9.10}$$

We continue to base the derivatives on the prices p_i^m and quantities X_i^m holding in the monopoly situation. From the analysis of section 3.2 we are able to write the second-order Taylor series expansion of the money-metric M as

$$\Delta M = \sum X_i^m (p_i^c - p_i^m)$$

$$- \frac{1}{2} \sum_i \sum_j \left(\frac{\partial X_i}{\partial p_j} - X_j \frac{\partial X_i}{\partial Y} \right) (p_i^c - p_i^m)(p_j^c - p_j^m) \tag{9.11}$$

If we define the income effect for each commodity in the monopoly situation as

$$b_i = p_i^m \frac{\partial X_i}{\partial Y} \tag{9.12}$$

and substitute (9.7), (9.9), (9.10), and (9.12) into (9.11), we obtain

$$\frac{1}{2} \sum_j \pi_j - \frac{1}{2} \sum_i \sum_j b_j \pi_j \frac{\pi_i}{R_i} \tag{9.13}$$

Note that both (9.8) and (9.10) will be positive, indicating that a move from the monopoly to the competitive solution yields a gain. In the case in which the elimination of only one monopoly is contemplated, (9.13) reduces to

$$\Delta M = \frac{1}{2} \pi_i \left[1 - \frac{b_i \pi_i}{R_i} \right] \tag{9.14}$$

In their calculations of the social cost of monopoly, Cowling and

Mueller simply added up monopoly profits and divided by one-half. Thus the expression

$$-\frac{1}{2}\sum_i \sum_j b_j \frac{\pi_i \pi_j}{R_i} \qquad (9.15)$$

represents a correction factor to their calculations. Because (9.15) is unambiguously negative, the Cowling-Mueller measure will overstate the extent of monopoly welfare loss, at least to a second-order approximation. Not surprisingly, an important role is played by the income effect b_i. If this is approximately zero, then the consumer surplus measure (9.8) may represent a reasonable approximation to (9.14). However, in the aggregate, income effects will not be zero, and hence the error (9.15) is likely to be significant in practice. Of course, this is not the only error involved. The expressions (9.8) and (9.14) both neglect the higher-order derivatives that, in general, are major sources of inaccuracy in second-order approximations. This problem can be clearly seen from the example that follows.

9.4   A simple model of monopoly practice

In order to highlight further the difficulties associated with the traditional measures, it is sufficient to construct a simple general equilibrium model similar in many respects to that of Bergson (1973). On the supply side, we assume that there are six industries, each producing homogeneous products. Costs are constant, with quantities measured in units such that average cost and marginal cost are equal to unity. Industry 1 is perfectly competitive, but the other five possess some leverage over their respective markets in the sense that they are capable of introducing a markup over costs. We shall assume that firms do not, in fact, attempt to maximize profits, but merely add a margin to their costs. For simplicity, we shall assume that this margin is the same across industries.

In the model, labor is the only factor of production. In total, there are 90 workers, each earning a constant wage of ten dollars per period. They are mobile, moving between industries in response to any change in the pattern of product demand. In addition, each of the monopoly industries has two managers, who earn a basic salary of ten dollars per period. They split the industry's profits between them. Because all of the industries in the following example are not equally profitable (i.e., in terms of gross profits), it follows that the remuneration to managers varies from industry to industry. These individuals, however, are not mobile between industries.

On the demand side, we assume that all (both workers and management) possess identical preference systems and that these take the Klein-Rubin form. The choice of this form is quite deliberate. As we indicated in Chapter 6, the approximation procedure proposed by Seade is valid only in the case of linear Engel curves, a property held by the Klein-Rubin system. By implication, this form is also marginally homothetic and hence reasonably close in structure to a strictly homothetic function for which consumer surplus procedures are valid.

If we denote each commodity by a subscript and each of the 100 individual consumers by a superscript, then a representative demand function can be written:

$$p_i X_i^j = b_i Y^j + c_i p_i - b_i \sum_{k=1}^{6} c_k p_k$$

$$(i = 1, \ldots, 6; j = 1, \ldots, 100) \tag{9.16}$$

Obviously, there is a wide pattern of parameter values that can be examined for this function. However, two will suffice for our purposes. Both will be based on the same values for the b_i parameters: $b_i = 0.5, b_2 = 0.033, b_3 = 0.067, b_4 = 0.1, b_5 = 0.133, b_6 = 0.167$. The differences will occur in the c_i parameters for each individual:

	Set A	Set B
c_1	-2.50	$+2.50$
c_2	-0.1667	$+0.1667$
c_3	-0.3333	$+0.3333$
c_4	-0.50	$+0.50$
c_5	-0.6667	$+0.1667$
c_6	-0.8333	$+0.8333$

The main implication of these alternative values in terms of the structure of demand is that set A generates elastic own-price elasticities, whereas set B generates elasticities that fall in the inelastic region.

9.5   A comparison of alternative welfare measures

Simulations for the foregoing parameter sets are presented in Tables 9.1 and 9.2 for profit markups of 10, 20, and 30 percent. In all cases examined, the supernumerary income is positive, thereby ensuring that consumer preferences possess the usual desirable properties (see Chapter 2). All price elasticities are reasonable. In other words, the parameters under examination do not generate any peculiar properties. Following the standard practice of many cost−benefit

Table 9.1. *Accuracy of proposed approximation procedures for calculation of the money-metric*

	Parameter set A			Parameter set B		
Profit rate	ΔM^a	Estimate	% Error	ΔM	Estimate	% Error
Modified Simpson's rule method						
0.1	−1.702	−1.702	b	−0.567	−0.567	b
0.2	−6.211	−6.212	b	−2.070	−2.070	b
0.3	−12.815	−12.820	b	−4.272	−4.269	b
Modified Taylor series method						
0.1	−1.702	−1.700	b	−0.567	−0.566	b
0.2	−6.211	−6.159	1	−2.070	−2.048	1
0.3	−12.815	−12.439	3	−4.272	−4.104	4

[a] ΔM indicates true change in value of money-metric.
[b] Error of less than one-half of 1 percent.

Table 9.2 *Accuracy of traditional approximation procedures for calculation of the money-metric*

	Parameter set A			Parameter set B		
Profit rate	ΔM^a	Estimate	% Error	ΔM	Estimate	% Error
Willig method						
0.1	−1.702	−2.860	68	−0.567	−1.751	209
0.2	−6.211	−10.513	52	−2.070	−6.565	217
0.3	−12.815	−21.815	70	−4.272	−13.901	225
Seade method						
0.1	−1.702	−2.574	51	−0.567	−1.458	157
0.2	−6.211	−9.436	52	−2.070	−5.444	162
0.3	−12.815	−19.538	52	−4.272	−11.479	169
Harberger method						
0.1	−1.702	−23.214	1,264	−0.567	−24.405	4,203
0.2	−6.211	−43.182	595	−2.070	−47.727	2,205
0.3	−12.815	−60.326	371	−4.272	−70.109	1,541

[a] ΔM indicates true change in value of money-metric.

analysts adhering to Harberger's third postulate, we have added gains and losses together irrespective of to whom they accrue. A highly revealing examination of the effects of monopoly practice on the distribution of income will be undertaken in Section 9.6.

The first thing to note is that the actual change in the money-metric is a relatively small proportion of national income. This result is consistent with many previously published studies attempting to measure the social cost of monopoly. Confirming our earlier theoretical discussion, the modified Simpson's rule method for approximating the money-metric generates errors of less than one-half of 1 percent. The modified Taylor series method also generates relatively small errors, although these are somewhat larger than those obtained with the Simpson's rule method.

These results stand in marked contrast to the calculations obtained by applying the formulas of Willig, Seade, or Harberger (Table 9.2). As explained in Chapter 6, the Willig approach involves calculating consumer surplus on the basis of a particular path of integration. In the cases under consideration here, any income variation is recorded first, and then the change in consumer surplus associated with the change in p_2 is calculated, with income at its new level and all other prices remaining at their initial levels. Then the effect of a change in p_3 is determined, with p_2 at its new level but other prices still at their original values. This procedure is repeated until all individual surpluses have been computed and summed. This is the same path used to calculate the Simpson's rule and Taylor series measures.

Unfortunately, Seade did not provide meaningful operational details for extending his approach to problems involving more than one price variation. However, because his method does involve approximating the integral

$$- \int_{p_i^0}^{p_i^*} \lambda X_i \, dp_i \tag{9.17}$$

the application of Willig's path of integration is, in principle, valid. Because an approximation to the integrating factor is incorporated in this approach (see Section 6.8), a priori we would expect Seade's approach to outperform that of Willig. This is indeed the case, but only marginally. For both parameter sets A and B, the values obtained by the two methods show substantial errors in comparison with the true aggregate welfare change. This is because both fail to take adequate account of the integrating factor. Indeed, as we noted in Chapter 6, Seade's approach would have enabled him to calculate this factor directly. However, he implicitly rejected this option in order to give prominence to the consumer surplus measure.

Because the Harberger approach outlined at the beginning of this chapter represents a second-order approximation to a measure that itself possesses substantial inaccuracy, the extremely high errors shown in Table 9.2 are not surprising. For the cases under consideration, the Harberger approach represents a substantial overestimate of the true change. However, the relationship depends on the characteristics of the function being evaluated as well as the magnitude of variable change, and hence this procedure can just as well generate an underestimate. Hence, no additional significance should be attributed to the results shown.

9.6   The effects of monopoly practices on the distribution of income

In Chapter 8, we argued that application of Harberger's third postulate of applied welfare economics involves a value judgment that must be made explicit. Simply adding up the gains and losses, irrespective of to whom they accrue, tells us very little about the desirability of alternative social states. Thus, it is instructive to examine (a) the impact of monopoly pricing policy on the distribution of income and (b) the ability of the various measures to accurately capture the redistribution of income involved. In Table 9.3, figures are presented for two cases involving parameter set A and a profit rate of 20 percent. In the first case, we are interested in evaluating the effect of a 100 percent tax on monopoly profits, the proceeds of which are redistributed to the work force. In the second, we examine the distribution effects when profits remain with the monopolists.

Because the Engel curves are linear, the summation of the measures over each individual remains unchanged, irrespective of how income is distributed. However, an analysis of the pattern of changes in the money-metric reveals substantial gains or losses, even though the aggregate measure is quite small. In the case in which profits are untaxed, the percentage change in income ranges between a loss of 8 percent for workers and a gain of 120 percent for the managers in industry 6. When profits are redistributed, there are negligible gains to workers, but losses to the managerial class of over 8 percent. In both cases, the small aggregate changes are averages of gains and losses that individually are quite substantial.

The implications of this pattern are far-reaching. In 1966, Stigler, commenting on Harberger's conclusion that the social costs of monopoly were small, wrote that "if this estimate is correct, economists might serve a more useful purpose if they fought fires or termites instead of monopoly" (Stigler, 1966, p. 34). The results derived earlier, however, suggest that Stigler's conclusion may have been reached too hastily. Instead, economists should have looked more closely at the income distributional effects of monopoly.

Table 9.3 *Comparative performances of alternative approximation methods by sector*

Sector ΔM	Modified Simpson's rule		Modified Taylor series		Willig measure		Seade measure	
	Estimate	% Error	Estimate	% Error	Estimate	% Error	Estimate	% Error
Parameter set A (profit rate 20%; all monopoly profits redistributed)								
1	0.0255	0.0255 [a]		0.0260	2	−0.0179	170	−0.0071	128
2–6	−0.8505	−0.8505 [a]		−0.8500 [a]		−0.8900	5	−0.8801	3
Parameter set A (profit rate 20%; no redistribution of profits)								
1	−0.8505	−0.8505 [a]		−0.8500 [a]		−0.8900	5	−0.8801	3
2	1.7775	1.7775 [a]		1.7781 [a]		1.7263	3	1.7391	2
3	4.4054	4.4054 [a]		4.4061 [a]		4.3427	1	4.3584	1
4	7.0334	7.0334 [a]		7.0342 [a]		6.9590	1	6.9778	1
5	9.6614	9.6613 [a]		9.6622 [a]		9.5754	1	9.5969	1
6	12.2893	12.2893 [a]		12.2903 [a]		12.1917	1	12.2161	1

[a] Error of less than one-half of 1 percent.

The results of disaggregation, as reported in Table 9.3, also provide us with more detailed information concerning the performances of the various alternative measures. If it is the case that large gains or losses accruing to individuals sum to a relatively small total, then it may very well be the case that the error associated with the total may not be a true reflection of the errors associated with the individual group measures. In regard to the modified Simpson's rule and modified Taylor series methods, both yield remarkably small errors across sectors. In contrast, the errors associated with the Willig and Seade methods can be quite substantial, depending on whether or not monopoly profits are taxed and redistributed to the work force. If profits are reallocated, then in the example under consideration the Willig and Seade methods yield a large percentage error, and worse yet *they generate the incorrect sign on the welfare change.* In point of fact, the work force gains from the redistribution; yet these two approximation procedures show that a loss has occurred.

9.7   Summary

This result brings us back to the basic thesis of this volume. Consumer surplus procedures neglect the marginal utility of money, which plays the crucial role of integrating factor in the construction of an exact welfare measure. Consequently, according to the path of integration used in the calculation of the surplus, different results will be generated, and these will, of course, vary from the correct value. Seade's approach attempts to take into account the integrating factor, but only in a very approximate fashion. Because it depends so explicitly on consumer surplus, it, too, does not adequately solve the problem arising from the fact that the calculation is path-dependent. In contrast, the procedures we proposed in Chapter 3 and used in the recent examples incorporate very precise approximations to the changes that occur in the integrating factor. By use of the modified Simpson's rule approach, the value of the integrating factor is calculated exactly to four decimal places, despite the fact that information about the derivatives of the demand function only up to the third order is used. This clearly goes a long way toward explaining why the capacity of this procedure to approximate changes in the money-metric is virtually error-free. This is not to deny that there may be cases in which the other approaches yield reasonable results; however, in general, this will not be the case.

In terms of informational requirements, all measures presume knowledge of the consumer demand function. In terms of complexity, all must be considered to be about equal. However, in terms of performance, the approximation procedure advanced here is unparalleled.

CHAPTER 10

A final comment and conclusion

In 1976, when Pearce and I showed that a well-behaved consumer preference function could be expanded as a Taylor series to represent the money-metric solely in terms of the parameters of ordinary demand functions, we wondered why this possibility had not been perceived earlier. Indeed, several colleagues and friends suggested that the general idea was well known, but when suitably challenged they were unable to come up with convincing references. It may very well be the case that many diligent readers who have struggled with the arguments contained in the previous chapters will be of the same opinion. Certainly, most first-year graduate students will be aware of the tools of analysis that have been used in this volume. The marginal utility of money emerges directly from the assumption that consumers maximize their satisfaction subject to a budget constraint. The cost-of-utility function is now well ensconced in the current generation of textbooks dealing with microeconomic theory. The numerical methods used are of a very basic kind. The only difference between the approach taken here and the conventional literature of applied welfare economics is the manner in which the constituent parts are assembled and developed.

Yet the question remains: If this is so, why have consumer surplus and related index-number techniques continued to attract such widespread attention and use? In the Preface to this book, and subsequently in Chapter 4, we noted that almost a century ago Alfred Marshall had become increasingly skeptical of consumer surplus. Samuelson, in his classic studies of integrability (1950) and the marginal utility of money (1942), provided a clear-cut analytic framework for appreciating the problems involved. But here we come to the crux of the matter. It is one thing to show that some concept contains a logical flaw; it is quite another to develop a superior alternative. As Corden (1971) said of the consumer surplus measure:

Officially, one might say, it died. And yet it would not stay in its grave. It has such strong intuitive appeal, and there is nothing better available, so people keep on measuring it. Indeed, with the overwhelming belief, characteristic of modern computer-age economics, in measurement as the proper activity of economists, it has had a revival. One suspects that the perfectionist theorists

177

gave up too quickly. They forgot that theory should be the handmaiden of applied economics. [p. 242]

Let us now attempt a somewhat broader perspective that should enable us to appreciate the evolution of economic thought in this area, on the one hand, but also to identify, on the other, a methodological confusion that persists in many areas of economics. It will be conjectured that this confusion has produced a form of "mind-set" that has prevented economists from fully understanding some of the problems with which they are dealing.

The development of economic science has proceeded in much the same way as for other branches of science via a series of gradual improvements involving (a) the reformulation of existing hypotheses and (b) the presentation of new hypotheses in an attempt to explain phenomena that were hitherto unforeseen. In the process of building logical structures designed to characterize some aspect of the economic environment, the economist becomes painfully aware that it is impossible to take into account all relevant effects. This inevitable fact has led to the development of two related methods. The first consists in the carrying out of one or more intellectual exercises designed to study the formal or logical interactions of a few variables, *ceteris paribus*. It would be a dubious exercise to attempt to trace an exact source for this approach. However, it certainly was a part of the tool kit of the fathers of modern economic analysis, Hume and Smith, and it reached significant heights in the writings of the great economists of the nineteenth century, Mill, Walras, and Marshall, to name but a few. The need to construct abstract models with little relationship to reality no doubt existed for two reasons. First, this approach paralleled the method of the physical scientist, who would attempt to isolate, under laboratory conditions, two (or perhaps more) variables in order to determine whether or not some interaction existed. Such an approach, however, is not, in general, available to the economist. From a pragmatic view, such experiments are likely to be extremely expensive and time-consuming. But perhaps a more important consideration is that such experiments will be viewed as ethically undesirable by the society being investigated. For this reason, an intellectual exercise based on mathematics or geometry provides an economist with an alternative. The interactions of interesting relationships can be studied in a vacuum by assuming that all other variables, whether deemed to be important or not, remain constant.

A second reason for the attractiveness of the *ceteris paribus* approach in the nineteenth and early twentieth centuries was that statistical econometric procedures were not sufficiently well developed to be of much assistance in examining the relationships among economic variables, even if the appropriate data had existed. Today, econometric methods have reached a high level of sophistication. But this does not mean that economists have gained the ability to describe economic activity to perfection. In a complex world clouded by uncertainty, the best that can be claimed is that econometric methods provide imperfect approximations to the phenomena being modeled. Nevertheless, given that we live in an uncertain world characterized by incomplete information, econometric procedures provide the only logical method for organizing existing data.

It is apparent that these two approaches, which we shall label the *pedagogic* and the *econometric*, respectively, have the common objective of enabling the economist to better understand the world in which we live. However, great care must be exercised in moving from the first to the second mode. The logical elegance and simplicity that often characterize the pedagogic model can trap the unwary economist into using the *ceteris paribus* model for empirical investigation almost without question. This is not to say that the gap between the two approaches should not or cannot be bridged. Ideas that arise from the study of pedagogic models can be incorporated into more general econometric models. Indeed, it may be possible to use the pedagogic model itself to create an approximate representation of actual economic behavior. In either case, however, it is imperative that the model builder make explicit, insofar as is possible, the nature of the *ceteris paribus* assumptions involved in any particular approximation.

It is in this area that consumer surplus advocates have, in my view, let the profession down in a very dramatic fashion. First, they have maintained a campaign to preserve this concept at almost any cost. Many of the modifications and modes of analysis used are so complicated as almost to swamp the basic simplicity of the surplus measure. Second, sufficient tests of the accuracy of the measure have not been undertaken. Yet, as we have seen, highly unrealistic assumptions have frequently been made in an attempt to justify its use as an approximation. It may very well be the case that consumer surplus methods do offer reasonable answers, although this is now difficult to believe, given the results that have been presented in this volume. Yet previous investigators have offered no systematic tests.

The basic problem can be appreciated somewhat more if we juxtapose two passages from Marshall's *Principles:*

If we shut our eyes to realities we may construct an edifice of pure crystal by imaginations, that will throw side lights on real problems at all like our own. Such playful excursions are often suggestive in unexpected ways: they afford good training to the mind: and seem to be productive only of good, so long as their purpose is clearly understood. [1961, p. 782]

The warning about the improper use of economic models was clearly raised. He then argued that

there arises a tendency towards assigning wrong proportions to economic forces; those elements being most emphasized which lend themselves most easily to analytical methods. No doubt this danger is inherent in every application not only of mathematical analysis, but of analysis of every kind, to the problems of real life. It is a danger which more than any other the economist must have in mind at every turn. [1961, p. 850]

These considerations clearly explain why Marshall persisted in his use of consumer surplus as a pedagogic device yet clearly rejected it as being of any great practicality.

In this volume we have drawn out the dangers about which Marshall so clearly warned. We can now conclude with considerable satisfaction that one of the major cornerstones of applied welfare economics, the consumer surplus integral,

$$\Delta CS = -\int_c \sum X_i \, dp_i \tag{10.1}$$

should be withdrawn and recast as

$$\Delta M = -\int_c \sum \lambda X_i \, dp_i \tag{10.2}$$

Our objective has been achieved. We now possess a monetary indicator of welfare that is operational and accurate and can be calculated to a high degree of accuracy from observable information.

References

Afriat, S. N. 1972. "The Theory of International Comparisons of Real Income and Prices." In D. J. Daley, ed., *International Comparisons of Prices and Outputs*, pp. 13–69. New York: National Bureau of Economic Research.

Allen, R. G. D. 1933. "The Marginal Utility of Money and Its Application." *Economica* 13:186–209.

——— 1949. "The Economic Theory of Index Numbers." *Economica* 16:197–203.

Antonelli, G. B. 1886. *Sulla teoria matematica della economia politica*. Pisa: Nella Tipografia del Fochetto (translated in J. S. Chipman, L. Hurwicz, M. K. Richter, and H. F. Sonnenschein, eds. 1971. *Preferences, Utility and Demand*, pp. 332–64. New York: Harcourt Brace).

Apostol, T. M. 1967. *Calculus*. Waltham, Mass.: Xerox.

Atkinson, A. B. 1970. "On the Measurement of Inequality." *Journal of Economic Theory* 2:244–63.

Bergson, A. 1973. "On Monopoly Welfare Losses." *American Economic Review* 63:853–70.

Bishop, R. 1943. "Consumer's Surplus and Cardinal Utility." *Quarterly Journal of Economics* 58:421–49.

Boadway, R. W. 1974. "The Welfare Foundations of Cost-benefit Analysis." *Economic Journal* 84:926–39.

Bowley, A. L. 1928. "Notes on Index Numbers." *Economic Journal* 38:216–37.

Burns, M. E. 1973. "A Note on the Concept and Measure of Consumer's Surplus." *American Economic Review* 53:335–44.

Champernowne, D. 1952. "The Graduation of Income Distribution." *Econometrica* 20:591–615.

Chipman, J. S., and Moore, J. C. 1980. "Compensating Variation, Consumer's Surplus, and Welfare." *American Economic Review* 70:933–49.

Corden, W. M. 1971. *The Theory of Protection*. Oxford University Press.

Courant, R. 1937. *Differential and Integral Calculus*. London: Blackie.

Cowling, K., and Mueller, D. C. 1978. "The Social Costs of Monopoly Power." *Economic Journal* 88:727–48.

Currie, J. M., Murphy, J. A., and Schmitz, A. 1971. "The Concept of Economic Surplus and Its Use in Economic Analysis." *Economic Journal* 81:741–99.

Deaton, A. S. 1978. "Specification and Testing in Applied Demand Analysis." *Economic Journal* 88:524–36.

——— 1979. "The Distance Function and Consumer Behaviour with Applications to Index Numbers and Optimal Taxation." *Review of Economic Studies* 46:391–405.

Deaton, A. S., and Muellbauer, J. 1980. *Economics and Consumer Behaviour*. Cambridge University Press.

Debreu, G. 1951. "The Coefficient of Resource Utilization." *Econometrica* 19:273–92.

——— 1954. "A Classical Tax-Subsidy Problem." *Econometrica* 22:14–22.

181

Diewert, W. E. 1976. "Harberger's Welfare Indicator and Revealed Preference Theory." *American Economic Review* 66:143–52.

——— 1980. "The Economic Theory of Index Numbers: A Survey." In A. S. Deaton, ed., *Essays in the Theory and Measurement of Consumer Behaviour,* pp. 163–208. Cambridge University Press.

Dixit, A. K. 1976. *Optimization in Economic Theory.* Oxford University Press.

Dixit, A. K., and Weller, P. A. 1979. "The Three Consumer's Surpluses." *Economica* 46:125–35.

Dupuit, J. 1844. "De la Mésure de l'utilité des travaux publics." *Annales des Ponts et Chausées, Mémoires et documents relatifs à l'art des constructions et au service de l'ingénieur* 8:332–75 (translated in K. J. Arrow and T. Scitovsky, eds., *Readings in Welfare Economics.* Homewood, Ill.: Irwin).

Eichhorn, W. 1976. "Fisher's Tests Revisited." *Econometrica* 44:247–56.

Fisher, I. 1922. *The Making of Index Numbers.* Boston: Houghton Mifflin.

Friedman, M. 1949. "The Marshallian Demand Curve." *Journal of Political Economy* 57:463–95.

Frisch, R. 1936. "Annual Survey of General Economic Theory: The Problem of Index Numbers." *Econometrica* 4:1–39.

——— 1959. "A Complete Scheme for Computing all Direct and Gross Demand Elasticities in a Model with Many Sectors." *Econometrica* 27:177–96.

Geary, R. C. 1950. "A Note on 'A Constant-Utility Index of the Cost of Living'." *Review of Economic Studies* 18:65–6.

Gorman, W. M. 1961. "On a Class of Preference Fields." *Metroeconomica* 13:53–6.

Harberger, A. C. 1954. "Monopoly and Resource Allocation." *American Economic Review* 49:77–87.

——— 1971. "Three Basic Postulates for Applied Welfare Economics: An Interpretative Essay." *Journal of Economic Literature* 9:785–97.

Hause, J. C. 1975. "The Theory of Welfare Measurement." *Journal of Political Economy* 83:1145–82.

Henderson, J. M., and Quandt, R. 1958. *Microeconomic Theory.* New York: McGraw-Hill.

Hicks, J. R. 1940. "The Rehabilitation of Consumers' Surplus." *Review of Economic Studies* 8:108–16.

——— 1942. "Consumers' Surplus and Index Numbers." *Review of Economic Studies* 9:126–37.

——— 1946. *Value and Capital.* Oxford University Press.

Hicks, J. R., and Allen, R. G. D. 1934. "A Reconsideration of the Theory of Value." *Economica* 1:52–75, 196–219.

Hildebrand, F. B. 1974. *Introduction to Numerical Analysis.* New York: McGraw-Hill.

Hotelling, H. S. 1938. "The General Welfare in Relation to the Problems of Taxation and of Railway and Utility Rates." *Econometrica* 6:269–72.

Householder, A. S. 1953. *Principles of Numerical Analysis.* New York: McGraw-Hill.

Houthakker, H. S. 1960. "Additive Preferences." *Econometrica* 28:244–56.

Hurwicz, L., and Uzawa, H. 1971. "On the Integrability of Demand Functions." In J. S. Chipman, L. Hurwicz, M. K. Richter, and H. F. Sonnenschein, eds., *Preferences, Utility and Demand,* pp. 114–48. New York: Harcourt Brace.

Jevons, W. S. 1871. *The Theory of Political Economy.* London: Macmillan.

Kamerschen, D. R. 1966. "An Estimation of the 'Welfare Losses' from Monopoly in the American Economy." *Western Economic Journal* 4:221–36.

Kannai, Y. 1974. "Approximation of Convex Preferences." *Journal of Mathematical Economics* 1:101–6.

Klein, L., and Rubin, H. 1947–8. "A Constant-Utility Index of the Cost of Living." *Review of Economic Studies* 15:84–7.

Konüs, A. A. 1924. "The Problem of the True Index of the Cost-of-Living" (in Russian). *The Economic Bulletin of the Institute of Economic Conjecture,* Moscow, No. 9–10, pp. 64–71 (English translation, 1939. *Econometrica* 7:10–29).

Leibenstein, H. 1966. "Allocative Efficiency vs. X-Efficiency." *American Economic Review* 56:392–415.

Lerner, A. P. 1934. "The Concept of Monopoly and the Measurement of Monopoly Power." *Review of Economic Studies* 1:157–75.

Little, I. M. D. 1960. *A Critique of Welfare Economics.* Oxford University Press.

McKenzie, G. W. 1974. *The Monetary Theory of International Trade.* London: Macmillan.

——— 1976. "Measuring Gains and Losses." *Journal of Political Economy* 84:641–6.

——— 1977. "Complementarity, Substitutability and Independence." *Oxford Economic Papers* 29:430–41.

——— 1979. "Consumer's Surplus Without Apology: A Comment." *American Economic Review* 69:465–8.

——— 1982. "Applied Welfare Indicators and the Economics of Exhaustible Resources." In W. Eichhorn, ed., *Economic Theory of Natural Resources.* Wurzberg-Wien: Physica-Verlag.

McKenzie, G. W., and Pearce, I. F. 1976. "Exact Measures of Welfare and the Cost of Living." *Review of Economic Studies* 43:465–8.

——— 1982. "Welfare Measurement — A Synthesis." *American Economic Review* 72: 669–82.

McKenzie, G. W., and Thomas, S. 1982. "Pitfalls in Modelling Consumer Behaviour." *Southampton discussion papers in economics and econometrics,* no. 8120.

McKenzie, L. W. 1957. "Demand Theory without a Utility Index." *Review of Economic Studies* 24:185–9.

Malmquist, S. 1953. "Index Numbers and Indifference Surfaces." *Tradajos de Estadistica* 4:209–41.

Marshall, A. 1890. *Principles of Economics.* London: Macmillan (also see the ninth variorum edition with annotations by C. W. Guillebaud, 1961, London: Macmillan).

Mas-Colell, A. 1974. "Continuous and Smooth Consumers: Approximation Theorems." *Journal of Economic Theory* 9:305–36.

Mishan, E. J. 1976. "The Use of Compensating and Equivalent Variations in Cost-Benefit Analysis." *Economica* 43:185–97.

Mohring, H. 1971. "Alternative Welfare Gain and Loss Measures." *Western Economic Journal* 9:349–68.

Muellbauer, J. 1976. "Economics and the Representative Consumer." In L. Solari and J. N. Du Pasquier, eds., *Private and Enlarged Consumption,* pp. 29–53. Amsterdam: North Holland.

Nicholson, J. S. 1902. *Principles of Political Economy.* London: Adam and Charles Black.

Pearce, I. F. 1964. *A Contribution to Demand Analysis.* Oxford University Press.

——— 1970. *International Trade.* London: Macmillan.

——— 1975. "Monopolistic Competition and General Equilibrium." In Michael Parkin and A. R. Nobay, eds., Proceedings of the A. U. T. E. Conference, *Current Economic Problems,* Cambridge University Press.

Pollak, R. A. 1971. "The Theory of the Cost-of-Living Index." Research Discussion Paper No. 11, Office of Prices and Living Conditions. Washington, D. C.: U. S. Bureau of Labor Statistics.

Reaume, D. M. 1973. "Cost-Benefit Techniques and Consumer Surplus: A Clarificatory Analysis." *Public Finance* 28:196–211.

Roy, R. 1942. *De l'utilité, contribution à la théorie des choix*. Paris: Herman.

Samuelson, P. A. 1942. "Constancy of the Marginal Utility of Income." In O. Lange, F. McIntyre, and T. O. Yntema, eds., *Studies in Mathematical Economics and Econometrics*, pp. 75–91. University of Chicago Press.

——— 1947. *Foundations of Economic Analysis*. Cambridge, Mass.: Harvard University Press.

——— 1950. "The Problem of Integrability in Utility Theory." *Economica* 17:355–85.

——— 1956. "Social Indifference Curves." *Quarterly Journal of Economics* 70:1–22.

——— 1974. "Complementarity—An Essay on the 40th Anniversary of the Hicks-Allen Revolution in Demand Theory." *Journal of Economic Literature* 12:1255–89.

Samuelson, P. A. and Swamy, S. 1974. "Invariant Economic Index Numbers and Canonical Duality: Survey and Synthesis." *American Economic Review* 64:566–93.

Say, J. B. 1880. *A Treatise on Political Economy*. New York: Augustus Kelley Editions (1970).

Schultz, H. 1939. "A Misunderstanding in Index-Number Theory: The True Konüs Condition on Cost-of-Living Index Numbers and Its Limitations." *Econometrica* 7:1–9.

Scitovsky, T. 1941. "A Note on Welfare Propositions in Economics." *Review of Economic Studies* 9:77–88.

Seade, J. 1978. "Consumer's Surplus and Linearity of Engel Curves." *Economic Journal* 88:411–523.

Sen, A. K. 1973. *On Economic Inequality*. Oxford University Press (Clarendon Press).

——— 1979. "The Welfare Basis of Real Income Comparisons: A Survey." *Journal of Economic Literature* 17:1–45.

Shephard, R. 1953. *Cost and Production Functions*. Princeton University Press.

Silberberg, E. 1972. "Duality and the Many Consumer's Surpluses." *American Economic Review* 62:942–52.

Stigler, G. 1956. "The Statistics of Monopoly and Merger." *Journal of Political Economy* 64:33–40.

Swamy, S. 1965. "Consistency of Fisher's Tests." *Econometrica* 33:619–23.

Varian, H. 1978. *Microeconomic Analysis*. New York, Norton.

Walras, L. 1954. *Elements of Pure Economics*. Homewood, Ill.: Irwin.

Willig, R. D. 1976. "Consumer's Surplus Without Apology." *American Economic Review* 66:589–97.

——— 1979. "Consumer's Surplus Without Apology: Reply." *American Economic Review* 69:469–74.

Wilson, E. B. 1939. "Pareto Versus Marshall." *Quarterly Journal of Economics* 53:645–50.

Worcester, D. A. 1973. "New Estimates of the Welfare Loss to Monopoly: U. S. 1956–69." *Southern Economic Journal* 40:234–46.

Index

185